Substance Abuse Assessment and Diagnosis

Substance Abuse Assessment and Diagnosis

A Comprehensive Guide for Counselors and Helping Professionals

Gerald A. Juhnke

Brunner-Routledge
New York and Hove

Published in 2002 by
Brunner-Routledge
29 West 35th Street
New York, NY 10001
www.brunner-routledge.com

Published in Great Britain by
Brunner-Routledge
27 Church Road
Hove, East Sussex
BN3 2FA
www.brunner-routledge.co.uk

Brunner-Routledge is an imprint of the Taylor & Francis Group.
Printed in the United States of America on acid-free paper.

10 9 8 7 6 5 4 3 2 1

Library of Congress Cataloging-in-Publication Data
Juhnke, Gerald A.
    Substance abuse assessment and diagnosis : a comprehensive guide for counselors and helping professionals / Gerald A. Juhnke.
        p. cm.
Includes bibliographical references and index.
    ISBN 1–58391–367–X (pbk.)
1. Substance abuse—Diagnosis.   I. Title.
RC564 .J84 2002
616.86'075—dc21

                                                     2002007321

Contents

Preface

As counselors and mental health professionals face greater numbers of persons experiencing addictions and addiction-related concerns, we continually strive to (a) more fully understand our clients and their specific needs and concerns, (b) accurately conceptualize clients' current alcohol and other drug (AOD) use within their overall drinking and drugging history, and (c) identify clients' potential strengths and resources so they may more effectively battle and achieve their ongoing recovery and sustained abstinence. Thus, this text is founded upon the assumption that addictions assessment is more than a one-time paperwork procedure, conducted at the onset of treatment to simply gather minimal facts and secure a *Diagnostic and Statistical Manual of Mental Disorders* (4th Edition)–Text Revision (2000) (*DSM–IV–TR*) diagnosis to fulfill Medicaid billing requirements. I view assessment and counseling as one. Neither is exclusive of the other or operating in a neutral vacuum. Instead, each impacts the other and is intertwined in complex ways as client, significant others, and counselor cocreate an effective, economical, and mutually respectful assessment and treatment.

Within the text I describe how to assess without becoming lost in the assessment process or losing sight of assessment's purpose—to help engender effective treatment. Too often, counselors and mental health professionals become myopic and fail to either remember the person behind the symptomatology or bridge effective treatment within the assessment process itself. Thus, the first two chapters provide readers a foundation on which to build the assessment process. Chapter 1 begins with a general introduction to the Clinical Interviews, Standardized Speciality, Drug Detection, and Personality Assessment (CLISD-PA) model. I describe the model's history and how I've used the CLISD-PA model with my clinical supervisees since 1991. Each of the four model tiers is described. Chapter 2, The *DSM–IV–TR* Multiaxial System and Common Substance-Related Disorders, provides readers with *DSM–IV–TR* diagnostic fundamentals. Here, readers learn how to use Vacc's (1982) continuous assessment construct, and compare and contrast immediate with past symptomatology. The end result provides a clinically relevant and thorough *DSM–IV–TR* diagnosis that helps counselor and client monitor counseling progress. This chapter further addresses two vitally important issues for counselors working with addicted persons—dual diagnosis and Axis I and Axis II disorders common to those who are AOD abusing.

The remaining chapters provide proven and practical directions on the assessment process itself. Chapter 3, Tier One: Individual Clinical Interviews, clarifies differences between clinical interviews and mere interpersonal conversations. Potential clinical interview benefits are noted and effective questioning techniques are described. Chapter 4, Significant Other Interviews: Understanding and Promoting Change through Others, provides a refreshing and clinically appropriate manner with which to gain vital information regarding clients and their concerns via their significant others. A six-phase model is outlined that ensures appropriate clinical perspective and encourages input from those most important to the client. Chapter 5, Standardized Alcohol and Other Drug (AOD) Speciality Assessment Instruments and Drug Detection Testing, provides a basic overview of important psychometric fundamentals and describes three of the most frequently used adult standardized AOD speciality instruments. These include the Alcohol Use Inventory, the Adult Substance Use Survey, and the Substance Abuse Subtle Screening Inventory–3. Standardized adolescent AOD instruments are also described, including the newest instrument from the SASSI Institute, the Adolescent Substance Abuse Subtle Screening Inventory (SASSI–A2). Finally, I have included pragmatic and practical information on drug detection testing—something that is absent from most addictions texts. This information helps counselors understand which drug detection testing is most appropriate for their clients and when to use it. Chapter 6, Personality Assessment and Therapeutic Feedback, provides readers with fundamentals related to the Minnesota Multiphasic Personality Inventory (MMPI–2) and the Minnesota Multiphasic Personality Inventory–Adolescent (MMPI–A). My main emphasis in this chapter is to provide no-nonsense basics of these fundamental personality assessment instruments and to explain how readers can explain results in a therapeutic and helpful manner. The book concludes with my closing remarks in chapter 7.

My intent throughout the text was to write a book that consistently reminds counselors and mental health professionals of the people behind the addiction diagnoses and disease. Each client is more than a diagnosis and deserves to be treated with utmost respect, dignity, and compassion. I trust you will find the book unique as it describes a multitiered assessment process that incorporates multiple assessment methods and describes how the assessment process works via clinical vignettes and examples. I sincerely trust the text is helpful to you as we change our world, one client at a time.

Jerry Juhnke

Chapter 1

The Clinical Interviews, Standardized Speciality, Drug Detection, and Personality Assessment (CLISD-PA) Model Overview

Chapter 1 Outline:
General CLISD-PA Overview
CLISD-PA Assumptions
Summary

Chapter 1 Learning Objectives:
Upon chapter completion, you should be able to:
• Provide a general description of the CLISD-PA model.
• Identify the purposes of each of the four tiers.
• Report the two basic CLISD-PA assumptions.

GENERAL CLISD-PA OVERVIEW

The four-tiered Clinical Interviews, Standardized Speciality, Drug Detection, and Personality Assessment (CLISD-PA) model is a progressive, stepwise substance abuse assessment model. The atheoretical model was developed by Juhnke in 1986 as he assessed and counseled alcohol and other drug (AOD) abusing clients and their families. The original CLISD-PA model was refined by the author's clinical experiences. By 1991, Juhnke began using the model as a means of training his master's and doctoral students in the art and science of substance abuse assessment. The current model, then, is founded upon the author's more than 16 years of clinical and clinical supervision experiences. The CLISD-PA model is used by clinical interns and staff supervised by Juhnke in his role as director of the Counseling and Consulting Services Clinic. The clinic is part of the Department of Counseling and Educational Development at the University of North Carolina at Greensboro. All AOD-adjudicated university students are required to participate in substance abuse assessments provided by Juhnke's counselors. Yearly, approximately 200 adjudicated students participate in AOD assessments and counseling services at the clinic under Juhnke's clinical supervision. Additionally, counselors at the clinic provide substance abuse assessment and counseling services to community clients who either have been recently arrested for AOD-related driving charges or are petitioning to reinstate their driving privileges after having their motor vehicle licenses revoked due to AOD-related driving violations.

Tier One of the CLISD-PA model begins with an individual clinical interview (Juhnke, 2000). At the conclusion of the clinical interview, counselors should have sufficient information to determine whether or not a clinical interview with the clients' significant others is warranted.[1] Tier Two is a clinical interview process with the clients' significant others. Persons participating in this clinical interview would typically include partners, close family members (e.g., a parent or sibling), or, depending on the situation, friends deemed supportive and important to the client's treatment. Only clients warranting further specific assessments progress to the third tier. Instruments used here consist of speciality assessments such as the Substance Abuse Subtle Screening Inventory–3 (SASSI–3). Tier Four includes general personality instruments such as the Minnesota Multiphasic Personality Inventory–2 (MMPI–2), or the Millon Clinical Multiaxial Inventory–II (MCMI–II). This tiered process (Table 1.1) insures adequate assessment and reduces both traditional testing costs and the time and energy required to administer, score, and interpret such traditional instrument experiences—especially when such testing is unwarranted.

CLISD-PA ASSUMPTIONS

The CLISD-PA model is founded on two general assumptions. First, multiple information sources provide superior assessments when compared to a single source. In other words, a face-to-face clinical interview with a client may provide valuable treatment information and suffice in providing needed information to accurately diagnose. However, when the face-to-face clinical interview is appropriately coupled with information from outside sources (e.g., partners, spouses, parents, siblings, etc.) or standardized assessment instruments, the assessment is likely to provide a greater context in which to view clients and their presenting symptomatology.

---

1. It is important that a release of confidential information be agreed to and signed by clients prior to interviewing their significant others. Speaking to significant others prior to gaining such releases will breach confidentiality. Therefore, the counselor may be in jeopardy of legal and ethical practice charges.

TABLE 1.1. Clinical Interviews Standardized Specialty, Drug Detection, and Personality Assessment (CLISD-PA) Model

---

Individual Clinical Interview

Sufficient information obtained to develop an accurate *DSM–IV–TR* diagnosis?
Sufficient information obtained to develop a thorough and effective treatment plan?

Yes: Proceed to significant other clinical   No: Identify needed information and
   interview   continue individual clinical interview

Diagnose and provide therapeutic feedback to client

Significant Other Clinical Interview

Sufficient information obtained to develop an accurate *DSM–IV–TR* diagnosis?
Sufficient information obtained to develop a thorough and effective treatment plan?

Yes: Proceed to standard alcohol and other   No: Identify needed information and
   drug specialty/drug detection   continue significant other clinical
   assessment individual clinical interview   interview

Review diagnosis and provide therapeutic feedback to client

Standardized Alcohol And Other Drug Specialty/Drug Detection Assessment

Sufficient information obtained to develop an accurate *DSM–IV–TR* diagnosis?
Sufficient information obtained to develop a thorough and effective treatment plan?

Yes: Proceed to personality assessment   No: Identify needed information and
                                                                      continue standardized alcohol and
                                                                      other drug specialty/drug detection
                                                                      assessment

Review diagnosis and provide therapeutic feedback to client

Personality Assessment

Sufficient information obtained to develop an accurate *DSM–IV–TR* diagnosis?
Sufficient information obtained to develop a thorough and effective treatment plan?

Yes: Review diagnosis, coestablish   No: Identify other information needed and
   treatment plan with client, and   conjointly determine with client
   initiate treatment   how to obtain it

Many times, clients will inadvertently or intentionally fail to present the full picture of their symptomatology. For example, an alcohol-abusing client may provide sufficient information for the counselor to accurately diagnose alcohol dependence. However, via an additional interview with the client's spouse, for example, the counselor may further learn that the onset of the client's alcohol and cocaine dependence began early in the client's life—as compared to only alcohol dependence portrayed by the client—and that the client was encouraged by legal counsel to seek counseling before his upcoming driving under the influence (DUI) court arraignment. Clearly, such added information gained by an additional interview will be helpful to the counselor providing treatment services to this client.

The second general CLISD-PA model assumption is that, when warranted, progressive "tiers" of intensive assessment are used. Thus, after the individual face-to-face clinical interview with a client, the counselor may perceive that a sufficient clinical picture has been developed to both provide an accurate diagnosis and effective treatment interventions. Hence, no further assessment would be warranted.

However, should the counselor perceive the need for more intensive assessment based on information gathered via the individual clinical interview, or the absence of it, the counselor may deem it important to complete all four assessment tiers. Thus, the counselor completes both individual and significant other clinical interviews, as well as specialty and broad-spectrum personality assessments. For example, within an individual clinical interview a client might present as emaciated, yet deny eating-disorder symptomatology. During Tier Two, the significant other interview, her parents might respond to posed eating disorder questions by stating, "Oh no, Sara is just naturally thin." Despite such claims by client and parents, the counselor may still suspect comorbid marijuana abuse and eating disorder diagnoses. Therefore, the counselor may logically move to the CLISD-PA model's third tier. Here, the counselor will administer additional specialty assessment instruments specific to AOD abuse (e.g., the Adult Substance Use Survey) and eating disorders (e.g., the Eating Disorders Inventory). Should either specialty instrument note the likely presence of one or both disorders, a broad-spectrum personality instrument such as the Millon Clinical Multiaxial Inventory–II (MCMI–II) will be administered to learn more about the client. Simply stated, then, when the counselor's clinical judgment suggests additional levels of assessment are warranted or when the assessments already utilized are incongruent or suspect, more intensive assessment tiers are used.

This second assumption also reminds counselors that all clients do not need each of the four assessment tiers, nor do all clients require the administration of identical assessment instruments. Basically, the CLISD-PA model encourages counselors to match both the levels and types of assessments to the client's specific needs. Stated differently, assessment instruments should form to the individual client's needs, not the other way around. Thus, this second assumption is in direct contrast to counselors and agencies that require all participating clients to complete the same assessment instruments regardless of individual concerns and presenting symptomatology.

SUMMARY

This brief introduction has given readers a succinct history and description of the CLISD-PA model. The next chapter begins with a rudimentary overview of substance-related disorders contained within the *Diagnostic and Statistical Manual of Mental Disorders* (4th Edition)–Text Revision (2000) (*DSM–IV–TR*) and progresses through each of the specific CLISD-PA model tiers. Thus, by the conclusion of the book, readers will have a practical understanding of substance-related disorders necessary for effective client treatment and a thorough understanding of how to use the CLISD-PA model when assessing client AOD.

REFERENCES

Juhnke, G. A. (2000). *Addressing school violence: Practical strategies and interventions.* Greensboro, NC: Educational Resources Information Center/Counseling and Student Services Clearinghouse (ERIC/CASS).

Chapter 2

The *DSM–IV–TR* Multiaxial System and Common Substance-Related Disorders

Other Axis I Diagnoses That Warrant Review
    Posttraumatic Stress Disorder
    Conduct Disorder
    Oppositional Defiant Disorder
    Axis V: The Global Assessment of Functioning (GAF) Scale
Summary

Chapter 2 Learning Objectives:
After reading this chapter, you should be able to:

- Describe potential diagnostic benefits of the *DSM–IV–TR*
- Describe the benefits of using the *DSM–IV–TR* Multiaxial Assessment System.
- Define dual diagnosis.
- Identify common Axis I substance-related disorders.
- Explain the differences between substance dependence and substance abuse.
- Describe the criteria necessary for substance intoxication.
- Identify frequently occurring comorbid Axis II personality disorders.
- Identify other, relevant Axis I disorders.
- Explain the use and structure of the Global Assessment of Functioning (GAF) Scale.

INTRODUCTION TO THE *DSM–IV–TR*

Reading this chapter will not make one an expert on the *Diagnostic and Statistical Manual of Mental Disorders* (4th Edition)–Text Revision (2000) (*DSM–IV–TR*) or its use. The *DSM–IV–TR*'s specific nomenclature and its idiosyncratic coding and reporting procedures warrant generalized instruction in the entire *DSM–IV–TR*. Such generalized instruction is outside this chapter's scope. However, this statement does not imply that addictions counselors should be *DSM–IV–TR* ignorant. In fact, the opposite is true.

All addictions counselors should have an overall rudimentary *DSM–IV–TR* understanding and specialized substance-related *DSM–IV–TR* knowledge. Addictions counselors, especially, must be skilled clinical diagnosticians who understand common substance-related disorders and frequently occurring comorbid personality disorders. Thus, the intent of this chapter is to help readers better understand potential client and counselor benefits resulting from accurately delivered *DSM–IV–TR* diagnoses and gain fundamental *DSM–IV–TR* Multiaxial System knowledge—especially knowledge regarding Axis I substance-related disorders, Axis II personality disorders, and dual diagnoses. The chapter also provides general information regarding the Global Assessment of Functioning Scale and its use with addicted persons. Four addictions-related vignettes are presented at the chapter's conclusion. These vignettes provide readers with an opportunity to practice their new *DSM–IV–TR* diagnostic skills with specific substance-using clients.

Potential Benefits of Accurate *DSM–IV–TR* Diagnoses

Accurately delivered *DSM–IV–TR* diagnoses help addictions counselors and their clients in a number of important ways. First, counselors who understand basic *DSM–IV–TR* diagnoses and associated criteria better comprehend the severity of their clients' presenting psychopathology and can use this understanding to facilitate continuous assessment opportunities (Vacc, 1982). Thus, in cases relevant to this addictions book, counselors using *DSM–IV–TR* diagnoses are able to continually assess their alcohol- and other drug-abusing clients. Here, clients' immediate symptomatology is compared to past levels and concurrently compared to established *DSM–IV–TR* criteria. Thus, continuous assessment helps clients and counselors note and track substance-related progress. Failure to note such progress warrants treatment review and requires counselors and clients to investigate other treatment options such as psychopharmacological interventions (e.g., Prozac, Antabuse) or intensive treatment occurring in more restrictive environmental or residential settings.

Additionally, the use of continuous assessment fosters counselors' and clients' knowledge regarding useful treatment interventions. Thus, treatment interventions identified as promoting positive outcomes can be continued, amplified, or redirected and generalized to other potential concern areas. For example, a client reporting the solution focused "miracle question" technique[2] (O'Hanlon and Weiner-Davis, 1989) helpful in promoting relevant alcohol abstinence goals and objectives may be encouraged to continue this technique in other addictive-relevant areas (e.g., marijuana abstinence) or generalize this technique to nonaddictive concerns such as parenting or relationships. Thus, the client could use the miracle question to identify desired behaviors perceived necessary to be an acceptable parent or partner. This in turn establishes a forum in which clients are affirmed for identifying how they want their behaviors, lives, and relationships changed. Such affirmation experiences are atypical for alcohol- and other drug-abusing clients and model appropriate self-directed goal identification and pursuit.

DSM–IV–TR assessment and diagnosis skills are also critical in securing appropriate client substance treatment. The advent of managed care has placed increased emphasis on standardized treatment protocols (Karon, 1995; Lawless, Ginter, & Kelly, 1999; Miller, 1996). Clients served by managed care services and presenting with similar symptomatology are more likely than not assigned to diagnostic-related groups (DRGs). These DRGs are used to group clients with similar diagnoses and symptom levels. Therefore, DRG placement frequently dictates the specific counseling theory to be used (e.g., behavioral therapy), the counseling modality (e.g., group counseling), and the number of preapproved or reim-

---

2. Counselors using the generic miracle question ask clients, "If a miracle happened tonight, and your immediate concerns disappeared, what would be the first thing you would notice upon awakening that would suggest your concerns were gone?" Clients then use the identified behaviors or occurrences suggesting the presenting concerns had disappeared as treatment goals.

bursable treatment sessions (Hawkins, 1991). Client inclusion in the most appropriate DRG requires addictions counselors to be knowledgeable of *DSM–IV–TR* substance-related diagnoses. Additionally, addictions counselors must be fully aware of the subtle yet significant differences among different substance-related diagnoses (e.g., alcohol abuse vis-à-vis alcohol dependence), especially when clients' clinical presentations and reported symptomatology may overtly appear identical to less skilled practitioners and laypersons. The more skilled addictions counselors are in assessment and diagnoses, the higher is the probability that clients will be assigned to the most representative DRG and therefore receive the necessary degree of managed-care-funded treatment.

Because many managed care companies are frugal and carefully regulate benefit allocations, only those clients whose diagnoses reflect greater severity are assigned to DRGs that allocate increased paid treatment sessions and services (e.g., detoxification, inpatient treatment, etc.). Misdiagnosed clients assigned to less severe DRGs are precertified for fewer reimbursed treatment sessions and typically are not provided inpatient or detoxification service opportunities. Thus, many of these clients may either fail to enter treatment due to initial financial concerns or prematurely discontinue treatment, which will require significant out-of-pocket expenses. Timely resolution to funding issues resulting from misdiagnosis and incorrect DRG placements is rare. Managed-care companies often challenge counselors seeking additional treatment session approval. This seems especially true when counselors are indicating previous misdiagnosis. Thus, addictions counselors need to be highly skilled in substance assessment and diagnosis. Such skill insures accurate DRG placement and often secures necessary client treatment access and adequate intervention levels, which match clients' addiction severity.

Additionally, private practice counselors contracting to purvey addictions counseling on local health-care provider panels who incorrectly assess or misdiagnose clients will likely be required by the contract's capitation clause[3] to provide continued addictions treatment to a misdiagnosed client without adequate reimbursement. Therefore, should the addictions counselor initially assess the client as having a less severe diagnosis with a corresponding truncated number of preapproved treatment sessions, the counselor may be required to continue treatment without charging either the client or provider panel for the additional sessions.

Thus, skilled *DSM–IV–TR* substance use assessment and diagnosis is vitally important to clients and counselors alike. For clients, accurate assessment promotes effective treatment and baseline data, which identify successful treatment interventions and goal achievement. Concomitantly, addictions counselors skilled

---

3. Capitation is an agreement between a counselor and a provider group (e.g., health maintenance organization, insurance company, etc.) in which the counselor agrees to purvey services at an agreed-on standard charge to provider group members for a set number of treatment sessions. Furthermore, the counselor agrees to continue to purvey necessary services beyond the agreed-on number of treatment sessions (e.g., 7) at no charge to either the provider group or provider group members.

in *DSM–IV–TR* diagnosis are able to advocate on their clients' behalfs for appropriate DRG placements. This helps insure that clients presenting with the most severe needs receive appropriate levels of care, thereby reducing the financial stressor and increasing the probability of treatment compliance and efficacy. Finally, counselors benefit from accurate *DSM–IV–TR* Substance Use diagnoses as well. Such accurate diagnosis enhances the probability of appropriate reimbursement for services provided and insures adequate quality and care.

THE *DSM–IV–TR* MULTIAXIAL ASSESSMENT

The *DSM-IV-TR*'s multiaxial system insures that counselors minimally assess clients according to five specific domain areas. These domain areas are called *axes* within the *DSM–IV–TR*. The multiaxial system discourages counselors from merely assessing clients' voiced concerns and promotes a broad understanding of factors that may contribute to or influence such concerns. This broad understanding aids addictions counselors in developing encompassing treatment plans, which increase the probability of successful treatment. These five axes include (APA, 2000, p. 27):

Axis I: The presenting clinical disorders or conditions that are the primary focus of clinical attention.

Axis II: Personality disorders or mental retardation.

Axis III: General medical conditions.

Axis IV: Psychosocial and environmental problems or concerns.

Axis V: A global functioning assessment.

Here, for example, a client presenting with depressed affect is not merely identified as being depressed, with treatment interventions designed to reduce depressed feelings. Instead, depression is viewed within the context of the client's life's axes. Thus, addictions counselors using the *DSM-IV-TR*'s multiaxial system would assess the client according to her: (a) presenting concerns or clinical disorders (including her noted depressed feelings as well as investigating other possibly nonvoiced areas of concern; e.g., her possible alcohol and marijuana abuse), (b) possible underlying personality constructs or mental retardation, which may be related to or influencing her presenting concerns, (c) general medical condition, especially medical factors that may contribute or influence her voiced concerns, (d) psychosocial and environmental problems that may engender stressors related to her depression, and (e) overall functioning level. In this example of a depressed female, it is likely that a counselor using the multiaxial system will attain a more complete clinical picture. Therefore, the counselor may learn via the multiaxial system assessment that the client's depressive symptomatology began shortly after her job termination. Furthermore, it might be noted that she has been abusing alcohol and marijuana as a means to cope with her depressed feelings and has few familial or social supports.

Some essential multiaxial system diagnostic features warrant discussion. For example, sometimes it is impossible to make an adequate diagnostic determination within a single, 50-minute interview. This seems especially true when substance abusing clients present: (a) limited intelligence, (b) many critical concerns that are noted by the client as equally acute, (c) multiple substances of abuse, (d) pressing legal issues that may either cause incarceration or influence sentencing determinations, and (e) chaotic interpersonal, social, and family relationships.

Should a counselor be unable to make an immediate Axis I disorder determination and need to defer diagnosis, the counselor would be able to indicate V799.9 Diagnosis or Condition Deferred on Axis I. Here, the counselor is merely indicating that inadequate information has been presented by the client or obtained by the counselor to make an informed and adequate Axis I determination. However, a deferred diagnosis should not continue indefinitely. Contrary to some misinformed or guarded clinicians who inappropriately continue a deferred diagnosis until treatment conclusion, an accurate diagnosis should be presented as early in the assessment and treatment process as possible. In most cases a clear diagnosis will be noted within one to three clinical interviews.

Also, many substance-abusing clients present with more than one Axis I presenting concern or clinical disorder. In the just noted example, if the client's reported depressed feelings occurred within 3 months of the onset of her job termination, included marked distress in excess of what would typically be expected from such a job termination, and the symptomatology is not severe enough to meet criteria for another specific Axis I disorder such as major depression or bereavement, she would likely qualify for an adjustment disorder with depressed mood diagnosis. Additionally, depending on the degree of severity and criteria met, this client would likely qualify for two additional Axis I disorders. These would include alcohol abuse or dependence, and cannabis abuse or dependence. Thus, she would likely have at least three Axis I disorders.

Further, it should be noted that multiple Axis I diagnoses are presented in descending order. Thus, the most pressing diagnosis is given first and the least pressing diagnosis is given last (APA, 2000, p. 27). An example of this is depicted in Table 2.1. Here, this depressed female client is given a principal diagnosis of adjustment disorder with depressed mood, because her most pressing concern and the impetus for her beginning counseling is her depressive symptomatology. Via the clinical interview, it was noted that the client primarily abuses alcohol and secondarily abuses marijuana to cope with her depressed feelings (her most pressing concern). Thus, these diagnoses are presented in descending order (i.e., depression first, alcohol second, marijuana third). Additionally, it may be that the client does not have an Axis II personality disorder. In such a case, the counselor would indicate "V71.09 No Diagnosis on Axis II," as demonstrated in Table 2.1.

As in the case of Axis I disorders, Axis II disorders are also presented in descending order. Therefore, should clients qualify for more than one Axis II personality disorder or mental retardation, all Axis II disorders are listed. Again, the most pressing Axis II disorder is listed first. Alcohol and other drug abusing

TABLE 2.1. *DSM–IV–TR* Multiaxial Report: Descending Order Axis I
and No Axis II Diagnosis Example

Axis I:	309.00	Adjustment Disorder with Depressed Mood
	305.00	Alcohol Abuse
	305.20	Cannabis Abuse
Axis II:	V71.09	No Diagnosis or Condition on Axis II
Axis III:	244.9	Hypothyroidism
Axis IV:	None	
Axis V:	GAF = 50 (on admission)	
	GAF = 62 (on discharge)	

clients commonly present with both Axis I and Axis II disorders. A frequent example of this includes clients fulfilling *DSM–IV–TR* Axis I criteria for alcohol dependence and Axis II criteria for antisocial personality disorder. Here, antisocial personality disordered persons' primary featured psychopathology is pervasive disregard for others and others' basic rights. The comorbid secondary feature frequently includes substance-related behaviors such as driving under the influence (DUI) or one of many substance-related disorders (e.g., alcohol abuse, cocaine dependence). Thus, they present both a clinical disorder, the Axis I disorder, and a personality disorder, the Axis II disorder. Each disorder warrants treatment. However, if the Axis II diagnosis is the principal reason for the interaction with the client, the specific notation "Principal Diagnosis" or "Reason for Visit" (APA, 2000, pp. 28–29) is indicated on the Axis II line of the multiaxial report. Table 2.2 demonstrates this Axis II primary disorder reference. Likewise, should a client not qualify for an Axis I diagnosis and the primary reason for the client's interaction be an Axis II personality disorder, the counselor would indicate "V71.09 No Diagnosis or Condition" on Axis I. An example of this is demonstrated in Table 2.3.

DUAL DIAGNOSES

Addictions counselors most often use the term *dual diagnosis* when clients present with comorbid Axis I substance-related and other mental health disorders. For example, clients presenting with Axis I inhalant dependence and Axis II border-

TABLE 2.2. *DSM–IV–TR* Multiaxial Report: Axis II Descending
Order with Principal Diagnosis Example

Axis I:	305.00	Alcohol Abuse
Axis II:	301.7	Antisocial Personality Disorder (Principal Diagnosis)
Axis III:	None	
Axis IV:	Job termination with pending incarceration	
Axis V:	GAF = 65 (Current)	

Table 2.3. *DSM–IV–TR* Multiaxial Report: No Axis I Diagnosis and
Axis II Principal Diagnosis Example

Axis I:	V71.06	No Diagnosis or Condition on Axis I
Axis II:	301.83	Borderline Personality Disorder (Principal Diagnosis)
Axis III:	967.00	Barbiturates Overdose
Axis IV:	Unemployment	
Axis V:	GAF = 68 (highest level past year)	
	GAF = 55 (lowest level past year)	

line personality disorders would be noted as "dually diagnosed" or fulfilling a dual diagnosis. In recent years, there have been increased efforts to provide more "seamless" mental health and addictions treatment services to such dually diagnosed clients—especially via systems of care philosophy and wraparound services treatments (Adams & Juhnke, 2001; Juhnke & Liles 2000; VanDenBerg & Grealish, 1996).

Previous to these dual diagnosis and seamless mental health services emphases, clients' presenting symptomatologies were compartmentalized as being either mental health or addictions specific. There was little unified effort to address the symbiotic relationship among the comorbid substance-related and other mental health disorder symptomatologies. Therefore, clients most often were treated separately by different mental health and addictions counselors. Many times no interactions occurred between the individual service providers and their agencies. Hence, clients fell between treatment gaps, because mental health counselors working within mental health treatment agencies were neither licensed nor reimbursed for addictions treatment. The reverse was true for addictions counselors. Often they wanted to provide treatment for comorbid depression, anxiety, or other mental health disorders, but were not allowed due to license limitations, reimbursement issues, or agency restrictions.

Thus, the intent of today's more seamless counseling emphasis is to address all client needs via a unified treatment body of collaborating specialists. The importance of such seamless counseling, the need for specialized services for dually diagnosed clients, and the gravity of accurate *DSM–IV–TR* diagnoses is clearly apparent in a previously used example. Here, the noted depressed female client began using alcohol and marijuana as a means to cope with her depressed symptomatology. This symptomatology initially resulted from her job termination. One would be foolish to treat this client's depression and psychoactive substance abuse separately. Each is tied to the other, and a symbiotic relationship among the three likely exists. Thus, the *DSM–IV–TR* Multiaxial System and accurate diagnoses provide vital information to addictions counselor as they generate diagnoses relevant to treatment goals and implement integrated interventions.

SUBSTANCE-RELATED DISORDERS

Approximately 124 Axis I substance-related disorders are contained within the *DSM–IV–TR* (APA, 2000, pp. 857–859, 863). Substance-related disorders range in frequency from those commonly presented (e.g., alcohol abuse) to those less frequently identified as troublesome (e.g., caffeine-related disorder NOS). Substance-related disorders are split into two separate categories (APA, 2000, p. 191). The first category is substance use disorders. These disorders generally describe maladaptive and dysfunctional psychoactive substance use patterns. The second category relates more specifically to behavioral, psychological, and cognitive changes occurring as a result of maladaptive psychoactive substance use.

Common Axis I Substance Use Disorders

Substance-related disorders use two generic terms. These terms are *substance abuse* (e.g., cannabis abuse, hallucinogen abuse, opioid abuse) and *substance dependence* (e.g., cocaine dependence, alcohol dependence, inhalant dependence). Counselors using the *DSM–IV–TR* apply the most relevant term (i.e., abuse or dependence) to a specific psychoactive substance (e.g., marijuana, alcohol). Thus, the appropriate term abuse or dependence is joined with the specific psychoactive substance classification category to which the client is abusing or dependent (e.g., marijuana abuse, alcohol dependence).

Substance Dependence Diagnoses

Substance dependence indicates persistent substance use despite occurring and reoccurring substance-related problems (APA, 2000, pp. 192–198). This persistent use pattern may also be associated with: (a) physical tolerance to the substance, manifest by the need to ingest or use increasing substance amounts to achieve a desired effect; (b) withdrawal symptomatology, where substance-dependent persons experience physical tremors, shaking, nausea, or vomiting, when the substance is not used or is used in a quantity that does not meet the substance-dependent persons' required use threshold, and (c) compulsive substance-using behaviors. The subjective desire to use a substance, otherwise known as "craving," is not required as a diagnosis criterion (APA). However, it is important to note that cravings typically accompany substance dependence diagnoses (APA, 2000, p. 192).

Although the *DSM–IV–TR* excludes caffeine from its list of dependent substances (APA, 2000), a substance dependence diagnosis can generally be applied across substances (e.g., alcohol, cocaine, nicotine, etc.). To qualify for a substance dependence diagnosis, three or more substance dependence criteria (see Table 2.4) must have been present within the preceding 12 months (APA).

Substance Dependence Specifiers

Either of two specifiers accompanies a substance dependence diagnosis. These specifiers include *with physiological dependence*, and *without physiological dependence* (APA, 2000, p. 195). As noted in Table 2.4, *with physiological dependence* is associated with tolerance or withdrawal symptomatology, whereas, *without physiological dependence* is unaccompanied by tolerance or withdrawal

TABLE 2.4. *DSM–IV–TR* (APA, 2000, pp. 197–198) Substance Dependence Criteria

A maladaptive pattern of substance use, leading to clinically significant impairment or distress, as manifested by three (or more) of the following, occurring at any time in the same 12-month period:

(1) tolerance, as defined by either of the following:
    (a) a need for markedly increased amounts of the substance to achieve intoxication or desired effect
    (b) markedly diminished effect with continued use of the same amount of the substance

(2) withdrawal, as manifested by either of the following:
    (a) the characteristic withdrawal syndrome for the substance (refer to Criteria A and B of the criteria sets for Withdrawal from the specific substances)
    (b) the same (or closely related) substance is taken to relieve or avoid withdrawal symptoms

(3) the substance is often taken in larger amounts or over a longer period than was intended

(4) there is a persistent desire or unsuccessful efforts to cut down or control substance use

(5) a great deal of time is spent in activities necessary to obtain the substance (e.g., visiting multiple doctors or driving long distances), use the substance (e.g., chain-smoking), or recover from its effects

(6) important social, occupational, or recreational activities are given up or reduced because of substance use

(7) the substance use is continued despite knowledge of having a persistent or recurrent physical or psychological problem that is likely to have been caused or exacerbated by the substance (e.g., current cocaine use despite recognition of cocaine-induced depression, or continued drinking despite recognition that an ulcer was made worse by alcohol consumption)

Specify if:

    With Physiological Dependence: evidence of tolerance or withdrawal (i.e., either Item 1 or 2 is present)
    Without Physiological Dependence: no evidence of tolerance or withdrawal (i.e., neither Item 1 or 2 is present)
    Course specifiers (see text for definitions):
    Early Full Remission
    Early Partial Remission
    Sustained Full Remission
    Sustained Partial Remission
    On Agonist Therapy
    In a Controlled Environment

symptomatology. It should be noted, however, that a compulsive desire for and behavior toward substance use might be present even when one does not have physiological dependence. This is often noted as Psychological Dependence, but is usually not noted within a multiaxial *DSM–IV–TR* report.

Other *DSM–IV–TR* course specifiers are also included in substance dependence diagnoses. These specifiers define abstinence length and may be used to more clearly portray the client's abstinence period—including factors that may have contributed to abstinence, such as controlled environments (e.g., incarceration, inpatient units) and agonist therapy (e.g., Antabuse). Course specifiers can be particularly useful when counselors are attempting to determine their clients' substance use improvements or decompensation. Four course specifiers are outlined here (APA, 2000, pp. 196–197):

> *Early Full Remission.* This specifier indicates the client has been free of any Substance Dependence or abuse diagnosis criteria for at least 1 month, but for less than 12 months.
>
> *Early Partial Remission.* Here, the client has met one or more Substance Dependence or Substance Abuse Diagnosis criteria for at least 1 month, but less than 12 months. However, the client has not met all criteria for a dependence or abuse diagnosis.
>
> *Sustained Full Remission.* If criteria for dependence or abuse have not been met for a period of 12 months or longer, this course specifier is applied.
>
> *Sustained Partial Remission.* If one or more criteria for dependence or abuse have been met for a period of 12 months or longer, but all criteria for dependence or abuse have not been met, then the using client can be described as in sustained partial remission (APA, 2000, p. 196).

For diagnostic purposes, if a client is engaged in agonist therapy or placed within a controlled environment, then the first four course specifiers just outlined may only be applied once the agonist therapy or controlled environment is no longer present (APA, 2000, p. 197).

Substance Abuse Diagnosis

The central corresponding theme within a substance abuse diagnosis is a maladaptive substance use pattern associated with occurring and reoccurring distressing consequences (Table 2.5). For instance, there may be significant failure to fulfill social and interpersonal obligations (e.g., home responsibilities, school attendance, job performance, etc.) or equally significant legal difficulties (e.g., DUI charges). Criteria for the substance abuse diagnosis must have occurred during the preceding 12 months. However, a substance abuse diagnosis would not include tolerance or withdrawal symptomatology, nor would there necessarily be any evidence of compulsive substance-using behaviors.

When assessing clients for substance abuse, it is important to note that a

TABLE 2.5. *DSM–IV–TR* (APA, 2000, p. 199) Substance Abuse Criteria

A. A maladaptive pattern of substance use leading to clinically significant impairment or distress, as manifested by one or more of the following, occurring within a 12-month period:

    (1) recurrent substance use resulting in a failure to fulfill major role obligations at work, school, or home (e.g., repeated absences or poor work performance related to substance use; substance-related absences, suspensions, or expulsions from school; neglect of children or household)

    (2) recurrent substance use in situations in which it is physically hazardous (e.g., driving an automobile or operating a machine when impaired by substance use)

    (3) recurrent substance-related legal problems (e.g., arrests for substance-related disorderly conduct)

    (4) continued substance use despite having persistent or recurrent social or interpersonal problems caused or exacerbated by the effects of the substance (e.g., arguments with spouse about consequences of intoxication, physical fights)

B. The symptoms have never met the criteria for Substance Dependence for this class of substance.

substance dependence diagnosis preempts the substance abuse diagnosis. Therefore, clients having the more severe *DSM–IV–TR* substance dependence diagnosis (e.g., alcohol dependence) cannot concurrently have the less severe substance abuse diagnosis (e.g., alcohol abuse). In other words, the more severe substance dependence diagnosis supersedes the less severe substance abuse diagnosis.

One additional point regarding general substance abuse diagnoses: It is important to note that neither caffeine nor nicotine is included among the list of substances typically associated with a substance dependence diagnosis (APA, 2000, pp. 199–200). Thus, persons cannot receive a substance dependence diagnosis to either of these psychoactive substance classification categories.

Polysubstance Dependence Diagnosis

One caveat to the generic dependence term is noteworthy. Should clients repeatedly use psychoactive substances from at least three different drug classification categories other than caffeine and nicotine (i.e., alcohol, amphetamines, cannabis, cocaine, hallucinogens, inhalants, opioids, phencyclidine, or sedative, hypnotics, or anxiolytics) within a 12-month period, with no single substance predominating, they may qualify for a polysubstance dependence diagnosis (APA, 2000, p. 293). To secure this diagnosis, clients must meet the substance dependence diagnosis criteria for "substances as a group but not for any specific substance" (p. 293). Hence, instead of indicating substance dependence disorder diagnoses for three or more drug classifications (e.g., alcohol, amphetamines, cannabis, etc.), the single polysubstance dependence diagnosis is given.

Common Substance-Induced Disorders

Substance-induced disorders are noted behavioral, psychological, and cognitive changes resulting from psychoactive substance use (i.e., substance use disorders) (APA, 2000, pp. 191–192). These disorders include substance intoxication, substance withdrawal, substance-induced delirium, substance-induced psychotic disorder, substance-induced mood disorder, substance-induced anxiety disorder, substance-induced sexual dysfunction, and substance-induced sleep disorder (APA, 2000, pp. 191–192). Similar to the previously described manner in which the generic terms *abuse* and *dependence* are applied to a specific psychoactive substance (e.g., alcohol) within the *DSM–IV–TR* substance use disorders, the terms *intoxication* (e.g., alcohol intoxication), *withdrawal* (e.g., amphetamine withdrawal), *psychotic disorder* (e.g., phencyclidine-induced psychotic disorder), *mood disorder* (e.g., hallucinogen-induced mood disorder), *anxiety disorder* (e.g., phencyclidine-induced anxiety disorder), *sexual dysfunction* (e.g., sedative-, hypnotic-, or anxiolytic-induced sexual dysfunction), and *sleep disorder* (e.g., caffeine-induced sleep disorder) are applied. However, not all terms (e.g., intoxication, withdrawal, etc.) are utilized within each specific psychoactive substance classification category. For example, no *DSM–IV–TR* diagnoses are used to indicate nicotine intoxication or caffeine withdrawal. Concomitantly, given the different psychoactive substances effects, withdrawal criteria may differ from one psychoactive substance to another. An example of this is alcohol withdrawal vis à vis amphetamine withdrawal. Here, criteria related to alcohol withdrawal may include autonomic hyperactivity (e.g., sweating or pulse rate above 100) (APA, p. 216), whereas amphetamine withdrawal may include different criteria such as dysphoric mood or increased appetite (p. 228).

SUBSTANCE INTOXICATION

Three essential criteria are necessary to establish a *DSM–IV–TR* substance intoxication disorder diagnosis (APA, 2000). The first criterion is the development of a reversible substance-specific syndrome due to the recent ingestion of (or exposure to) a substance (p. 199). To fulfill this first criterion, the noted syndrome will be reversed and disappear once the substance is metabolized and completely eliminated from clients' systems. Thus, psychoactive substances effects of "disturbances of perception, wakefulness, attention, thinking, judgment, psychomotor behavior, and interpersonal behavior" (p. 200) will disappear once the clients' systems are void of the ingested psychoactive substances.

The second criteria relates to "clinically significant maladaptive behavioral or psychological changes associated with intoxication . . . due to the direct physiological effects of the substance on the central nervous system and develop during or shortly after use of the substance" (p. 200). Thus, clients who present for services after ingesting a psychoactive substance, such as alcohol, and behave belligerently and whose affects are depressed may fulfill this second criterion.

However, their belligerent behaviors and depressed affects must be a direct result of psychoactive substance ingestion. Therefore, it is important to learn whether or not these persons typically behave belligerently and demonstrate depressed affects when not under psychoactive substance influence. Should their belligerent behaviors and depressed affects be eliminated once the alcohol is metabolized and eliminated from their systems, the second criterion for substance intoxication is met. However, should their belligerence and depression continue even after the alcohol has been eliminated from their bodies, and should family members and acquaintances indicate that the clients typically are belligerent and depressed—even when no psychoactive substances have been ingested—this second criterion will not have been adequately demonstrated.

The third and final criterion for substance intoxication indicates "The symptoms are not due to a general medical condition and are not better accounted for by another mental disorder" (APA, 2000, p. 201). In other words, if the client's symptoms are the result of factors other than the substances taken, the final criterion is not fulfilled. An example of this might be a diabetic perceived by others as being intoxicated, yet who has not ingested any psychoactive substance. Here, the diabetic's misperceived symptoms resembling alcohol intoxication (e.g., slurred speech, memory impairment, etc.) are a result of internal physiological factors, which have nothing to do with ingested psychoactive substances.

Securing histories from friends, acquaintances, and family members can help the counselor more accurately determine whether the client's presenting symptomatology is substance induced or whether such mimicking symptomatology stems from other causes. Persons bringing clients to treatment often have a fairly accurate understanding of events leading to the clinical assessment and can provide significant details regarding the types and amounts of substances ingested. They can also provide information related to the time of ingestion. This information can be augmented by blood, urine, and/or breath analyses. Ancillary signs are often present as well. For example, metallic paint noted in and around the nose and mouth or present on clothes and hands, something often associated with inhaling paint vapors, or the smell of alcohol emanating from the client, including the smell of alcohol on her breath and clothes, provides significant clues as to the types of psychoactive substances used and their most recent use. Such informa-

---

TABLE 2.6. *DSM–IV–TR* (APA, 2000, p. 201) Substance Intoxication Criteria

A. The development of a reversible substance-specific syndrome due to recent ingestion of (or exposure to) a substance. Note: Different substances may produce similar or identical syndromes.

B. Clinically significant maladaptive behavioral or psychological changes that are due to the effect of the substance on the central nervous system (e.g., belligerence, mood lability, cognitive impairment, impaired judgment, impaired social or occupational functioning) and develop during or shortly after use of the substance.

C. The symptoms are not due to a general medical condition and are not better accounted for by another mental disorder.

tion is vital in determining whether clients fulfill substance intoxication diagnoses.

SUBSTANCE WITHDRAWAL

The primary features of substance withdrawal typically include clinically significant distress or impairment resulting from the reduction in or cessation of the use of psychoactive substances, which have been heavily used for a prolonged period. In other words, clients presenting with substance withdrawal-related symptomatology would likely demonstrate or report noxious or troublesome cognitive, behavioral, and/or physiological factors. The onset of these factors will likely be correlated to a client's reduction in or cessation of use after a long and chronic substance use history. Given the significant differences in psychoactive substance effects among major psychoactive substance classification categories (e.g., alcohol, amphetamines, cocaine, etc.), withdrawal criteria vary accordingly, and there are no withdrawal diagnoses for caffeine, cannabis hallucinogens, inhalants, or phencyclidine. It is important to note that withdrawal symptomatology is typically associated with persons fulfilling a substance dependence diagnosis, and that the most enduring withdrawal experience manifests itself as a craving to ingest previously used substances in an effort to eliminate noxious withdrawal symptoms (APA, 2000, p. 201).

The *DSM–IV–TR* describes three general substance withdrawal criteria. The first criterion is "The development of a substance specific syndrome due to the cessation of (or reduction in) substance use, which has been heavy and prolonged" (APA, 2000, p. 202). Here, the emphasis is on the cessation of or reduction in heavy and prolonged substance use. Clients experiencing the first substance withdrawal criterion will generally present long-term psychoactive substance use and identify withdrawal symptomatology occurring after either discontinuing or reducing the quantity or frequency of substance use. The second *DSM–IV–TR* substance withdrawal criterion states, "The substance-specific syndrome causes clinically significant distress or impairment in social, occupational, or other important areas of functioning." (p. 202). Therefore, clients will report that their withdrawal symptoms disrupt or debilitate at least one important life area. These areas could be with their partners, friends, or related to adequate functioning at work or school. Finally, the third criterion states, "The symptoms are not due to a general medical condition and are not better accounted for by another mental disorder" (p. 202). This final criterion merely reflects the need to insure that symptomatology is the direct result of substance withdrawal vis-à-vis other medical, social, or environmental factors (Table 2.7).

SUBSTANCE-INDUCED INTOXICATION DELIRIUM

The *DSM–IV–TR* denotes 10 different psychoactive substance group classifications, which have separate intoxication delirium diagnoses. These include: (a) alcohol, (b) amphetamines, (c) cannabis, (d) cocaine, (e) hallucinogens, (f) inhalants, (g) opioids, (h) phencyclidine, (i) sedatives, hypnotics, or anxiolytics, and

TABLE 2.7. *DSM–IV–TR* (APA, 2000, p. 202) Substance Withdrawal Criteria

A. The development of a substance-specific syndrome due to the cessation of (or reduction in) substance use that has been heavy and prolonged.
B. The substance-specific syndrome causes clinically significant distress or impairment in social, occupational, or other important areas of functioning.
C. The symptoms are not due to a general medical condition and are not better accounted for by another mental disorder.

(j) other [or unknown] substance (APA, 2000, p. 193). These diagnoses indicate that clients have experienced disturbances of consciousness and changes in their cognitions resulting from specific substance use (e.g., hallucinogen intoxication delirium). Such disturbances typically develop within a short time period, often within hours or days, and manifest themselves in a number of ways. These include, but are not limited to, a reduction in environmental clarity (e.g., bewilderment, disorientation, or confusion regarding the interactions occurring within the immediate environment), short-term memory impairment (e.g., an inability to recall items read from a list), language disturbance (especially, dysnomia [impaired ability to name objects] and dysgraphia [impaired ability to write]), problems focusing on immediate interpersonal interactions or communications, and an inability to "focus, sustain, or shift attention" (p. 136). Additionally, some may present with rambling, pressured speech, or incoherence (p. 137).

Perceptual disturbances may also manifest themselves. Thus, clients diag-

TABLE 2.8. *DSM–IV–TR* (APA, 2000, p. 145) Substance Intoxication
Delirium Criteria

A. Disturbance of consciousness (i.e., reduced clarity of awareness of the environment) with reduced ability to focus, sustain, or shift attention.
B. A change in cognition (such as memory deficit, disorientation, language disturbance) or the development of a perceptual disturbance that is not better accounted for by a preexisting, established, or evolving dementia.
C. The disturbance develops over a short period of time (usually hours to days) and tends to fluctuate during the course of the day.
D. There is evidence from the history, physical examination, or laboratory findings of either (1) or (2):
(1) the symptoms in Criteria A and B developed during Substance Intoxication
(2) medication use is etiologically related to the disturbance*

Note: This diagnosis should be made instead of a diagnosis of substance intoxication only when the cognitive symptoms are in excess of those usually associated with the intoxication syndrome and when the symptoms are sufficiently severe to warrant independent clinical attention.

*Note: The diagnosis should be recorded as Substance-Induced Delirium if related to medication use.

Code [Specific Substance] Intoxication Delirium:

(291.0 Alcohol; 292.81 Amphetamine [or Amphetamine-Like Substance]; 292.81 Cannabis; 292.81 Cocaine; 292.81 Hallucinogen; 292.81 Inhalant; 292.81 Opioid; 292.81 Phencyclidine [or Phencyclidine-Like Substance]; 292.81 Sedative, Hypnotic, or Anxiolytic; 292.81 Other [or Unknown] Substance [e.g., cimetidine, digitalis, benztropine])

nosed with substance-induced intoxication deliriums may experience hallucinations where clients see people's faces looking at them from behind windows, or may make misinterpretations of environmental stimuli. Here, for example, they may hear actual human voices from the next room and misinterpret these voices as being God's attempt to converse with them. Table 2.8 indicates specific substance-induced intoxication delirium criteria.

SUBSTANCE-INDUCED PSYCHOTIC DISORDER

Ten different psychoactive substance classification categories qualify for the substance-induced psychotic diagnosis within the *DSM–IV–TR* and include: (a) alcohol, (b) amphetamines, (c) cannabis, (d) cocaine, (e) hallucinogens, (f) inhalants, (g) opioids, (h) phencyclidine, (I) sedatives, hypnotics, or anxiolytics, and (j) other [or unknown] substances (APA, 2000, p. 193). Clients qualifying for one of these diagnoses experience prominent hallucinations or delusions, which are directly attributed to psychoactive substances. These diagnoses are different from other psychotic disorders, because they are substance-induced. Therefore, they only occur when clients are either using or withdrawing from psychoactive substances (pp. 338–339). Given that withdrawal from some psychoactive substances can be lengthy, persons qualifying for these diagnoses may experience psychotic symptomatology up to 4 weeks after substance discontinuance (p. 339). It is important to note that these diagnoses require evidence to support the position that the psychotic symptomatology is substance induced. Thus, clients' self-reports, psychosocial histories, physical examinations, or laboratory findings must support either substance intoxication or withdrawal diagnoses (p. 338) (Table 2.9).

Substance-Induced Psychotic Disorders Subtypes and Specifiers. One of two subtypes must be noted with substance-induced psychotic disorders (APA, 2000, p. 339). These include *with delusions* or *with hallucinations*. Here, the predominant symptom is used. For example, if clients predominantly experienced delusions (e.g., the number of delusions was greater than the number of hallucinations), they would receive the subtype *with delusions* or vice versa. Additionally, one of two specifiers is required (i.e., *with onset during intoxication* or *with onset during withdrawal*) (p. 339). Basically, these specifiers indicate when the psychotic symptoms occurred. Thus, counselors use specifiers to note that delusions or hallucinations were predominately experienced during the intoxication or withdrawal phase.

Table 2.9 indicates specific substance-induced psychotic disorders with their subtypes and specifiers.

SUBSTANCE-INDUCED MOOD DISORDER

The substance-induced mood disorder diagnosis is given when clients present with a prominent and persistent mood disturbance directly resulting from recent or long-term psychoactive substance use (APA, 2000, p. 405). Clients exposed to toxins may also qualify for a substance-induced mood disorder, if it is determined that such toxin exposure has induced the mood disorder. Substance-induced mood

TABLE 2.9. *DSM–IV–TR* (APA, 2000, pp. 342–343) Substance-Induced
Psychotic Disorder Criteria

A. Prominent hallucinations or delusions. Note: Do not include hallucinations if the person has insight that they are substance induced.
B. There is evidence from the history, physical examination, or laboratory findings of either (1) or (2):
   (1) the symptoms in Criterion A developed during, or within a month of, Substance Intoxication or Withdrawal
   (2) medication use is etiologically related to the disturbance
C. The disturbance is not better accounted for by a Psychotic Disorder that is not substance induced. Evidence that the symptoms are better accounted for by a Psychotic Disorder that is not substance induced might include the following: the symptoms precede the onset of the substance use (or medication use); the symptoms persist for a substantial period of time (e.g., about a month) after the cessation of acute withdrawal or severe intoxication, or are substantially in excess of what would be expected given the type or amount of the substance used or the duration of use; or there is other evidence that suggests the existence of an independent non-substance-induced Psychotic Disorder (e.g., a history of recurrent non-substance-related episodes).
D. The disturbance does not occur exclusively during the course of a delirium.

Note: This diagnosis should be made instead of a diagnosis of Substance Intoxication or Substance Withdrawal only when the symptoms are in excess of those usually associated with the intoxication or withdrawal syndrome and when the symptoms are sufficiently severe to warrant independent clinical attention.

Code [Specific Substance]-Induced Psychotic Disorder:

(291.5 Alcohol, With Delusions; 291.3 Alcohol, With Hallucinations; 292.11 Amphetamine [or Amphetamine-Like Substance], With Delusions; 292.12 Amphetamine [or Amphetamine-Like Substance], With Hallucinations; 292.11 Cannabis, With Delusions; 292.12 Cannabis, With Hallucinations; 292.11 Cocaine, With Delusions; 292.12 Cocaine, With Hallucinations; 292.11 Hallucinogen, With Delusions; 292.12 Hallucinogen, With Hallucinations; 292.11 Inhalant, With Delusions; 292. Inhalant, With Hallucinations; 292.11 Opioid, With Delusions; 292.12 Opioid, With Hallucinations; 292.11 Phencyclidine [or Phencyclidine-Like Substance] With Delusions; 292.12 Phencyclidine [or Phencyclidine-Like Substance], With Hallucinations; 292.11 Sedative, Hypnotic, or Anxiolytic, With Delusions; 292.12 Sedative, Hypnotic, or Anxiolytic, With Hallucinations; 292.11 Other [or Unknown] Substance, With Delusions; 292.12 Other [or Unknown} Substance, With Hallucinations)

Specify

   With Onset During Intoxication: if criteria are met for Intoxication with the substance and the symptoms develop during the intoxication syndrome
   With Onset During Withdrawal: if criteria are met for Withdrawal from the substance and the symptoms develop during, or shortly after, a withdrawal syndrome

disorder symptomatology can only occur during intoxication or withdrawal (p. 405). Furthermore, it should be noted that mood disturbance symptomatology might occur up to 4 weeks after psychoactive substance abstinence. Such symptomatology may include "depressed mood or markedly diminished interest or pleasure or elevated, expansive, or irritable mood" (p. 405).

A substance-induced mood disorder may resemble other diagnoses such as

major depressive, manic, mixed, or hypomanic episode (APA, 2000, p. 405). However, all criteria for the major depressive episode need not be fulfilled, and the
distinguishing feature will be that the substance-induced mood disorder symptomatology results from psychoactive substance or toxin exposure (Table 2.10).

TABLE 2.10. *DSM–IV–TR* (APA, 2000, p. 409) Substance-Induced Mood
Disorder Criteria

A. A prominent and persistent disturbance in mood predominates in the clinical picture
    and is characterized by either (or both) of the following:
    (1) depressed mood or markedly diminished interest or pleasure in all, or almost all,
         activities
    (2) elevated, expansive, or irritable mood
B. There is evidence from the history, physical examination, or laboratory findings of
    either (1) or (2):
    (1) the symptoms in Criterion A developed during, or within a month of, Substance
         Intoxication or Withdrawal
    (2) medication use is etiologically related to the disturbance
C. The disturbance is not better accounted for by a Mood Disorder that is not substance
    induced. Evidence that the symptoms are better accounted for by a Mood Disorder
    that is not substance induced might include the following: the symptoms precede the
    onset of the substance use (or medication use); the symptoms persist for a substantial
    period of time (e.g., about a month) after the cessation of acute withdrawal or severe
    intoxication or are substantially in excess of what would be expected given the type or
    amount of the substance used or the duration of use; or there is other evidence that
    suggests the existence of an independent non-substance-induced Mood Disorder (e g ,
    a history of recurrent Major Depressive Episodes).
D   The disturbance does not occur exclusively during the course of a delirium.
E. The symptoms cause clinically significant distress or impairment in social, occupa-
    tional, or other important areas of functioning.

Note: This diagnosis should be made instead of a diagnosis of Substance Intoxication or Substance
Withdrawal only when the mood symptoms are in excess of those usually associated with the intoxication or withdrawal syndrome and when the symptoms are sufficiently severe to warrant independent clinical attention.

Code [Specific Substance]-Induced Mood Disorder:

(291.8 Alcohol; 292.84 Amphetamine [or Amphetamine-Like Substance]; 292.84 Cocaine; 292.84 Hallucinogen; 292.84 Inhalant; 292.84 Opioid; 292.84 Phencyclidine [or
Phencyclidine-Like substance]; 292.84 Sedative, Hypnotic, or Anxiolytic; 292.84 Other
[or Unknown] Substance)

Specify Type:

   With Depressive Features: if the predominant mood is depressed
   With Manic Features: if the predominant mood is elevated, euphoric, or irritable
   With Mixed Features: if symptoms of both mania and depression are present and nei-
      ther predominates

Specify if:

   With Onset During Intoxication: If the criteria are met for Intoxication with the sub-
      stance and the symptoms develop during the intoxication syndrome
   With Onset During Withdrawal: if criteria are met for withdrawal from the substance
      and the symptoms develop during, or shortly after, a withdrawal syndrome

Substance-Induced Mood Disorder Subtypes and Specifiers.   Three substance-induced mood disorder subtypes are noted. Each indicates that specific features predominant (i.e., depressive, manic, or mixed features). The first of these subtypes is *with depressive features* and notes that the predominant mood exhibited by the client is depressive (APA, 2000, p. 406). Thus, these persons may report feeling, sad, blue, discouraged, depressed or hopeless (p. 409).[4] *With depressive features* may also be noted by clients as an inability to feel or a lack of caring about the present or future (pp. 406–410). Discontinued social or hobby-related activities may also be noted with this feature, as well as low energy or fatigue, and an inability to concentrate (pp. 406–410).

With *manic features* is another subtype. Here, the predominant mood is elevated, euphoric, or irritable (APA, 2000, p. 406). Thus, clients presenting with this feature may demonstrate psychomotor agitation and report exaggerated feelings of happiness or bliss, unwarranted optimism, decreased need for sleep, or increased goal-directed behaviors (p. 357). They may also be loquacious and demonstrate pressured speech, or, if irritable, may demonstrate angry outbursts, openly communicated hostility, or angry tirades (p. 358).

The final subtype is *with mixed features*. This feature denotes both depressive and manic features and indicates that neither the depressive or manic features dominate (APA, 2000, p. 409). Here, for example, clients may demonstrate significant psychomotor agitation and excessive talking while concomitantly reporting feelings of excessive discouragement and hopelessness.

Four psychoactive substance classification categories have specifiers. These include alcohol, amphetamines, cocaine, and sedatives, hypnotics, or anxiolytics. Specifiers for these psychoactive substance classification categories are used to indicate whether the onset of symptomatology began during intoxication or withdrawal. The specifier *with onset during intoxication* indicates that the substance-induced mood disorder's genesis developed during the intoxication syndrome (APA, 2000, p. 409). Conversely, the specifier *with onset during withdrawal* denotes symptomatology developing during or shortly after the withdrawal syndrome (p. 409).

SUBSTANCE-INDUCED ANXIETY DISORDER

Ten psychoactive substance classification categories denote the substance-induced anxiety disorder (APA, 2000, p. 193). These categories include alcohol, amphetamines, caffeine, cannabis, cocaine, hallucinogens, inhalants, phencyclidine, sedatives, hypnotics, or anxiolytics, and other [or unknown] substance. The prominent feature of this disorder is anxiety symptomatology directly attributed to psychoactive substances, including medications and toxins. Such symptomatology includes panic attacks, phobias, and obsessions or compulsions. As is the case with

---

4. Hopeless feelings are strongly correlated with suicidal behaviors. Thus, clients indicating hopeless feelings should be assessed for immediate suicide risk and appropriate interventions should be initiated to insure safety.

substance-induced mood disorder, substance-induced anxiety disorder symptomatology must occur during either intoxication or withdrawal (p. 480) and may resemble other disorders (e.g., panic disorder, generalized anxiety disorder, etc.). However, complete criteria fulfillment of these other disorders is not required. Likewise, symptomatology may develop within 4 weeks of substance intoxication or withdrawal (p. 480) and the symptomatology should not be better accounted for by another more accurate diagnosis (e.g., agoraphobia, generalized anxiety disorder, posttraumatic stress disorder, etc.). Furthermore, a substance-induced anxiety disorder diagnosis should not be made if the anxiety symptomatology only occurs during delirium (p. 480). Concomitantly, the symptomatology must be noted as problematic for the client (p. 480) (Table 2.11).

Substance-Induced Anxiety Disorder Specifiers. Six specifiers are noted under the substance-induced anxiety disorder (APA, 2000, p. 483). These include: (a) *with generalized anxiety*, (b) *with panic attacks*, (c) *with obsessive–compulsive symptoms*, (d) *with phobic symptoms*, (e) *with onset during intoxication*, and (f) *with onset during withdrawal*. The first four of these specifiers indicate the predominate symptomatology, whereas the last two describe the anxiety's genesis. Each is described in greater detail next.

The specifier *with generalized anxiety* indicates excessive anxiety and worry. Here, clients find their anxiety and worry difficult to control and problematic. Key features often include restlessness, being easily fatigued, difficulty concentrating, and sleep disturbance (APA, 2000, p. 472). Often persons experiencing this specifier will experience worry related to routine life circumstances and the worry circumstance is perceived by clients as far more likely to occur than the actual probability of occurrence (p. 473). Concomitantly, the feared impact of the event is significantly greater than the actual impact would likely be (p. 473). An example of such generalized anxiety might be an undergraduate student who has successfully passed all of her courses with a 4.0 grade point average and is worried beyond what typically is expected among college students that she will not graduate because of some unknown yet lurking concern. Furthermore, the student notes that when this unknown concern occurs, it will end her college career, and she will be unable to either complete her degree or find anything other than unacceptable, low-paying jobs in which she would be unable to experience any form of contentment.

The second specifier is *with panic attacks*. Here the chief presenting clinical concern resulting from the substance-induced disorder is a sudden onset of intense fear (APA, 2000, p. 431). When panic attacks are experienced, persons sense imminent danger and often sense they are dying, losing control, or having a stroke (p. 394). Many times those experiencing panic attacks note an urgent desire to flee or attempt escaping the immediate situation that they are experiencing (p. 431).

With obsessive–compulsive symptoms is the specifier that indicates clients are predominately experiencing obsessions or compulsions resulting from the disorder. Thus, the person is: (a) having intrusive, anxiety-provoking thoughts, im-

TABLE 2.11. *DSM–IV–TR* (APA, 2000, p. 483) Substance-Induced Anxiety
Disorder Criteria

A. Prominent anxiety, Panic Attacks, or obsessions or compulsions predominate in the
clinical picture.
B. There is evidence from the history, physical examination, or laboratory findings of
either (1) or (2):
  (1) the symptoms in Criterion A developed during, or within one month of, Substance
      Intoxication or Withdrawal
  (2) medication use is etiologically related to the disturbance
C. The disturbance is not better accounted for by an Anxiety Disorder that is not substance induced. Evidence that the symptoms are better accounted for by an Anxiety
Disorder that is not substance induced might include the following: the symptoms
precede the onset of the substance use (or medication use); the symptoms persist for a
substantial period of time (e.g., about a month) after the cessation of acute withdrawal
or severe intoxication or are substantially in excess of what would be expected given
the type or amount of the substance used or the duration of use; or there is other
evidence suggesting the existence or an independent non-substance-induced Anxiety
Disorder (e.g., a history of recurrent non-substance-related episodes).
D. The disturbance does not occur exclusively during the course of a delirium.
E. The disturbance causes clinically significant distress or impairment in social, occupational, or other important areas of functioning.

Note: This diagnosis should be made instead of a diagnosis of Substance Intoxication or Substance
Withdrawal only when the anxiety symptoms are in excess of those usually associated with the
intoxication or withdrawal syndrome and when the anxiety symptoms are sufficiently severe to warrant independent clinical attention.

Code [Specific Substance]-Induced Anxiety Disorder

(291.8 Alcohol; 292.89 Amphetamine (or Amphetamine-Like Substance); 292.89 Caf-
feine; 292.89 Cannabis; 292.89 Cocaine; 292.89 Hallucinogen; 292.89 Inhalant; 292.89
Phencyclidine (or Phencyclidine-Like Substance); 292.89 Sedative, Hypnotic, or
Anxiolytic; 292.89 Other [or Unknown] Substance)

Specify if:

  With Generalized Anxiety: if excessive anxiety or worry about a number of events or
      activities predominates in the clinical presentation
  With Panic Attacks: if Panic Attacks predominate in the clinical picture
  With Obsessive-Compulsive Symptoms: if obsessions or compulsions predominate in
      the clinical presentation
  With Phobic Symptoms: if phobic symptoms predominate in the clinical presentation

Specify if:

  With Onset During Intoxication: if the criteria are met for Intoxication with the sub-
      stance and the symptoms develop during the intoxication syndrome
  With Onset During Withdrawal: if criteria are met for Withdrawal from the substance
      and the symptoms develop during, or shortly after, a withdrawal syndrome

ages, or impulses which are reoccurring, persistent, and based on something other
than normal, excessive worries regarding "real-life" concerns, and/or (b) demon-
strating repetitive behaviors (e.g., rechecking a radio to make certain it is turned
off) or mental acts (e.g., silently saying words which begin with the letter "a")
separate from and unrelated to a dreaded event, in an effort to inhibit the dreaded
event from occurring (APA, 2000, p. 456).

The specifier *with phobic symptoms* is used when phobic symptomatology is the chief concern resulting from the substance-induced anxiety disorder. This specifier indicates clients are fearful of objects (e.g., razors) or situations (e.g., riding in city buses), attempt to avoid such objects or situations, and the anxiety related to encountering such objects or situations intrudes on their daily living, occupational functioning, or social life (p. 444). Additionally, it should be noted that the diagnoses should not be better documented by another *DSM–IV–TR* diagnosis (p. 443). Often clients' anxiety levels increase as they move closer to the noted object or begin engaging in the situation (p. 444).

With onset during intoxication indicates that substance-induced anxiety's onset developed during the intoxication syndrome (APA, 2000, p. 483). In other words, the anxious symptomatology was initiated during intoxication. *With onset during withdrawal,* however, notes that the anxious symptomatology developed during or shortly after (i.e., within 4 weeks) the withdrawal syndrome (p. 483).

SUBSTANCE-INDUCED SEXUAL DYSFUNCTION

The key substance-induced sexual dysfunction feature is "a clinically significant sexual dysfunction that results in marked distress or interpersonal difficulty" (APA, 2000, p. 562). Such dysfunction may include impaired sexual desire, arousal, or orgasm, or sexual pain, and must be determined as resulting from psychoactive substance use or toxin exposure (p. 562). Thus, through clinical interviews, physical examinations, and laboratory findings, counselors must determine that either substance use or toxins have engendered the sexual dysfunction. Addictions counselors should remember that illicit psychoactive substances as well as prescribed medications often impact sexual functioning. Therefore, clients using prescribed medications and reporting sexual dysfunction resulting from psychoactive substance use qualify for this diagnosis. As with other diagnoses, the substance-induced sexual dysfunction diagnosis should be used only when another *DSM–IV–TR* diagnoses does not better account for the presenting symptomatology. Counselors can state on the Multiaxial Assessment *with onset during intoxication* (p. 562) to note that the clients' reported substance-induced sexual dysfunctions occur when they are under psychoactive substance influence (Table 9.12).

Substance-Induced Sexual Dysfunction Specifiers. One of four specifiers is used when making the substance-induced sexual dysfunction diagnosis. Each specifier provides enhanced sexual dysfunction symptom descriptions. *With impaired desire* indicates that the predominant substance-induced sexual dysfunction feature is an absence of sexual desire (APA, 2000, p. 562). Here, clients may indicate that they no longer experience a desire for sexual activity or note that they have not instigated sexual behaviors due to their lack of sexual desire. The specifier *with impaired arousal* notes that the central concern revolves around an inability to experience normal arousal responses (p. 562). This specifier is used when clients indicate that they experience things such as erectile dysfunction or impaired lubrication resulting from psychoactive substance use. The specifier *with impaired*

TABLE 2.12. *DSM–IV–TR* (APA, 2000, p. 565) Substance-Induced Sexual
Dysfunction Criteria

A. Clinically significant sexual dysfunction that results in marked distress or interpersonal difficulty predominates in the clinical picture.
B. There is evidence from the history, physical examination, or laboratory findings that the sexual dysfunction is fully explained by substance use as manifested by either (1) or (2):
    (1) the symptoms in Criterion A developed during, or within a month of, Substance Intoxication
    (2) medication use is etiologically related to the disturbance
C. The disturbance is not better accounted for by a Sexual Dysfunction that is not substance induced. Evidence that the symptoms are better accounted for by a Sexual Dysfunction that is not substance induced might include the following: the symptoms precede the onset of the substance use or dependence (or medication use); the symptoms persist for a substantial period of time (e.g., about a month) after the cessation of intoxication, or are substantially in excess of what would be expected given the type or amount of the substance used or the duration of use; or there is other evidence that suggests the existence of an independent non-substance-induced Sexual Dysfunction (e.g., a history of recurrent non-substance-related episodes).

Note: This diagnosis should be made instead of a diagnosis of Substance Intoxication only when the sexual dysfunction in excess of that usually associated with the intoxication syndrome and when the dysfunction is sufficiently severe to warrant independent clinical attention.

Code [Specific Substance]-Induced Sexual Dysfunction:

(291.8 Alcohol; 292.89 Amphetamine [or Amphetamine-Like Substance]; 292.89 Cocaine; 292.89 Opioid; 292.89 Sedative, Hypnotic, or Anxiolytic; 292.89 Other [or Unknown] Substance)

Specify if:

    With Impaired Desire
    With Impaired Arousal
    With Impaired Orgasm
    With Sexual Pain

Specify if:

    With Onset During Intoxication: if the criteria are met for Intoxication with the substance and the symptoms develop during the intoxication syndrome

---

orgasm is used when clients have an inability to experience orgasm or when orgasm is difficult to achieve due to psychoactive substance use (p. 562). *With sexual pain* is the fourth substance-induced sexual dysfunction specifier. The predominant feature of this specifier is pain associated with intercourse (p. 562).

SUBSTANCE-INDUCED SLEEP DISORDERS

This diagnosis is used when clients using psychoactive substances experience sleep disturbances severe enough to require clinical intervention (APA, 2000, p. 655). Therefore, clients will note that symptomatology affiliated with this diagnosis is severe enough to engender distress or impairment within social, occupational, or other areas of the clients' lives (p. 655). To qualify for this diagnosis, another *DSM–IV–TR* diagnosis does not more appropriately account for the presenting symptomatology. The diagnosis should not be used if the sleep disturbance occurs only during delirium (p. 655) (Table 2.13).

Substance-Induced Sleep Disorder Subtypes and Specifiers.   Four subtypes exist within this *DSM–IV–TR* diagnosis. The intent of the subtypes is to describe the type of sleep disturbance resulting from the psychoactive substance or toxin exposure. *Insomnia type* indicates that the primary complaint will revolve around issues regarding difficulties in falling asleep, maintaining sleep, or related to

TABLE 2.13. *DSM–IV–TR* (APA, 2000, pp. 660–661) Substance-Induced Sleep Disorder Criteria

A. A prominent disturbance in sleep that is sufficiently severe to warrant independent clinical attention.
B. There is evidence from the history, physical examination, or laboratory findings of either (1) or (2):
    (1) the symptoms in Criterion A developed during, or within a month of, Substance Intoxication or Withdrawal
    (2) medication use is etiologically related to the sleep disturbance
C. The disturbance is not better accounted for by a Sleep Disorder that is not substance induced. Evidence that the symptoms are better accounted for by a Sleep Disorder that is not substance induced might include the following: the symptoms persist for a substantial period of time (e.g., about a month) after the cessation of acute withdrawal or severe intoxication, or are substantially in excess of what would be expected given the type or amount of the substance used or the duration of use; or there is other evidence that suggests the existence of an independent non-substance-induced Sleep Disorder (e.g., a history of recurrent non-substance-related episodes).
D. The disturbance does not occur exclusively during the course of a delirium.
E. The sleep disturbance causes clinically significant distress or impairment in social, occupational, or other important areas of functioning.

Note: This diagnosis should be made instead of a diagnosis of Substance Intoxication or Substance Withdrawal only when the sleep symptoms are in excess of those usually associated with the intoxication or withdrawal syndrome and when the symptoms are sufficiently severe to warrant independent clinical attention.

Code [Specific Substance]-Induced Sleep Disorder:

(291.8 Alcohol; 292.89 Amphetamine; 292.89 Caffeine; 292.89 Cocaine; 292.89 Opioid; 292.89 Sedative, Hypnotic, or Anxiolytic; 292.89 Other [or Unknown] Substance)

Specify type:
    Insomnia Type: if the predominant sleep disturbance is insomnia
    Hypersomnia Type: if the predominant sleep disturbance is hypersomnia
    Parasomnia Type: if the predominant sleep disturbance is a Parasomnia
    Mixed Type: if more than one sleep disturbance is present and none predominates

Specify if:
    With Onset During Intoxication: if the criteria are met for Intoxication with the substance and the symptoms develop during the intoxication syndrome
    With Onset During Withdrawal: if criteria are met for Withdrawal from the substance and the symptoms develop during, or shortly after, a withdrawal syndrome

nonrestorative sleep (e.g., feeling as though the client has not slept) (APA, 2000, p. 656). Thus, clients presenting with this subtype typically complain that they are unable to sleep or indicate that they awaken throughout their typical sleeping time and that once awakened they are unable to sleep again. On the other end of the continuum, the *hypersomnia type* subtype indicates excessive sleepiness during regular wake hours. These clients report sleeping beyond previously normal amounts and excessive sleepiness during waking hours (p. 656). The *parasomnia type* subtype indicates that clients experience abnormal behavioral events that are associated with sleep or sleep transitions (p. 656). For example, clients could indicate the predominant complaint is substance-induced fighting or walking behaviors when asleep. The final subtype is *mixed type*. This subtype is used when the substance-induced sleep disorder has multiple types but no one subtype is predominant.

Two substance-induced sleep disorder specifiers are used. These specifiers indicate whether the sleep disorder occurs during the intoxication syndrome (*with onset during intoxication*) (APA, 2000, p. 656) or during or shortly following the withdrawal syndrome (*with onset during withdrawal*) (p. 656). Major psychoactive substance classifications which most commonly promote substance-induced sleep disorders during intoxication include: (a) alcohol, (b) amphetamine and related substances, (c) caffeine, (d) cocaine, (e) opioids, and (f) sedatives, hypnotics, and anxiolytics (pp. 656–657). Psychoactive substance classification categories that commonly induce substance-induced sleep disorder in association with withdrawal include: (a) alcohol, (b) amphetamine and related stimulants, (c) cocaine, (d) opioids, and (e) sedatives, hypnotics, and anxiolytics (p. 657). This is not to say that other psychoactive substances from other classifications cannot engender substance-induced sleep disorders in the intoxication or withdrawal syndrome. Rather, the noted correlations between psychoactive substance classifications and substance-induced sleep disorders within the intoxication and withdrawal syndromes are more typical.

Axis II Personality Disorders Commonly Occurring with Substance Related Disorders

As previously indicated, Axis II disorders reflect personality disorders or mental retardation. Given the prevalence of comorbid substance-related disorders (e.g., alcohol abuse) with three Axis II personality disorders (antisocial personality disorder [APA, 2000, p. 703], borderline personality disorder [p. 708], and narcissistic personality disorder [p. 716]), it is important for addictions counselors to understand the basic personality disorder construct and become familiar with personality disorders which frequently appear with concurrent psychoactive substance use issues. Thus, each of the three personality disorders commonly occurring with substance-related disorder diagnoses is described in greater detail next.

What Is a Personality Disorder?

The *DSM–IV–TR* (1994) indicates, "A personality disorder is an enduring pattern of inner experience and behavior that deviates markedly from the expectations of the individual's culture, is pervasive and inflexible, has an onset in adolescence or early adulthood, is stable over time, and leads to distress or impairment" (p. 685). Many times, personality disordered persons either create emotional distress for others or they experience emotional stress themselves. This is due to their maladaptive ways of behaving or their dysfunctional ways of living and experiencing life. Depending on the associated psychopathology of the personality disorder, disordered persons have a history checkered with disappointments and hardships. This is typically due to others' harsh responses to the personality disordered persons' maladaptive behaviors or their maladaptive and enduring inner experiences.

Personality disorders are separated into three distinct clusters (APA, 2000, p. 685). The first cluster includes persons who present as odd or eccentric (p. 685). This cluster includes paranoid, schizoid, and schizotypal personality disorders. Another cluster includes persons who frequently present as anxious or fearful and includes avoidant, dependent, and obsessive–compulsive personality disorders (p. 685). Many persons within these first two clusters, as well as many nonpersonality disordered persons, present with substance-use and substance-related disorders. However, the third cluster is particularly important to addictions counselors as it includes three personality disorders (antisocial, borderline, and narcissistic personality disorders to which substance-related disorders are so notably common (p. 685). This third cluster includes the antisocial, borderline, histrionic, and narcissistic personality disorders (p. 685). Persons presenting in this cluster often present as erratic, emotional, or dramatic. Although not all personality-disordered persons in this third cluster fulfill substance-use and substance-related disorders, many are substance abusing or substance dependent.

It is important to remember that persons fulfilling criteria for a substance-related disorder should not be given a personality disorder diagnosis entirely based on substance intoxication or withdrawal consequences or associated with antisocial behaviors related to gaining either money for purchasing drugs or access to drugs (e.g., robbery) (APA, 2000, pp. 688–689). Personality disorder diagnoses must be based on prominent, maladaptive features, which broadly describe the person, not just her substance-using or substance-seeking behaviors.

ANTISOCIAL PERSONALITY DISORDER

Those qualifying for antisocial personality disorder have an enduring pattern and history of violating and disregarding others' rights (APA, 2000, p. 701). Onset of these patterns begins in childhood or early adolescence (p. 701). Many times the initial childhood or early adolescence behaviors will demonstrate a disregard for societal norms or rules (p. 702) and evidence of a conduct disorder[5] existed prior

---

5. The *DSM–IV–TR* conduct disorder diagnosis is discussed in detail starting on p. 38.

to age 15 years. As adults, antisocial personality disordered persons often demonstrate unlawful behaviors (p. 702). Such behaviors may include stealing or deceiving others for personal gain, destroying others' property, fighting, or participating in illegal activities or occupations (p. 702). Concomitantly, they may demonstrate a history of age inappropriate impulsivity and irresponsibility, which frequently result in negative consequences (e.g., poor work attendance resulting in frequent job losses, assaultive or violent behaviors resulting in multiple incarcerations, etc.). Criteria necessary to fulfill antisocial personality disorder are noted in Table 2.14.

Two caveats related to the antisocial personality disorder are especially important for addictions counselors. First, should a client fulfill a substance-related disorder and demonstrate antisocial behaviors, the antisocial personality disorder diagnosis should not be used unless antisocial symptomatology began during childhood and continued into adulthood (APA, 2000, p. 705). This, then, suggests that certain behaviors commonly associated with antisocial personality disorder and occurring in adulthood with no previous manifest antisocial behaviors during childhood may be substance rather than personality engendered. Here, substance-abusing persons may be behaving in ways that mimic antisocial personality disorder criteria. However, these mimicking behaviors are either a result of their substance use (e.g., acting aggressively due to the effects of cocaine) or their attempts to gain access to substances (e.g., stealing to obtain money to purchase substances). Thus, these persons' behaviors are substance engendered, and they do not fulfill antisocial personality disorder criteria. Second, should clients indicate the presence of both substance use and antisocial behaviors in childhood, which continued into adulthood, and criteria for both substance-related disorder and antisocial personality disorders are concurrently met, the client should receive both diagnoses.

TABLE 2.14. *DSM–IV–TR* (APA, 2000, p. 706) Antisocial Personality Disorder Criteria

A. There is a pervasive pattern of disregard for and violation of the rights of others occurring since age 15 years, as indicated by three (or more) of the following:
   (1) failure to conform to social norms with respect to lawful behaviors as indicated by repeatedly performing acts that are grounds for arrest
   (2) deceitfulness, as indicated by repeated lying, use of aliases, or conning others for personal profit or pleasure
   (3) impulsivity or failure to plan ahead
   (4) irritability and aggressiveness, as indicated by repeated physical fights or assaults
   (5) reckless disregard for safety of self or others
   (6) consistent irresponsibility, as indicated by repeated failure to sustain consistent work behavior or honor financial obligations
   (7) lack of remorse, as indicated by being indifferent to or rationalizing having hurt, mistreated, or stolen from another
B. The individual is at least age 18 years.
C. There is evidence of Conduct Disorder with onset before age 15 years.
D. The occurrence of antisocial behavior is not exclusively during the course of Schizophrenia or a Manic Episode.

BORDERLINE PERSONALITY DISORDER

Key factors of this personality disorder revolve around unstable and intense, over-valuing and devaluing, interpersonal relationships in which the borderline personality disordered person experiences significant distress when feeling abandoned by others (APA, 2000, pp. 706–709). Such abandonment could be real or imagined. Nevertheless, either can promote intense fear of being alone and inappropriate anger toward the person or persons perceived as abandoning the client (p. 706). Often borderline personality disordered persons perceive such abandonment as a direct result of their being "bad" (p. 706). Clients fulfilling this personality disorder quickly shift from idealizing persons to devaluing those previously idealized (p. 707). Thus, their interpersonal relationships are often strained.

Also, many borderline personality disordered persons will self-mutilate by cutting their bodies with razors or other sharp objects. It is believed that self-mutilating behaviors may bring borderline personality disordered persons "relief by reaffirming [their] ability to feel or by expiating the individual's sense of being evil" (APA, 2000, p. 707). They also tend to use suicidal behaviors as a means to escape intolerable abandonment feelings or as an attempted means to gain others' nurturing behaviors or relationship continuation. However, such sensational behaviors quickly lose their dramatic effect on friends and family members. This typically requires borderline personality disordered persons to increase the lethality of their behaviors to again gain family and friend support and further escalates a life-threatening cycle, which often intentionally or unintentionally leads to death.

Additionally, a significant percentage of borderline personality disordered persons present with an unstable sense of self and experience dramatic shifts in their self-images (APA, 2000, p. 707). Thus, they may demonstrate significant and sudden shifts in their career, relationship, and educational goals. Often such shifts are short-lived, and clients move quickly to another unfulfilling shift. This seems especially true when borderline personality disordered persons are using psychoactive substances, which increase impulsivity.

Such impulsivity is noted as a hallmark trait of borderline personality disordered persons (APA, 2000, p. 707). Many times these impulsive behaviors can be potentially dangerous or self-damaging. Substance abuse is just one of the impulsive behaviors noted within the *DSM–IV–TR* for this population. Others include gambling, spending money irresponsibly, driving recklessly, and engaging in unsafe sex (p. 707). Suicidal ideation, behaviors, and threats are also noted as recurrent with borderline personality disordered persons and frequently are correlated with others' threats of abandonment or expectations of increased responsibilities (p. 707).

Criteria necessary to fulfill Borderline Personality Disorder are noted in Table 2.15.

NARCISSISTIC PERSONALITY DISORDER

The central focus of narcissistic personality disordered persons is to be admired. These persons demonstrate a pervasive pattern of grandiosity, a sense of inflated

TABLE 2.15. *DSM–IV–TR* (APA, 2000, p. 710) Borderline Personality
Disorder Criteria

A pervasive pattern of instability of interpersonal relationships, self-image, and affects, and marked impulsivity beginning by early adulthood and present in a variety of contexts, as indicated by five (or more) of the following:

   (1) frantic efforts to avoid real or imagined abandonment. Note: Do not include suicidal or self-mutilating behavior covered in Criterion 5.
   (2) a pattern of unstable and intense interpersonal relationships characterized by alternating between extremes of idealization and devaluation
   (3) identify disturbance: markedly and persistently unstable self-image or sense of self
   (4) impulsivity in at least two areas that are potentially self-damaging (e.g., spending, sex, substance abuse, reckless driving, binge eating). Note: Do not include suicidal or self-mutilating behavior covered in Criterion 5.
   (5) recurrent suicidal behavior, gestures, or threats, or self-mutilating behavior
   (6) affective instability due to a marked reactivity of mood (e.g., intense episodic dysphoria, irritability, or anxiety usually lasting a few hours and only rarely more than a few days)
   (7) chronic feelings of emptiness
   (8) inappropriate, intense anger or difficulty controlling anger (e.g., frequent displays of temper, constant anger, recurrent physical fights)
   (9) transient, stress-related paranoid ideation or severe dissociative symptoms

self-importance, and a lack of empathy toward others (APA, 2000, p. 714), thereby projecting a sense of "emotional coldness" (p. 715). They generally overinflate their accomplishments and boastfully overestimate their skills and abilities, while devaluing others' contributions (p. 715). Thus, they are usually perceived as being arrogant, conceited, artificial, and pretentious (p. 715). Often narcissistic personality disordered persons believe they are superior to others and entitled to special privileges and recognition. Given their need for excessive admiration, when such expected privileges and recognitions are slow to come or absent, they often are bewildered and feel slighted.

Despite their external presentation of boastful self-importance, extreme self-confidence, and arrogance, narcissistic personality disordered persons' self-esteems are relatively fragile (APA, 2000, p. 714). Therefore, they are quite vulnerable to criticism (p. 715), especially when such criticism comes from persons regarded as successful or privileged. Addictions counselors need to be keenly aware that this population may be at risk of substance-using behaviors when experiencing or anticipating criticism from important others. Furthermore, it should be noted that cocaine use could produce symptomatology that may mimic certain narcissistic personality disorder criteria (e.g., grandiosity [p. 244], extreme self-confidence [Taylor & Gold, 1990]) (p. 244). Therefore, addictions counselors must make certain that a diagnosis is founded on the personality disorder's established criteria vis-à-vis mimicking psychoactive substance-engendered behaviors. Thus, narcissistic personality disorder criteria must be fulfilled even when the client is not under psychoactive substance influence (Table 2.16).

TABLE 2.16. *DSM–IV–TR* (APA, 2000, p. 717) Narcissistic Personality Disorder Criteria

A pervasive pattern of grandiosity (in fantasy or behavior), need for admiration, and lack of empathy, beginning by early adulthood and present in a variety of contexts, as indicated by five (or more) of the following:

(1) has a grandiose sense of self-importance (e.g., exaggerates achievements and talents, expects to be recognized as superior without commensurate achievements)

(2) is preoccupied with fantasies of unlimited success, power, brilliance, beauty, or ideal love

(3) believes that he or she is "special" and unique and can only be understood by, or should associate with, other special or high-status people (or institutions)

(4) requires excessive admiration

(5) has a sense of entitlement, i.e., unreasonable expectations of especially favorable treatment or automatic compliance with his or her expectations

(6) is interpersonally exploitative, i.e., takes advantage of others to achieve his or her own ends

(7) lacks empathy: is unwilling to recognize or identify with the feelings and needs of others

(8) is often envious of others or believes that others are envious of him or her

(9) shows arrogant, haughty behaviors or attitudes

Other Axis I Diagnoses That Warrant Review

Three additional Axis I diagnoses warrant review, as they frequently are associated with substance use disorders. These include posttraumatic stress disorder (PTSD), conduct disorder, and oppositional defiant disorder. Although PTSD can be diagnosed in adults or children, the latter two disorders are typically noted in childhood or adolescence (APA, 2000, p. 39). This is because adults with these types of behaviors will more often than not present with greater psychopathology and will typically fulfill the antisocial personality disorder.

Posttraumatic Stress Disorder

Given both the noted prevalence and risk of comorbid PTSD and substance use disorders (APA, 2000, p. 465; Dansky, Byrne, & Brady, 1999; Engdahl, Dikel, Eberly, & Blank, 1998; Epstein, Saunders, Kilpatrick, & Resnick, 1998; Zlotnick, 1997), it is important that addictions counselors be familiar with PTSD criteria. Prominent PTSD features include: (a) reexperiencing the distressing event (e.g., recurrent and intrusive memories of the event), (b) avoidance of stimuli associated to the trauma experience (e.g., attempts to avoid thoughts or feelings associated with the trauma), and arousal symptoms (e.g., difficulty falling asleep) that occur after exposure to a traumatic stressor (APA, 2000, p. 468). Such exposure could be: (a) experienced (e.g., being raped or beaten), (b) witnessed (e.g., observing the violent death of a loved one), or (c) learned (e.g., learning via a police officer that one's child was tortured and killed). Persons suffering from PTSD may attempt to escape such symptomatology via substance-abusing behaviors.

Three specifiers are used with the PTSD diagnosis. The *acute specifier* is used when symptom duration is less then three months (APA, 2000, p. 465). When the symptoms last three months or more the *chronic specifier* is used (p. 465). Finally, the specifier *with delayed onset* is used when the experienced trauma and associated PTSD symptoms began 6 or more months following the incident (p. 465) (Table 2.17).

Conduct Disorder

The *DSM–IV–TR* indicates, "Conduct Disorder is often associated with an early onset of sexual behavior, drinking, smoking, use of illegal substance, and reckless and risk-taking acts. Illegal drug use may increase the risk that Conduct Disorder will persist" (APA, 2000, p. 96). Thus, this disorder warrants special attention by addictions counselors. The diagnosis's foremost and most predominant characteristic is a pattern of persistent behaviors in which children or adolescents deny others' rights (e.g., initiate physical fights) or ignore major age-appropriate societal norms (e.g., break into homes or cars) (APA, 2000, pp. 93–99). In particular, a conduct disorder diagnosis includes four main categories: (a) aggressive behaviors that threaten or harm other people or animals, (b) behaviors that cause damage to property, (c) lying and stealing, and (d) full violation of societal rules or norms (pp. 98–99) (Table 2.18).

A conduct disorder diagnosis requires the presence of three or more characteristic behaviors (e.g., bullying) within the last 12 months. Minimally, one characteristic behavior must have been present during the preceding 6 months. Although persons over age 18 years can be diagnosed with conduct disorder, it is more likely that those over age 18 will fulfill antisocial personality disorder criteria.

CONDUCT DISORDER SUBTYPES

Two conduct disorder subtypes exist. *Childhood-onset subtype* is often identified as the most persistent subtype. Adolescents diagnosed with this Subtype tend to fulfill antisocial personality disorder in adulthood (APA, 2000, p. 95). *Childhood-onset subtype* minimally requires the presence of one criterion for diagnosis prior to age 10 (p. 95). Males typically are identified with this subtype. They often are physically aggressive toward others and have "disturbed peer relationships" (p. 95). Furthermore, many who are oppositional defiant disordered (see Table 2.19) in early childhood, also fulfill conduct disorder criteria prior to puberty (p. 95).

Adolescent-onset is the second subtype. These adolescents have an absence of any conduct disorder criteria prior to age 10. Furthermore, they are less likely to exhibit openly aggressive behaviors and tend to participate in more normative peer relationships (p. 95).

Conduct disorder severity specifiers help counselors note treatment progress (or lack thereof). Three specifiers (mild, moderate, and severe) are affiliated with conduct disorder and are noted in the *DSM–IV–TR* (p. 95).

TABLE 2.17. *DSM–IV–TR* (APA, 2000, pp. 467–468) Posttraumatic Stress
Disorder Criteria

A. The person has been exposed to a traumatic event in which both of the following were
present:
  (1) the person experienced, witnessed, or was confronted with an event or events that
      involved actual or threatened death or serious injury, or a threat to the physical
      integrity of self or others
  (2) the person's response involved intense fear, helplessness, or horror. Note: In chil-
      dren, this may be expressed instead by disorganized or agitated behavior
B. The traumatic event is persistently reexperienced in one (or more) of the following
   ways:
  (1) recurrent and intrusive distressing recollections of the event, including images,
      thoughts, or perceptions. Note: In young children, repetitive play may occur in
      which themes or aspects of the trauma are expressed.
  (2) recurrent distressing dreams of the event. Note: In children, there may be fright-
      ening dreams without recognizable content.
  (3) acting or feeling as if the traumatic event were recurring (includes a sense of
      reliving the experience, illusions, hallucinations, and dissociative flashback epi-
      sode, including those that occur on awakening or when intoxicated). Note: In
      young children, trauma-specific reenactment may occur.
  (4) intense psychological distress at exposure to internal or external cues that sym-
      bolize or resemble an aspect of the traumatic event
  (5) physiological reactivity on exposure to internal or external cues that symbolize or
      resemble an aspect of the traumatic event
C. Persistent avoidance of stimuli associated with the trauma and numbing of general
   responsiveness (not present before the trauma) as indicated by three (or more) of the
   following:
  (1) efforts to avoid thoughts, feelings, or conversations associated with the trauma
  (2) efforts to avoid activities, places, or people that arouse recollections of the trauma
  (3) inability to recall an important aspect of the trauma
  (4) markedly diminished interest or participation in significant activities
  (5) feeling of detachment or estrangement from others
  (6) restricted range of affect (e.g., unable to have loving feelings)
  (7) sense of a foreshortened future (e.g., does not expect to have a career, marriage,
      children, or a normal life span)
D. Persistent symptoms of increased arousal (not present before the trauma), as indicated by two (or more) of the following:
  (1) difficulty falling or staying asleep
  (2) irritability or outbursts of anger
  (3) difficulty concentrating
  (4) hypervigilance
  (5) exaggerated startle response
E. Duration of the disturbance (symptoms in Criteria B, C, and D) is more than 1 month.
F. The disturbance causes clinically significant distress or impairment in social, occupational, or other important areas of functioning.

Specify if:
  Acute: if duration of symptoms is less than 3 months
  Chronic: if duration of symptoms is 3 months or more

Specify if:
  With Delayed Onset: if onset of symptoms is at least 6 months after the stressor

TABLE 2.18. *DSM–IV–TR* (APA, 2000, pp. 98–99) Conduct Disorder Criteria

A. A repetitive and persistent pattern of behavior in which the basic rights of others or major age-appropriate societal norms or rules are violated, as manifested by the presence of three (or more) of the following criteria in the past 12 months, with at least one criterion present in the past 6 months.

Aggression to people and animals

    (1) often bullies, threatens, or intimidates others
    (2) often initiates physical fights
    (3) has used a weapon that can cause serious physical harm to others (e.g., a bat, brick, broken bottle, knife, gun)
    (4) has been physically cruel to people
    (5) has been physically cruel to animals
    (6) has stolen while confronting a victim (e.g., mugging, purse snatching, extortion, armed robbery)
    (7) has forced someone into sexual activity

Destruction of Property

    (8) has deliberately engaged in fire setting with the intention of causing serious damage
    (9) has deliberately destroyed others' property (other than by fire setting)

Deceitfulness or theft

    (10) has broken into someone else's house, building, or car
    (11) often lies to obtain goods or favors or to avoid obligations (i.e., "cons" others)
    (12) has stolen items of nontrivial value without confronting a victim (e.g., shoplifting, but without breaking and entering; forgery)

Serious violations of rules

    (13) often stays out at night despite parental prohibitions, beginning before age 13 years
    (14) has run away from home overnight at least twice while living in parental or parental surrogate home (or once without returning for a lengthy period)
    (15) is often truant from school, beginning before age 13 years

B. The disturbance in behavior causes clinically significant impairment in social, academic, or occupational functioning.

C. If the individual is age 18 years or older, criteria are not met for Antisocial Personality Disorder.

Specify type based on age at onset:

    Childhood-Onset Type: onset of at least one criterion characteristic of Conduct Disorder prior to age 10 years
    Adolescent-Onset Type: absence of any criteria characteristic of Conduct Disorder prior to age 10 year

Specify severity:

    Mild: few if any conduct problems in excess of those required to make the diagnosis and conduct problems cause only minor harm to others
    Moderate: number of conduct problems and effect on others intermediate between "mild" and "severe"
    Severe: many conduct problems in excess of those required to make the diagnosis or conduct problems cause considerable harm to others

Severe. This specifier indicates that the client is exhibiting an abundance of conduct problems and that the number of problems clearly exceeds the criteria needed for a conduct disorder diagnosis.

Moderate. The moderate specifier indicates adolescent placement in an intermediate or midpoint category. Here, the adolescent's presenting symptomatology and predominant behavioral patterns are neither limited nor extreme.

Mild. This specifier indicates the adolescent met minimal conduct disorder diagnosis criteria. This specifier's use suggests dangerousness to others is relatively low and that the behaviors identified as meeting conduct disorder criteria were minor. An example of this might be truancy, where there is little risk that truancy in and of itself is dangerous.

Oppositional Defiant Disorder

Oppositional defiant disorder criteria (Table 2.19) are less severe in nature than conduct disorder and do not include acts of aggression, property destruction, or theft or deceit patterns (APA, 2000, pp. 101–102). However, the *DSM–IV–TR* (2000) states those qualifying for oppositional defiant disorder have a "precocious use of alcohol, tobacco, or illicit drugs" (p. 100). Should a child or adolescent qualify for the conduct disorder diagnosis, they are not dually diagnosed with oppositional defiant disorder. This is because the oppositional defiant disorder criteria are subsumed under the conduct disorder diagnosis (p. 102). Due to the noted correlation between oppositional defiant disorder and substance use, addictions counselors should be careful to assess those children and adolescents fulfilling the oppositional defiant disorder for substance use.

TABLE 2.19. *DSM–IV–TR* (APA, 2000, p. 102) Oppositional Defiant Criteria

A. A pattern of negativistic, hostile, and defiant behavior lasting at least 6 months, during which four (or more) of the following are present:
   (1) often loses temper
   (2) often argues with adults
   (3) often actively defies or refuses to comply with adults' requests or rules
   (4) often deliberately annoys people
   (5) often blames others for his or her mistakes or misbehavior
   (6) is often touchy or easily annoyed by others
   (7) is often angry and resentful
   (8) is often spiteful or vindictive

Note: Consider a criterion met only if the behavior occurs more frequently than is typically observed in individuals of comparable age and developmental level.

B. The disturbance in behavior causes clinically significant impairment in social, academic, or occupational functioning.
C. The behaviors do not occur exclusively during the course of a Psychotic or Mood Disorder.
D. Criteria are not met for Conduct Disorder, and, if the individual is age 18 years or older, criteria are not met for Antisocial Personality Disorder.

Axis V: The Global Assessment of Functioning (GAF) Scale

As indicated at the chapter's beginning, Axis V indicates clients' overall functioning levels (APA, 2000, p. 32). The Global Assessment of Functioning (GAF) Scale provides scores between 0 and 100 (Table 2.20). A score of 0 indicates inadequate information has been obtained. Thus, the addictions counselor must obtain more information before an accurate Axis V score can be identified. Scores of 1 suggest that clients are an acute danger to themselves or others, or have acutely decompensated. Clearly, persons with such low scores warrant inpatient hospitalization at the most restricted and observed level. Conversely, scores of 100 suggest superior functioning and total psychopathic freedom. Thus, this axis merely reflects clients' functioning as it relates to psychological, social, and occupational functioning (p. 32). In other words, physical or environmental impairments should not be reflected in relationship to this axis (p. 32). Thus, it is likely that addictions counselors working in outpatient treatment programs will have typical client GAF scores between 40 and 72, whereas those counseling at inpatient or residential programs will likely have clients who score lower (e.g., 25 to 65).

Finally, it should be noted that the GAF scores could be used to indicate clients' functioning at different times. For example, when a single GAF score is indicated and the term "Current" is placed next to the score, the immediate functioning level of the client is being noted (Table 2.2). However, should the addictions counselor wish to indicate the client's highest and lowest levels of functioning within a year, both numbers could be indicated with a notation indicating this (Table 2.3). Additionally, some addictions counselors may wish to indicate both the client's GAF score on entering treatment and a posttreatment GAF scores as well. This is demonstrated in Table 2.1.

SUMMARY

Vacc's (1982) continuous assessment construct, where counselors compare their clients' immediate symptomatology to both past levels and established *DSM–IV–TR* diagnostic criteria, was described within this chapter. Additionally, this chapter noted how *DSM–IV–TR* diagnostic criteria are often used to prescribe clients' treatment and reimbursable services via diagnostic-related group placements. Readers also were provided a rudimentary overview of the *DSM–IV–TR* Multiaxial System as well as potential *DSM–IV–TR* diagnostic benefits for counselors and clients alike. Of particular importance within this chapter was the information on Axis I substance-related disorders and common Axis II personality disorders, which addictions counselors will most likely encounter. Clearly, addictions counselors must be quite familiar with these disorders and able to skillfully diagnose clients presenting with correlated *DSM–IV–TR* diagnostic criteria. Additionally, information was presented on the Global Assessment of Functioning Scale and the need to address dually diagnosed clients in a manner that addresses symbiotic substance abuse and mental health symptomatology.

TABLE 2.20. *DSM–IV–TR* (APA, 2000, p. 34) Global Assessment of Functioning (GAF) Scale

Consider psychological, social, and occupational functioning on a hypothetical continuum of mental health-illness. Do not include impairment in functioning due to physical (or environmental) limitations.

Code

100 Superior functioning in a wide range of activities, life's problems never seem to get out of hand, is sought out by others because of his or her many positive qualities. No symptoms.

91

90 Absent or minimal symptoms (e.g., mild anxiety before an exam), good functioning in all areas, interested and involved in a wide range of activities, socially effective, generally satisfied with life, no more than everyday problems or concerns (e.g., an occasional argument with family members).

81

80 If symptoms are present, they are transient and expectable reactions to psychosocial stressors (e.g., difficulty concentrating after family argument); no more than slight impairment in social, occupational, or school functioning (e.g., temporarily falling behind in schoolwork).

71

70 Some mild symptoms (e.g., depressed mood and mild insomnia), OR some difficulty in social, occupational, or school functioning (e.g., occasional truancy, or theft within the household), but generally functioning pretty well, has some meaningful interpersonal relationships.

61

60 Moderate symptoms (e.g., flat affect and circumstantial speech, occasional panic attacks) OR moderate difficulty in social, occupational, or school functioning (e.g., few friends, conflicts with peers or co-workers).

51

50 Serious symptoms (e.g., suicidal ideation, severe obsessional rituals, frequent shoplifting) OR any serious impairment in social, occupational, or school functioning (e.g., no friends, unable to keep a job).

41

40 Some impairment in reality testing or communication (e.g., speech is at times illogical, obscure, or irrelevant) OR major impairment in several areas, such as work or school, family relations, judgment, thinking, or mood (e.g., depressed man avoids friends, neglects family, and is unable to work; child frequently beats up younger children, is defiant at home, and is failing at school).

31

30 Behavior is considerably influenced by delusions or hallucinations OR serious impairment in communication or judgment (e.g., sometimes incoherent, acts grossly inappropriately, suicidal preoccupation) OR inability to function in almost all areas (e.g., stay in bed all day; no job, home, or friends)

21

20 Some danger of hurting self or others (e.g., suicide attempts without clear expectation of death; frequently violent; manic excitement) OR occasionally fails to maintain minimal personal hygiene (e.g., smears feces) OR gross impairment in communication (e.g., largely incoherent or mute).

11

10 Persistent danger of severely hurting self or others (e.g., recurrent violence) OR persistent inability to maintain minimal personal hygiene OR serious suicidal act with clear expectation of death.

1

0 Inadequate Information.

DSM–IV–TR ADDICTIONS DIAGNOSTIC SKILL BUILDER

The primary focus of this chapter has been to provide readers a rudimentary overview of the *DSM–IV–TR* Multiaxial System, especially commonly occurring Axis I substance-related disorders and Axis II personality disorders, as well as information regarding the Global Assessment of Functioning Scale. Here are four clinical vignettes that readers can use to practice their *DSM–IV–TR* addictions diagnostic skills. Read the vignettes and complete the accompanying blank Axes I, II, and V lines on the *DSM–IV–TR* Multiaxial Reports (Axes III and IV are completed for readers). Use Tables 2.21 and 2.22 (at the end of the chapter) to identify the *DSM–IV–TR* numbers that correspond to each vignette associated diagnoses. Readers can then compare their diagnostic findings to the answers provided on pages 48 through 49

DSM–IV–TR Addictions Diagnostic Skill Builder Vignette 1: Andrew

Andrew presented as a lucid, articulate, and intelligent 15-year-old African-American male. His high school counselor and juvenile probation officer referred him to your agency. Andrew was accompanied by his 40-year-old mother, Violet, who indicated that Andrew was expelled from school on Monday. Violet stated, "They found less than a half an ounce of marijuana in his locker along with a few marijuana rolling papers." Violet further indicated that Andrew had been suspended three times earlier in the year for similar marijuana-related school infractions.

When you individually interviewed Andrew, he stated, "My grades have dropped from mostly A's and B's at the beginning of the school year to D's." Andrew reported his academic difficulties were related to attending classes while being under the influence of marijuana and his frequent absences. The absences were noted as times when he was either "too stoned on weed to get to class" or times when he was "just hanging around my buddies and getting high on weed." Each of his previous school suspensions was marijuana related and resulted in both court hearings and fines.

Andrew denied the use of other psychoactive substances and his urine analysis was negative for substances other than cannabis. Thus, Andrew's urine analysis supported his claim of exclusively using marijuana. When asked about alcohol use, Andrew stated, "Hate the stuff. It tastes bad. You've got to drink a lot before you feel anything, and it makes you puke. Weed is the only way to go. A couple of puffs of weed, and you're flying."

Andrew denied feelings of depression or anxiety. He denied sleep problems, concentration difficulties, or interpersonal problems between himself and other family members. Andrew also stated he had "5 or 6 pretty close friends—I do everything with them." Furthermore, he denied the need to increase the amount of cannabis, which he typically used to achieve his desired "high," and denied possible diminished effects when he used the same amount of cannabis. Concomitantly, Andrew indicated that he has not experienced any cannabis withdrawal symptoms.

DSM–IV–TR Multiaxial Report: Andrew
Axis I: _____
Axis II: _____
Axis III: None
Axis IV: School expulsion
Axis V: GAF = 71 (current)

DSM–IV–TR Addictions Diagnostic Skill Builder Vignette 2: Mickee

Thirty-four-year-old Mickee, a Caucasian female, was referred by Child Protective Services and her court-assigned probation officer. Information provided by Mickee's probation officer indicated that Mickee's recent child abuse and cocaine possession charges were plea-bargained and reduced to a child neglect conviction. The initial charges would be reinstated against Mickee and her children removed from her home should she not comply with weekly counseling sessions and attend a 16-week parenting class.

During your initial meeting, Mickee stated, "My stuck-up princess neighbor called the cops on me for doing a little cocaine and whipping my oldest when he mouthed off to my friend." Mickee notes that as a youngster she had numerous interactions with the criminal justice system for fighting, breaking into houses, purse snatching, and truancy. At age 14, she was arrested, convicted on aggravated assault charges, and incarcerated in a state juvenile corrections facility. She was released upon turning age 18. Mickee then enlisted in the U.S. Army, but was discharged before completing basic training. She stated, "I had a bad-butt sergeant, who gave me nothing but grief. When I jacked him in the mouth and threatened to sue the Army for discrimination, they offered me a discharge." Mickee has a checkered job history. She has worked numerous odd jobs and typically has been terminated for interpersonal difficulties with her supervisors and peers. "I don't know what it is. People think they can walk on you and that you'll just keep eating their cram." Mickee reported that her previous relationships with others were "short lived, but that is fine with me."

Approximately 2 years ago, Mickee was convicted on grand larceny charges and placed on house arrest. She stated, "It was stupid. Instead of going to jail, I got to stay home, watch television, and play cards. I could have been growing marijuana in my bedroom for all they cared." Mickee continued, "I took the money, because they had lots of it. It's people like me who work hard, but never get the money we deserve." She also was jailed earlier in the year on a driving under the influence conviction. Mickee stated, "The cops are always watching me. I had just been out drinking with my friends. There was no way I was drunk."

Mickee reported that she "infrequently" used psychoactive substances other than alcohol. "I don't use cocaine that often, but when someone has it and wants to share, I'm one party girl." She reported, "I never buy beer. Instead, I just drink whatever people have at their house." Concomitantly, Mickee reported that she often argues with people or her children when she "drinks too much."

Mickee denied depressed or anxious feelings, and stated, "I don't get depressed. I make others depressed if they mess with me." She denied sleep problems or concentration difficulties. Additionally, she denied: (a) the need to increase the amount of cocaine or alcohol she needed to use to become high, (b) possible diminished effects when she used the same amounts of cocaine or alcohol, and (c) withdrawal symptoms when not using psychoactive substances. Also noteworthy was the client's report that she had "acute bronchitis.

DSM–IV–TR Multiaxial Report: Mickee
Axis I: _____

              V61.21 Physical Abuse of Child[6]
Axis II: _____

              _____
Axis III: 466.0 Bronchitis, Acute
Axis IV: Threat of incarceration/possible threat of losing custody of a
              nonminor child
Axis V: GAF = 62 (Current)

DSM–IV–TR Addictions Diagnostic Skill Builder Vignette 3: Clinton

Clinton indicated he was 24 years of age and worked as an emergency-room nurse at a large metropolitan hospital. He reported that his father died when Clinton was approximately 8 years old, "Then my overbearing grandmother raised me and life has been miserable ever since." Clinton stated that he often feels "abandoned, chronically empty, chronically lonely, and always unlovable." During the interview, Clinton reported that he has difficulty controlling his anger, especially when he feels others have "abandoned me or hurt me."

Although Clinton is an emergency-room nurse who knows the dangerous effects of driving under the influence of psychoactive substances, Clinton reported that, when angered, he frequently ingests LSD and drives "as fast as I can." When asked whether his intent on those occasions was to commit suicide, Clinton stated, "I almost always want to die. I sometimes cut my neck with surgical razors to see how close I can come to cutting my jugular vein, or I inject small amounts of vegetable oil into my veins with a hypodermic needle to see if I can cause my heart to stop."

---

6. This "V Code" of Physical Abuse of Child indicates that as a perpetrator of physical abuse, Mickee warrants clinical attention to this area. However, Mickee's other multiple mental disorders are related to this act of child physical abuse, and the other multiple mental disorders warrant distinct clinical treatment as well.

When asked about friends and social supports, Clinton stated, "I usually love people when I first meet them. Then they inevitably hurt me and although I want to be around them. But I can't be around them, because it hurts too much." Clinton indicated that his interpersonal difficulties began at approximately age 14 and have continued to the present.

When asked if he felt depressed, Clinton noted, "I feel miserable all the time. I don't think it's depression. I just feel so very alone, empty and abandoned." He denied: (a) a poor appetite or overeating, (b) insomnia or hypersomnia, (c) hopelessness, or (d) low energy or fatigue. He also denied sleep problems or concentration difficulties. He did indicate "low self-esteem, which rarely if ever disappears."

Related to his LSD use, Clinton reported that he has had to increase LSD amounts to get the "experience" he likes. Yet he denied the need to use LSD to relieve or avoid noxious withdrawal symptoms. Clinton reported that within the last 2 months he has begun using LSD more frequently and for longer time periods. He indicated that he has attempted to stop using LSD but "I fall off the wagon and use more than I did before." Clinton further noted that most of his nonwork time is spent using LSD or purchasing the drug. Additionally he stated, "I believe my LSD use has negatively impacted my work in the emergency room. I received a warning for my continued absences and have been told that I will be terminated if I don't arrive ready to work when scheduled." Furthermore, he denotes having "hypertensive heart disease." When asked about this, Clinton responded, "It really doesn't matter to me. I will die by it or with it. Either way, it is my life. I'll live it the way I want to without changing my lifelong habits."

> *DSM–IV–TR* Multiaxial Report: Clinton
> Axis I: _____
> Axis II: _____
> Axis III: 402.90 Hypertensive heart disease without congestive heart
>   failure
> Axis IV: Possible threat of job loss
> Axis V: GAF = 50 (Current)

DSM–IV–TR Addictions Diagnostic Skill Builder Vignette 4: Rosa

A local health maintenance Organization (HMO) referred 45-year-old Rosa. As a district manager for a local department store chain, she and four of her colleagues were held at gunpoint and repeatedly struck and threatened during a recent store robbery. At the time of her interview, 1 month after the robbery, two of her two colleagues were still hospitalized. Rosa reported that since the trauma, she has been bothered by images of the robbers and anxiety-provoking dreams, which culminate in her awakening by her own screams and tears. During the interview, Rosa noted that she is able to think of little except the robbery, and indicated she has no interest in continuing her work. She especially noted that she could not enter into the building where the trauma occurred and felt detached from those with whom she socialized prior to the trauma. Furthermore, she reported that even previously enjoyed hobbies like backpacking were no longer of interest.

Rosa also noted concerns related to her irritability: "I've never been so angry as I have been since the robbery. I have difficulty concentrating, and then suddenly I find myself yelling at my husband or son for no reason. I never did that before and am quite embarrassed by my behaviors." Rosa indicated that she has begun drinking three to four glasses of wine at night. The intent of this alcohol consumption is to induce restful sleep. However, she reported this has not yet happened.

DSM–IV–TR Multiaxial Report: Rosa

Axis I:	_____
Axis II:	_____
Axis III:	None
Axis IV:	Recent victim of life-threatening robbery
Axis V:	GAF = 48 (Current)

COMPLETED *DSM–IV–TR* MULTIAXIAL REPORTS

DSM–IV–TR Multiaxial Report: Andrew

Axis I:	305.20 Cannabis Abuse
Axis II:	V71.09 No Diagnosis
Axis III:	None
Axis IV:	School expulsion
Axis V:	GAF = 71 (Current)

DSM–IV–TR Multiaxial Report: Mickee

Axis I:	305.60 Cocaine Abuse
	305.00 Alcohol Abuse
	V61.21 Physical Abuse of Child
Axis II:	301.7 Antisocial Personality Disorder
	(Principal Diagnosis)
Axis III:	None
Axis IV:	Threat of incarceration/possible threat of losing custody of a nonminor child
Axis V:	GAF = 62 (Current)

DSM–IV–TR Multiaxial Report: Clinton

Axis I:	304.50 Hallucinogen Dependence
	With Physiological Dependence
Axis II:	301.83 Borderline Personality Disorder
	(Principal Diagnosis)
Axis III:	None

Axis IV: Possible threat of job loss

Axis V: GAF = 50 (Current)

DSM–IV–TR Multiaxial Report: Rosa

Axis I: 309.81 Posttraumatic Stress Disorder
          Acute

Axis II: V71.09 No Diagnosis

Axis III   None

Axis IV: Recent victim of life-threatening robbery

Axis V: GAF = 48 (Current)

TABLE 2.21. *DSM–IV–TR* (APA, 2000, pp. 857–866) Numerical Listing of DSM–IV–TR Substance-Related Diagnoses and Codes

291.0	Alcohol Intoxication Delirium
291.0	Alcohol Withdrawal Delirium
291.1	Alcohol-Induced Persisting Amnestic Disorder
291.2	Alcohol-Induced Persisting Dementia
291.3	Alcohol-Induced Psychotic Disorder, With Hallucinations
291.5	Alcohol Induced Psychotic Disorder, With Delusions
291.8	Alcohol-Induced Anxiety Disorder
291.8	Alcohol-Induced Mood Disorder
291.8	Alcohol-Induced Sexual Dysfunction
291.8	Alcohol-Induced Sleep Disorder
291.8	Alcohol Withdrawal
291.9	Alcohol-Related Disorder Not Otherwise Specified
292.0	Amphetamine Withdrawal
292.0	Cocaine Withdrawal
292.0	Nicotine Withdrawal
292.0	Opioid Withdrawal
292.0	Other (or Unknown) Substance Withdrawal
292.0	Sedative, Hypnotic, or Anxiolytic Withdrawal
292.11	Amphetamine-Induced Psychotic Disorder, With Delusions
292.11	Cannabis-Induced Psychotic Disorder, With Delusions
292.11	Cocaine-Induced Psychotic Disorder, With Delusions
292.11	Hallucinogen-Induced Psychotic Disorder, With Delusions
292.11	Inhalant-Induced Psychotic Disorder, With Delusions
292.11	Opioid-Induced Psychotic Disorder, With Delusions
292.11	Other (or Unknown) Substance-Induced Psychotic Disorder, With Delusions
292.11	Phencyclidine-Induced Psychotic Disorder, With Delusions
292.12	Amphetamine-Induced Psychotic Disorder, With Hallucinations
292.12	Cannabis-Induced Psychotic Disorder, With Hallucinations
292.12	Cocaine-Induced Psychotic Disorder, With Hallucinations
292.12	Hallucinogen-Induced Psychotic Disorder, With Hallucinations
292.12	Inhalant-Induced Psychotic Disorder, With Hallucinations
292.12	Opioid-Induced Psychotic Disorder, With Hallucinations
292.12	Other (or Unknown) Substance-Induced Psychotic Disorder, With Hallucinations
292.12	Phencyclidine-Induced Psychotic Disorder, With Hallucinations

(*Continued*)

TABLE 2.21. Continued

292.12	Sedative-, Hypnotic-, or Anxiolytic-Induced Psychotic Disorder, With Hallucinations
292.81	Amphetamine Intoxication Delirium
292.81	Cannabis Intoxication Delirium
292.81	Cocaine Intoxication Delirium
292.81	Hallucinogen Intoxication Delirium
292.81	Inhalant Intoxication Delirium
292.81	Opioid Intoxication Delirium
292.81	Other (or Unknown) Substance-Induced Intoxication Delirium
292.81	Phencyclidine Intoxication Delirium
292.81	Sedative, Hypnotic, or Anxiolytic, Intoxication Delirium
292.81	Sedative Hypnotic, or Anxiolytic Withdrawal Delirium
292.82	Inhalant-Induced Persisting Dementia
292.82	Other (or Unknown) Substance-Induced Persisting Dementia
292.82	Sedative-, Hypnotic-, or Anxiolytic-Induced Persisting Dementia
292.83	Sedative-, Hypnotic-, or Anxiolytic-Induced Persisting Amnestic Disorder
292.84	Amphetamine-Induced Mood Disorder
292.84	Cocaine-Induced Mood Disorder
292.84	Hallucinogen-Induced Mood Disorder
292.84	Inhalant-Induced Mood Disorder
292.84	Opioid-Induced Mood Disorder
292.84	Other (or Unknown) Substance-Induced Mood Disorder
292.84	Phencyclidine-Induced Mood Disorder
292.84	Sedative-, Hypnotic-, or Anxiolytic-Induced Mood Disorder
292.89	Amphetamine-Induced Anxiety Disorder
292.89	Amphetamine-Induced Sexual Dysfunction
292.89	Amphetamine-Induced Sleep Disorder
292.89	Amphetamine Intoxication
292.89	Caffeine-Induced Anxiety Disorder
292.89	Caffeine-Induced Sleep Disorder
292.89	Cannabis-Induced Anxiety Disorder
292.89	Cannabis-Induced Intoxication
292.89	Cocaine-Induced Anxiety Disorder
292.89	Cocaine-Induced Sexual Dysfunction
292.89	Cocaine-Induced Sleep Disorder
292.89	Cocaine-Induced Intoxication
292.89	Hallucinogen-Induced Anxiety Disorder
292.89	Hallucinogen Intoxication
292.89	Hallucinogen-Persisting Perception Disorder
292.89	Inhalant-Induced Sleep Disorder
292.89	Inhalant Intoxication
292.89	Opioid-Induced Sleep Disorder
292.89	Opioid-Induced Sexual Dysfunction
292.89	Opioid Intoxication
292.89	Other (or Unknown) Substance-Induced Anxiety Disorder
292.89	Other (or Unknown) Substance-Induced Sexual Dysfunction
292.89	Other (or Unknown) Substance-Induced Sleep Disorder
292.89	Other (or Unknown) Substance Intoxication
292.89	Phencyclidine-Induced Anxiety Disorder
292.89	Phencyclidine Intoxication

(Continued)

TABLE 2.21. Continued

292.89	Sedative-, Hypnotic-, or Anxiolytic-Induced Anxiety Disorder
292.89	Sedative-, Hypnotic-, or Anxiolytic-Induced Sexual Dysfunction
292.89	Sedative-, Hypnotic-, or Anxiolytic-Induced Sleep Disorder
292.89	Sedative-, Hypnotic-, or Anxiolytic Intoxication
292.9	Amphetamine-Related Disorder Not Otherwise Specified
292.9	Caffeine-Related Disorder Not Otherwise Specified
292.9	Cannabis-Related Disorder Not Otherwise Specified
292.9	Cocaine-Related Disorder Not Otherwise Specified
292.9	Hallucinogen-Related Disorder Not Otherwise Specified
292.9	Inhalant-Related Disorder Not Otherwise Specified
292.9	Nicotine-Related Disorder Not Otherwise Specified
292.9	Opioid-Related Disorder Not Otherwise Specified
292.9	Other (or Unknown) Substance-Related Disorder Not Otherwise Specified
292.9	Phencyclidine-Related Disorder Not Otherwise Specified
292.9	Sedative-, Hypnotic-, or Anxiolytic-Related Disorder Not Otherwise Specified
302.9	Sexual Disorder Not Otherwise Specified
303.00	Alcohol Intoxication
303.90	Alcohol Dependence
304.00	Opioid Dependence
304.10	Sedative, Hypnotic, or Anxiolytic Dependence
304.20	Cocaine Dependence
304.30	Cannabis Dependence
304.40	Amphetamine Dependence
304.50	Hallucinogen Dependence
304.60	Inhalant Dependence
304.80	Polysubstance Dependence
304.90	Other (or Unknown) Substance Dependence
304.90	Phencyclidine Dependence
305.00	Alcohol Abuse
305.10	Nicotine Dependence
305.20	Cannabis Abuse
305.30	Hallucinogen Abuse
305.40	Sedative, Hypnotic, or Anxiolytic Abuse
305.50	Opioid Abuse
305.60	Cocaine Abuse
305.70	Amphetamine Abuse
305.90	Caffeine Intoxication
305.90	Inhalant Abuse
305.90	Other (or Unknown) Substance Abuse
305.90	Phencyclidine Abuse

Table 2.22. *DSM–IV–TR* (APA, 2000, pp. 857–866) Numerical Listing of DSM–IV–TR Personality Disorders Discussed Within This Chapter

301.7	Antisocial Personality Disorder
301.83	Borderline Personality Disorder
301.81	Narcissistic Personality Disorder

REFERENCES

Adams, J. R., & Juhnke, G. A. (2001). Using the systems of care philosophy within counseling to promote human potential. *Journal of Humanistic Counseling, Education & Development, 40*, 225–232.

American Psychiatric Association. (2000). *Diagnostic and statistical manual of mental disorders* (4th ed., text revision). Washington, DC: Author.

Dansky, B. S., Byrne, C. A., & Brady, K. T. (1999). Intimate violence and post-traumatic stress disorder among individuals with cocaine dependence. *American Journal of Drug and Alcohol Abuse, 25*, 257–268.

Engdahl, B., Dikel, D. N., Eberly, R., & Blank, A., Jr. (1998). Comorbidity and course of psychiatric disorders in a community sample of former prisoners of war. *American Journal of Psychiatry, 155*, 1740–1745.

Epstein, J. N., Saunders, B. E., Kilpatrick, D. G., & Resnick, H. S. (1998). PTSD as a mediator between childhood rape and alcohol use in adult women. *Child Abuse and Neglect, 22*, 223– 234.

Hawkins, J. L. (1991). Utilization review: How to live with it. *Family Therapy News, 22*, 9–10.

Juhnke, G. A., & Liles, R. G. (2000). Treating adolescents presenting with comorbid violent and addictive behaviors: A behavioral family therapy model. In D. S. Sandu & C. B. Aspy (Eds.), *Violence in American schools: A practical guide for counselors* (pp. 319–333). Alexandria, VA: American Counseling Association.

Karon, B. P. (1995). Provision of psychotherapy under managed health care: A growing crisis and national nightmare. *Professional Psychology: Research and Practice, 26*, 5–9.

Lawless, L. L., Ginter, E. J., & Kelly, K. R. (1999). Managed care: What mental health counselors need to know. *Journal of Mental Health Counseling, 21*, 50–63.

Miller, I. J. (1996). Managed care is harmful to outpatient mental health services: A call for accountability. *Professional Psychology: Research and Practice, 27*, 349–363.

O'Hanlon, W. H. & Weiner-Davis, M. (1989). *In search of solutions: A new direction in psychotherapy.* New York: Norton.

Taylor, W. A., & Gold, M. S. (1990). Pharmacologic approaches to the treatment of cocaine dependence. *Western Journal of Medicine, 152*, 573–578.

Vacc, N. A. (1982). A conceptual framework for continuous assessment of clients. *Measurement and Evaluation in Guidance, 15*, 40–48.

VanDenBerg, J. E., & Grealish, E. M. (1996). Individualized services and supports through the wraparound process: Philosophy and procedures. *Journal of Child and Family Studies, 5*, 7–21.

Zlotnick, C. (1997). Posttraumatic stress disorder (PTSD), PTSD comorbidity, and childhood abuse among incarcerated women. *Journal of Nervous and Mental Disease, 12*, 761–763.

Chapter 3

Tier One:
Individual Clinical Interviews

Chapter 3 Learning Objectives:
After reading this chapter, readers should be able to:

- Describe Tier One of the CLISD-PA model.
- Identify differences between clinical interviews and conversations.
- Discuss potential benefits of clinical interviews.
- Describe specific questioning techniques used in individual clinical interviews.
- Discuss the relevant information that can be obtained by establishing a historical perspective.
- Describe specific standardized individual clinical interview techniques.
- Discuss potential disadvantages of clinical interviewing

Typically, clinical interviews have been used to address one of two primary purposes: diagnostic assessment or descriptive assessment (Edelbrock & Costello, 1990). Clinical interviews have significant assessment utility and are frequently used in research and practice (Hodges, 1993; Vacc & Juhnke, 1997). In general, clinical interviews consist of a list of relevant behaviors, symptoms, and events to be addressed during face-to-face interviews. Additionally, they typically include guidelines for conducting the interview, and procedures for recording and analyzing obtained data. Therefore, clinical interviews may define what questions are asked, how the questions will be asked, and in what sequence. These factors may influence client responses through the choice of a particular line of inquiry (Vacc & Juhnke, 1997). Concomitantly, the amount of clinical knowledge required by counselors using clinical interviews greatly varies. Some clinical interviews require vast knowledge of the field, whereas others require only rudimentary interview technique training (Gutterman, O'Brien, & Young, 1987).

Although some may believe there exists little difference between daily conversation and individual clinical interviews, Kadushin (1983) identified eight distinct differences. These differences include:

1. The individual clinical interview has a specific intent and purpose.
2. The counselor directs the clinical interview and selects the content to be explored.
3. There exists a nonreciprocal relationship between the counselor and the client in which the counselor questions the client and the client responds.
4. The counselor formally arranges the clinical interview meeting.
5. The clinical interaction mandates sustained attention to the clinical interview.
6. The counselor's behaviors are planned and organized.
7. In the majority of situations, the counselor accepts the client's request for a clinical interview.
8. Discussion regarding emotionally charged and traumatic experiences is not avoided; rather, these are discussed in detail.

In contrast, daily conversation does not typically seek to gather personal or historical data for the purposes of diagnosis or mental health treatment. Additionally, daily conversation has less structure and is more spontaneous (Sattler, 1988).

Potential Individual Interview Benefits

Lanyon and Goodstein (1982) identified four significant clinical interview benefits. These benefits support their use and make interviews valuable when assessing clients. First, even highly structured clinical interviews are more flexible than paper-and-pencil or computer-generated assessments. Therefore, clinical interviews allow for the possibility of further examination of unclear responses. Thus, if counselors are uncertain about client-indicated responses, counselors can restate the question or request that client responses be further explained or amplified. Second, counselors are able to establish basic rapport with interviewed clients—something that is less than likely with paper-and-pencil or computer-generated instruments. Third, confused or distressed clients are better able to relate to counselors during interviews than when completing written questionnaires. Thus, counselors can verbally direct clients to slow down or relax when necessary. Additionally, counselors can verbally encourage frustrated, anxious, or depressed clients to continue the assessment process or recommend short client recesses before returning to the assessment process. Therefore, confused or distressed clients receive support that helps validate them[7] and enhances the probability of successful data gathering.

An additional benefit is that clinical interviews permit counselors to observe clients' nonverbal reactions to various subjects and topics during the interview. Undoubtedly, this is one of the most important benefits of face-to-face clinical interviews. For example, clients who turn away or avoid eye contact when queried about possible drug use or who become tearful when asked about domestic violence or child abuse issues convey robust nonverbal information. These nonverbal reactions clearly warrant further investigation and inquiry to insure that the best counseling treatment and support services are rendered.

Finally, during the course of the clinical interview clients have the freedom to openly express their concerns. This is particularly relevant for racial and ethnic minority persons. Here, clinical interviews present opportunities for nonmajority persons to provide a cultural context when expressing themselves (Hodges & Cools, 1990). Given that racial and ethnic minority persons frequently believe they may be misrepresented by traditional paper-and-pencil instruments that are normed and conceptualized primarily on the dominant culture (Sabnani & Ponterotto, 1992), an opportunity to provide a cultural context for expression seems particu-

---

7. Remember that validating clients is different than validating their presenting perceptions. Clients' perceptions may or may not be accurate. Therefore, validation of such perceptions may not be in the clients' best interests. However, validating and valuing clients as people is always important.

larly important. Thus, clinical interviews promote vital two-way communications between counselors and clients and encourage clients to provide a culturally relevant context in which to frame their presenting concerns and treatment requests. In other words, clients are not merely being assessed by an external source. They are actively contributing and participating in the process itself by teaching counselors about the cultural context in which concerns occur. Hence, clinical interviews encourage clients to mold counseling to their needs. Thus, clients learn that they both direct treatment and are the locus for change. This, then, accurately depicts counselors not as change agents, but rather client-directed expert coaches or teachers. The importance of establishing such client-directed treatment and internal vis-à-vis external change expectations has significant relevance for the upcoming counseling process. Thus, clients learn at the onset of the assessment process that they construct their goals and that goal attainment is a mutual client–counselor responsibility.

Standardized Individual Clinical Interviews

Depending on the client's presenting symptomatology and voiced concerns, one of many standardized clinical interviews can be used within the CLISD-PA model.[8] Examples of such individual clinical interviews include the Form 90: Drinking Assessment Interview-Intake (National Institute on Alcohol Abuse and Alcoholism [NIAAA], 1996), an assessment interview that provides alcohol consumption data for a specific 90-day period; the CAGE (Ewing & Rouse, 1970), a screening instrument for alcohol-related problems; and the SUBSTANCE-Q Addictions Scale (Juhnke & Scholl, 1997), an AOD assessment interview founded on the clustering effect of 10 high-risk factors. These clinical interviews provide a direct means for interviewing clients and learning about their presenting symptomatology. Furthermore, for counselors working with AOD-abusing clients, such clinical interviews help counselors and clients better understand the often intertwined and symbiotic relationship between clients' AOD-abusing behaviors and other presenting concerns (e.g., domestic violence, depression, etc.).

For example, it is common for anxious or depressed persons to self-medicate on psychoactive substances in an attempt to control or reduce their anxious or depressed symptoms. However, they often do not perceive their new AOD-abusing behaviors or their physical dependence on these substances as being a primary concern. Many times these clients will merely report their anxious or depressed symptoms and actually fail to note the connection between their debilitating AOD use and their florid interpersonal difficulties. Thus, counselors can use clinical

---

8. It should be noted that when clients present with more than one pressing concern, two or more separate standardized clinical interviews may be used. For example, if a client voices concerns related to both suicidal ideation and substance dependence, the counselor may wish to use both the Adapted SAD PERSONS Suicide Assessment Scale (Juhnke, 1996) and the SUBSTANCE-Q Addictions Scale (Juhnke & Scholl, 1997) to determine immediate risk for both suicide and substance abuse, and ascertain correlated intervention recommendations.

interviews as a forum for increasing clients' understanding regarding these inter-twined and symbiotic relationships.

In addition to gaining highly relevant and clinically useful information re-garding AOD-abusing clients and their concerns, standardized clinical interviews often engage clients and provide an opportunity for clients to interact within a safe and inviting professional relationship. In general, AOD-abusing clients readily participate in clinical interviews, even when they have flatly refused to participate in more traditional paper-and-pencil or computer-scored psychological assess-ments. Thus, when using the CLISD-PA model, counselors typically engage cli-ents in general, concern-relevant conversation first, and then ask if clients would be willing to participate in a "clinical interview." After responding to any indi-cated questions related to the proposed interview, counselors describe the purpose of the interview and indicate how obtained information will be used.

Informing the Client of the Clinical Interview's Intended Purpose and Use

It is important to indicate that the clinical interview's purpose is to learn how counselors can help clients. Additionally, counselors convey that clinical inter-views are used to identify possible counseling goals and determine if clients pose a significant threat or danger to themselves or others. It is best to indicate that perceived threats or dangers will require counselors to respond accordingly. Such responses may include: (a) breaking client–counselor confidentiality, (b) warning potentially endangered persons (e.g., spouses, work place supervisors, peers, etc.), (c) making required reports to agencies such as Child Protective Services, and (d) placing clients in restrictive environments to insure their safety. Clients are also informed how the obtained information will be used. Generally, it is indicated that the information gathered via the clinical interview will be used to: (a) estab-lish a diagnosis that will be presented to client-identified insurers or other third parties for reimbursement, (b) increase the probability of relevant and effective treatment, (c) determine clients' and others' safety needs and intervene appropri-ately, (d) ascertain whether or not further assessment is warranted, and (e) learn whether or not physician-supervised, inpatient detoxification or a more secure, structured environment such as a hospital setting is warranted. If information de-rived from the assessment is to be used in any other manner, it must be clearly delineated and clients should be informed of this alternative use.

Describing Potentially Negative Consequences of Interview Participation

Some assessments may engender negative client consequences. One example of such negative consequences might be if the assessment information was requested by Child Protective Services and the issues revolved around continued parental custody. In other words, Child Protective Services may be seeking an AOD assessment to determine whether or not a referred father has a diagnosable AOD disorder. Should such a disorder be diagnosed, Child Protective Services will likely ask the counselor to provide a professional opinion related to commonly associated behavioral, cognitive, and emotional dysfunctions associated with the disorder. Specifically, Child Protective Services will want to determine whether these commonly associated dysfunctions will pose a danger to this father's children. If the risk is high, this father may be removed from the home or lose parental custody. In such a case, possible negative assessment consequences should be made clear to the father before embarking upon the assessment. Specifically, the father should be apprised that the assessment findings may result in being evicted from the home or loss of child custody. Furthermore, despite laws enacted to protect those seeking AOD treatment from losing custody, he should be informed that the assessment could be subpoenaed and a judge could order the assessment to be used even if the assessment is not released by the father. Although such behaviors by a judge are highly improbable, they could occur if child endangerment is suspected. Given that most counselors are not licensed attorneys, the father should be strongly encouraged to speak to legal counsel before participating in the assessment.

Management of Noncompliant, Court-Mandated Clients

Because the impetus for clients seeking to enter treatment is so varied and diverse, it would be foolish to attempt to describe the management of each situation where a client may decline clinical interview participation. This is especially true for voluntary clients (e.g., clients not ordered into treatment by the judicial system). Many times these individuals feel coerced into treatment by family members or employers, only to withdraw from offered counseling services. Others will discontinue early in the treatment process because they perceive that the traditional recovery process does not match their specific AOD-abusing needs.

However, the situation is somewhat different for clients mandated by judicial systems to participate in counseling services. This is especially true when court-mandated clients have voluntarily submitted a valid release of confidential information indicating that the counselor is to provide specific court-requested assessment findings. Depending on the specific circumstances of the client's refusal to be assessed, the counselor can generally indicate that nonparticipation typically guarantees the elimination of previous agreements with the judicial system and may result in paying the original levied fines or completing incarceration sentences.[9] Again, counselors should encourage clients to speak with legal counsel should clients either have legal concerns or refuse to participate.

The intent of indicating possible incarceration or fines is not to threaten or intimidate. Rather, the statement merely reflects reality. Judges and prosecuting

---

9. Such statements should only be made if true. In most cases, counselors providing addictions counseling are not part of the judicial system and are not employed as court investigators. Therefore, the counselor should not act on behalf of the judicial system as a police officer or informant. Nor should the counselor act as the client's legal counsel. Instead, the intent here is to explain available client options and describe possible consequences resulting from nonparticipation.

attorneys frequently offer first-time AOD-abusing offenders the opportunity to participate in counseling in lieu of incarceration or fines. Those offered such opportunities have generally been arrested for relatively minor crimes (e.g., drunk and disorderly conduct, urinating in a public place, etc.) and are not viewed by the courts as being a significant public threat. Therefore, should clients breech their court agreements by refusing to participate in the assessment process, clients likely must either pay the original fine or be incarcerated. Once this is verified by clients' attorneys, clients have a high rate of "voluntary" participation.

Empowering the Client During the Individual Clinical Interview

It is important to inform clients that they control the clinical interview and may stop the interview at any time. Rarely do clients actually stop clinical interviews. However, informing them that they have the opportunity to do so seems to dispel most concerns and reminds clients that they control the assessment process.[10]

Should clients request that their interviews be stopped, comply with the request and query the clients as to the reasons for the request. Counselors may always advocate for a brief break and encourage clients to continue the clinical interview afterward. During breaks, counselors may attempt to build continued rapport by purchasing for clients sodas or snacks and initiating more general conversation to reduce client distress. Given that many AOD-abusing clients smoke tobacco, a cigarette break is often welcomed as well. During such breaks, counselors can engender general conversation. Once clients regain their composure, counselors suggest the clinical interview begin again. Should the clients refuse or be too emotionally distraught to continue the clinical interview, counselors should note what questions resulted in the clients' request to discontinue the clinical interview. For example, were the questions related to family relationships, career, or previous incarcerations or psychiatric hospitalizations? If so, further assessment and data gathering related to this area are likely warranted. Should clients refuse to continue the interview or respond to queries related to the disconcerting subject area, clarifying data might be obtained via clinical interviews with family members and friends or via more traditional paper-and-pencil or computer-generated assessment instruments via CLISD-PA model Tier Two through Tier Four.

THE USE OF PROJECTIVE, CIRCULAR, AND DIRECTIVE QUESTIONING WITHIN THE CLINICAL INTERVIEW PROCESS

Three particularly effective clinical interview techniques are used in the first CLISD-PA model tier. These techniques include projective, circular, and direc-

---

10. Contrary to the beliefs of some professionals, clients always control clinical interviews as well as their self-endorsements on traditional paper-and-pencil and computer-scored instruments. For example, clients can respond accurately to posed questions, or they can attempt to present themselves in a more positive or negative manner. Therefore, counselors are not surrendering control to clients when they make such statements. Counselors are merely reporting the fact that clients do control their responses to the assessment process.

tive questioning. Each provides significant information regarding clients' perceptions of significant others and perceived potential support during the intervention and recovery processes. The techniques are easily implemented and take relatively little time to employ. Yet their potential benefits are great.

Counselors are cautioned to remember, however, that clients' responses are frequently based on perceptions, not fact. In other words, despite the fact that clients' perceptions may be completely inaccurate, these perceptions can significantly influence treatment. Thus, even floridly inaccurate perceptions must be taken into consideration when devising an effective treatment plan and building treatment alliances. Indifference or failure to consider even faulty perceptions can result in flawed treatment planning and inappropriate treatment alliances which will ultimately hinder treatment progress.

Interestingly, attempting to correct inaccurate perceptions may not always be best. In fact, there are times when attempting to change such inaccurate perceptions may actually rob clients of precious treatment time, resources, and energy. For example, as a counselor working in a community mental health setting, I once counseled an AOD-abusing client who perceived that his wife of 6 years was intent on sabotaging his newly initiated recovery. Even her most benign behaviors, such as offering to participate in marital counseling sessions, were interpreted as part of his wife's conspiracy to incite his relapse. Despite functional relationships with coworkers, supervisors, family members, and neighbors, he was unable to accept his wife's treatment support or verbalized commitment to aid his sobriety.

After considerable effort to confront his faulty perception, it became apparent that my efforts were actually impeding his recovery and reducing the remaining number of preauthorized insurance treatment sessions. Thus, instead of building an alliance between this client and his spouse designed to support his specific recovery needs, I implemented projective questioning to learn who his most trusted friends and family members were. The client readily agreed to treatment alliances with these perceived friends and family members, and the client's abstinence was long term.

Projective Questioning

Counselors using projective questioning typically ask clients to use from one to five words to describe someone (a spouse), an experience (being mandated by the court to participate in hospital detoxification), or a thing (a psychoactive substance). When counseling AOD-abusing clients, the primary intent of projective questioning is to gain increased understanding of clients' perceptions and beliefs and to better understand how these perceptions and beliefs can be addressed or used to promote effective treatment.

Therefore, a common projective questioning query would be, "What three words would you use to describe your husband?" Here, the intent is to learn how the client perceives her husband. Responses provide greater insight as to the degree to which the client's husband should be initially involved in treatment and whether or not ancillary forms of assessment and intervention may be warranted. For example, should the client respond by describing her husband as "abusive," "violent," and "punishing," the counselor might wish to ask additional assessment questions related to possible domestic violence and child abuse. Furthermore, questions related to the husband's use of AODs such as cocaine or alcohol might be asked as well. Should information gathered from projective questioning and other noted data (e.g., lacerations and abrasions to the client's face) suggest that the husband's initial involvement in treatment is likely to impede progress, the counselor may choose not to encourage couples counseling or seek the husband's support in the initial stages of the client's addictions treatment. On the other hand, should the client describe her husband as "loving," "caring," and "supportive," his inclusion in the treatment might be helpful. Such positive spouse perceptions may indicate that the husband would be a resource to aid his wife's abstinence.

Client responses to projective questioning can also promote counselors' understanding related to the treatment experience and the client's pressing treatment needs. Here, for example, the counselor might ask:

> "If a woman very similar to you, who was addicted to cocaine and who had been severely abused by her husband, asked you to use just one single word to describe what it is like to walk into a clinic like this and begin the addictions treatment process, what word do you believe she would use?"

Should the client use the word, "overwhelming," the counselor might respond by asking: "Tell me how you think she would have found the treatment process overwhelming." After the client's explanation had been thoroughly explored, the counselor might then ask, "What three things could we do for her that would make her recovery experience less overwhelming?" Thus, projective questioning has served as a means for the client to describe her experience via projection and to indicate what can be done to address her most pressing needs.

Another projective questioning use is to promote client insight and garner increased client support for personal recovery. Here, the counselor might ask something like,

> "Given that you have been addicted to alcohol since you were a teenager and you indicate that your alcohol abuse has cost you the relationship with your husband and the business which you founded, what three things would you like to say to this drug?"

Should the client indicate, "I hate you," "You disgust me," and "I will never consume you again," the counselor might reply with a statement such as "It seems that you have much to lose should you begin to abuse alcohol again. Describe for me the ways in which you choose to commit yourself to fighting this disease." Thus, projective questioning has encouraged an opportunity for the client to think about her substance of choice and project verbalize feelings about this psychoactive substance. This in turn created a chance to identify ways in which she believes she can effectively treat her disease.

Circular Questioning

Circular questioning is similar to projective questioning in that each solicits clients' perceptions and beliefs. However, this time, clients are asked to describe themselves as they believe others would describe them. Here, the intent is not to learn clients' perceptions of others. Rather, the intent is to learn how clients believe others perceive them. Circular questioning is invaluable within the clinical interview process, because it helps clients identify and build on strengths they perceive others see in them. Furthermore, clients can consider and address weaknesses they perceive others believe they demonstrate.

Frequently clients will give great credence to others' perceptions and beliefs about them. In general, clients are quick to dismiss others' compliments. Yet unfavorable remarks and caustic statements are often given considerable weight. The clinical interview process via circular questioning affords counselors the opportunity to learn what clients think others believe about them. Noted strengths can be utilized and built on. Unfavorable perceptions can be considered and dismissed, or needed improvements can be defined.

When initiating circular questioning, it is important to learn whom clients consider most important. This can be accomplished by asking a simple question, such as "Jane, which five people mean the very most to you?" Once these persons are identified, circular questioning can be used to understand how clients believe each of the five persons perceive them. Here, circular questioning begins with the most important person and continues to the fifth most important person. Thus, counselors might state something similar to:

> "You indicate that your son is the most important person in your life. If your son were sitting here right now, what would he indicate are your most positive attributes and skills?"

This question is important because it encourages clients to identify attributes and skills that they believe persons important to them would identify. Counselors can then begin building on such noted attributes and skills within the counseling process. For example, should this mother state, "Sean would say that I am caring, compassionate, and trustworthy," counselors might ask how she could initiate her positive attributes and skills in other ways to successfully battle her addiction. Thus, the intent is to use such perceived attributes and skills to address clients' addictions and pressing needs. On the other hand, should clients be unable to state positive attributes or skills that they believe others perceive in them, counselors might ask something like:

> "It sounds as though you don't know what attributes or skills this very impor-
> tant person might see in you. Let's think about it in another way. What at-
> tributes or skills would you like them to see in you?"

Here, the intent is to learn how clients wish to be perceived by significant others. Once these attributes and skills are listed, counselors might continue by asking a question like:

> "What things would you need to begin doing so others could begin noticing
> the existing favorable attributes and skills you have or the ones you would like
> these important people to see in you?"

At this point, counselors can help clients identify ways in which such attributes and skills can be demonstrated.

Finally, counselors can use circular questioning to encourage new client behaviors by having clients describe their perceptions of how their drugs of choice perceive them. For example, a counselor might say:

> "Charlie, you have used cocaine since you were 30. You say you've wasted
> your money purchasing this drug from people who cared less whether you
> lived or died. You say you purchased cocaine with your daughter's college
> money, and that your marriage has suffered because of your cocaine use. Given
> all of this, if cocaine could talk, how would it describe you?"

Should Charlie indicate that cocaine would describe him as "weak" and "stupid," the counselor might then ask, "How would you need to begin acting so that cocaine would know you are strong and smart?"

The intent is to have clients identify new behaviors that would serve as indicators that they are initiating their long term recovery and are committed to same.

Directive Questioning

Directive questioning queries clients about themselves and their presenting concerns. In other words, instead of asking clients how they believe others perceive them or how counselors could be helpful to persons presenting with similar needs, clients directly respond to counselor-engendered questions about clients and their symptomatology. Thus, a likely query might be:

> "John, I've heard you say that you believe others perceive you as being co-
> caine addicted. However, I want to know whether you are addicted to cocaine.
> Therefore, my question to you is 'Are you addicted to cocaine?'"

Such questions have particular merit in that they provide counselors direct client self-report. Self-report is vital to any clinical interview, because self-report allows counselors to confront illogical beliefs. Additionally, self-report provides counselors greater knowledge of their clients and their clients' circumstances.

Thus, using the above example, if John stated, "No, I'm not addicted to cocaine." the counselor might respond by stating something like, "I'm confused. You indicate that you are not addicted to cocaine despite your three arrests for driving under the influence of cocaine this month." Here the counselor is using directive questioning to confront the client. Should John state, "However, unlike cocaine addicted persons who are homeless and jobless, I have an apartment and still have my job," directive questioning has provided crucial information regarding the client's definition of cocaine addiction. John believes cocaine-addicted persons must be both homeless and jobless. The counselor might then respond:

> "John, you report that you have been spending all your income to purchase this drug, even though it means you have not had sufficient money to pay your rent or eat. Furthermore, you indicate that you have failed a second work-related random drug screen and have been absent from work due to your drug use. Aren't you meeting your own definition of cocaine addiction?"

It is hoped that such direct confrontation can open treatment opportunities.

Of course, if John continued to be unwilling to participate in counseling and was not mandated into treatment, the counselor would present to John information related to cocaine addiction, including the counselor's professional recommendation for immediate cocaine treatment. Furthermore, John would be encouraged to return when he loses both his apartment and job. The intent is not to abandon the client or ignore his dangerous symptomatology. Instead, given that John is unwilling to voluntarily participate in treatment, the counselor is attempting to establish a positive relationship and build rapport. Hopefully, at a later time, when John admits his addiction or is mandated into treatment, he will have a favorable perception of the counselor, the experience, and the agency, and thus desire to return.

Establishing Treatment Goals, a Historical Perspective, and AOD Baseline Data

Establishing Treatment Goals

As previously indicated, individual clinical interviews have great data-gathering utility. This is especially true when learning about AOD-abusing persons' goals, substance histories, and current AOD abuse. Effective treatment requires counselors to possess sufficient information related to clients and their presenting. Typically, within individual clinical interviews, information is gathered regarding the primary presenting concerns that clients wish to address (e.g., alcohol abuse and marital discord). To help clients describe both concerns and the goals that they wish to use in addressing these concerns, the counselor might ask, "Shawna, people often indicate to me that they want specific things to change in their lives. Help me understand how you wish to change your life." Here, the counselor is attempting to learn what things Shawna wishes to accomplish via counseling. Should Shawna indicate an overwhelming number of changes that she wishes to immediately implement, the counselor might respond by stating something like:

> "I'm impressed. You really know all the things you wish to change. It has been my experience, however, that often we need to initially limit ourselves to just two or three important changes. Once those changes are established, then we can progress to other areas. Help me understand, what two or three changes that you mentioned are most important for you."

Here the counselor helps Shawna focus the treatment toward her most pressing needs, thus increasing the probability of successful goal attainment.

Conversely, should Shawna report she has no concerns or goals, the counselor might use the "crystal ball technique" (O'Hanlon & Weiner-Davis, 1989). Here the counselor states something like:

> "I'm wondering how you want things to be, Shawna. If I had a magic crystal ball that would let us see the future, tell me how you see yourself behaving, thinking, or experiencing life differently upon the conclusion of our successful counseling."

The intent of this technique is to have Shawna describe how she would like to be at the conclusion of treatment. These descriptors of her post-treatment life, then, become her goals.

A Historical Perspective

It is imperative that counselors understand their clients' AOD and psychiatric histories. Common AOD questions that establish a historical perspective revolve around symptomatology onset. Specifically, counselors learn: (a) when clients first began using AODs, (b) times clients don't use AODs or times they use AODs less, and (c) times clients use AODs more frequently or in greater amounts. This historical perspective usually begins with clients listing all psychoactive substances they have ever used (e.g., alcohol, marijuana, cocaine, tobacco). They report also their first and last use dates. This historical perspective is also established within Tier One of the CLISD-PA model. Thus, counselors might begin this historical perspective by asking something like:

> "Carla, we find it important to identify what drugs people have used. Would you be so kind as to help me learn what drugs you have used and when you began using them? Let's start with alcohol. When did you first and last consume alcohol?"

Given that most AOD-abusing clients have used alcohol, this is a non-anxiety-provoking manner in which to engage clients in the historical perspective of the clinical interview. A thorough review of common AODs (e.g., alcohol, tobacco, marijuana, etc.) then begins. Thus, counselors may wish to investigate these more commonly abused AODs first and then move onto less generally used AODs (e.g., steroids, hallucinogenic mushrooms, etc.). Next, counselors investigate times when clients note increased or decreased AOD use or abstinence. Here, counselors may ask something like:

> "Often our clients will note times when they used more or less AODs than usual, or times when they discontinued using AODs. Tell me about the times when you used more AODs than normal."

This question is stated in a fashion that first indicates what information is being sought (e.g., times when the client used more or less AODs) and then indicates that most clients report such AOD abuse aberrations. Thus, the question implies that this client has likely had similar experiences. Therefore, the question encourages direct report of these aberrant consumption times vis-à-vis denial that such times occurred. Although the list of occasions doesn't need to be totally exhaustive, it is thorough enough to identify times within recent months when the client used AODs more than usual. Such historical data identifies AOD abuse precipitators (e.g., break-ups with partners, arguments with parents, job dissatisfaction). Additionally, questions providing information related to decreased use or abstinence highlight important resources or strengths that can be used during the client's upcoming treatment. For example, should a client report that his AOD abuse stopped when his wife threatened that she would leave if he did not seek AOD treatment, this suggests she may be important in treatment.

Once sufficient overall identification of all previously used drugs has been obtained, counselors investigate AODs used within a specific period immediately preceding treatment. Often this reviewed period will be 1 year or less (e.g., 1 year, 6 months, 1 month, etc.). Here, clients report routes of AOD administration used (e.g., oral ingestion, sniffing, huffing, injection), money typically spent on the substance per week, and quantity of each substance used.

The route of administration often correlates with the intensity in which the drug was experienced (e.g., the peak effect of injected drugs occurs more rapidly than the peak effect of drugs ingested orally), the degree of invasiveness that the client was willing to accept to experience the drug (e.g., needle injection vs. oral consumption), and potential secondary health hazards to which the client might have been exposed (e.g., there is greater HIV infection risk for those who use unsterile needles during the act of injection, etc.). Additionally, counselors learn how the AODs were experienced (e.g., what did clients like most when being under the influence), methods used to pay for the AODs, and persons commonly present when using. Thus, the counselor might ask, "Maria, it is important for us to learn how you were taking the crack and the amount of money you spent on crack in a typical week. Can you first tell me how you would take the crack?"

Once Maria has indicated that she would free-base the crack, the counselor would then attempt to determine the amount of money typically spent during the week on the substance. The counselor might ask:

"Some of our clients report spending approximately $25 to purchase cocaine during the last week they used. Others tell us they used $100 worth of crack during their last week of use. Still others indicate they used over $400 or $600 worth of crack a week before they entered treatment. How much money did you spend on crack the last week in which you used?"

In addition to learning the amount of money Maria spent purchasing crack per week, this question is designed to indirectly inform Maria that whether she used a little or a lot, her response would be acceptable and valued. Furthermore, it demonstrates that people with varying levels of cocaine addiction have sought treatment. This implies hope for Maria's success.

The counselor might further ask the amount of crack consumed in a typical sitting and during a typical week. Here, the counselor might ask something like, "Maria, can you help me understand how much crack you used in a typical sitting?" Once this information is obtained, the counselor might follow up with a question like, "Given that you typically free-based crack each day of the week and that you used about an eighth of an ounce of crack each time you used, how much crack would you consume during most weeks?"

Comparing the money reported as typically spent per week to the amount of substance consumed per week allows counselors to note incongruent data. For example, should Maria state that she was spending at least $600 per week on crack, yet report that she used less than an ounce of crack in an average week, the counselor might wish to clarify her response. Thus, the counselor might ask, "You say that in an average week you used less than an ounce of crack per week. Yet, you usually bought more than $600 worth of crack per week. Can you help me understand? It seems that $600 dollars would purchase more than an ounce of crack." The intent here is not to badger the client or to make the clinical interview into an interrogation. Instead, the counselor is merely attempting to learn whether or not Maria was using more cocaine than she originally reported and learn what she was doing with the unused crack (e.g., was Maria selling the remainder of the unused crack to pay for her drug habit?).

Other AOD information is also sought. For example, counselors make special note of pleasurable, "under the influence" experiences reported by clients. Regrettably, some counselors continue to believe that AOD abuse only produces negative and caustic effects. If this were the case, clients would not use. The truth is often perplexing. Most clients report significant positive experiences related to their AOD abuse. To effectively treat their clients, counselors must fully understand these positive experiences and help clients learn how to cope with the loss of these. Here the counselor might ask, "Malachi, what did you like most when you were under cocaine's influence?" This question helps clients describe pleasurable experiences derived via their AOD abuse and provides clients an opportunity to examine potential grief issues related to their forthcoming abstinence: "It sounds as though you enjoyed feeling 'free' and 'alive' when you were using. How will you cope with the loss of these drug-induced feelings as you continue your abstinence?"

Gaining additional AOD-related information is important as well. For example, has the client ever participated in previous AOD treatment? If so, the counselor seeks information regarding treatment dates, prescribed medications, and positive or negative effects of such treatment. Here the counselor might ask, "Many times our clients report they attended substance abuse treatment prior to coming here. Have you ever seen a counselor or health care professional for your AOD abuse or AOD-related concerns?" Should the client report she received previous AOD treatment, the counselor might ask, "Would you be so kind as to tell me when and where the treatments occurred, and what things you found most helpful or unhelpful in your treatment experience? Let's start with treatment dates. What year did you first begin AOD counseling?"

Learning when treatment began can help counselors understand treatment precipitators. In other words, did the client begin treatment following a DUI charge or was the impetus for treatment her fear related to losing her children to Child Protective Services? These factors may continue to be relevant reasons for attempting to reestablish AOD abstinence. Thus, they still may be helpful in initiating and securing abstinence. Learning when treatment occurred is also important. If treatment occurred many years ago, discussions of new therapies and increased percentages of successful client outcomes builds hope for current success. Furthermore, such discussions can be used to inoculate clients against despair. Clients often feel that if previous treatment wasn't successful, the probability of future success is diminished as well. Therefore, the goal is to encourage clients to recommit to the treatment processes. On the other hand, if failed treatment was relatively recent, discussions regarding the clients' demonstrated tenacity, strengths, and commitment would be warranted. For example, the counselor might state something like:

> "Many people might have give up after such a recent treatment and relapse experience. However, you seem to see the experience for what it is, a step to moving closer to your continued abstinence. Clearly, you have the tenacity that others wish they had and an inner strength and commitment to succeed."

Understanding where treatment was received is helpful too. Specifically, a release of confidential information is sought and treatment records from the previous treatment provider are obtained. Such information provides data regarding clients and what helped secure previous abstinence and recovery periods. The emphasis is on what went well. Previously successful practices that clients report as helpful can then be reimplemented. Hence, if clients learned to use "I" statements in their previous treatment (e.g., I feel frustrated when you don't pay attention to me) and found them effect in curbing their AOD abuse, counselors build on these previously learned and helpful practices. Conversely, should the clients report, "Nothing was helpful in my previous counseling," counselors respond by asking how the clients informed their previous counselors that treatment was ineffective. The intent is to help clients learn that it is their responsibility both to inform counselors when they perceive treatment as ineffective and to manage treatment. Thus, the verbal interaction might go something like this.

Counselor: How did you let your previous counselor know that treatment was ineffective?

Client: I didn't.

Counselor: I'm confused, was it helpful not to tell your previous counselor that treatment was ineffective?

Client: It wasn't.

Counselor: So, you lost an opportunity to gain the effective treatment that you sought? How can we make certain that doesn't happen within our treatment?

Client: Beats me.

Counselor: Should you begin to find treatment ineffective, how will you let me know?

Client: I don't know.

Counselor: I know that some clients will look their counselors square in the eyes and state, "I'm not finding this treatment helpful." Others will say, "I don't think this is working." Still others will write letters or leave voice mails. Which of these or other methods will you use?

Client: I guess I'd tell you or write you a letter.

Counselor: Good, because I need to know if things aren't working so we can implement new strategies for your successful treatment. That is what you want, right? Successful treatment.

Client: Yeah, I guess.

Counselors: You guess? I think I'm confused here, Joe. Are you coming here so you can take control of your life and stop your alcohol addiction, or are you just wasting your time and mine?

Client: I don't want to waste your time. I want to stop drinking.

Counselor: Good, because I need to know how you will inform me if you begin to perceive you are wasting your time or if treatment isn't helping you attain your abstinence goals. I want treatment to be successful for you, Joe. However, should you fail to inform me that things aren't working, I will be unable to help you implement new treatment strategies that have a high probability of working for you. You wouldn't be here if you didn't want to stop drinking, am I right?

Client: Yes, you are right.

Counselor: Then help me understand specifically how you will let me know when things you learn in here are helpful or when you don't think you are making the progress that you want.

Client: O.K., man. I'll look you square in the eyes and let you know what is and isn't working.

Counselor: Are you being truthful? Because I want and need to know what is and isn't helpful. This is the only way we can help you achieve your abstinence goals.

Client: I'm being square with you, man. I want to be sober.

Counselor: O.K., Joe. Now what things will I begin seeing you do within the next week that will let me know that you are initiating your long-term recovery and making progress toward your abstinence goals?"

Client: I don't know, man. What do you want me to say?

Counselor: I want you to tell me what new behaviors I will see you beginning which show that you are starting your recovery and making progress on your abstinence goals.

Client: You'll see that my urine screen will be clean and that I'm attending Alcoholics Anonymous [AA]."

Counselor: How soon will I see these things?

Client: Well, I've already had a clean urine screen today, and I'm going to AA when I leave here.

Counselors: That's exactly what I need to know, Joe. I know this is hard work, but I don't want you to spend all this energy and time on treatment if you're not going to see benefits. I know you can beat this thing. Thanks for your commitment to making this treatment effective for you and for your willingness to stick this process out by identifying what new behaviors I will see that will demonstrate you are making progress.

The intent of this vignette is to demonstrate that assessment is not merely gaining information. It is also treatment. Furthermore, as the vignette demonstrates, assessment is demanding work for clients and counselors alike. For example, when Joe indicated his previous treatment was ineffective, the counselor asked Joe how he informed the previous counselor that treatment was ineffective. Instead of ignoring Joe's statement that he hadn't informed the previous counselor regarding the treatment's ineffectiveness, the counselor both confronted Joe and attempted to inoculate Joe from repeating these noninforming behaviors. This was done by directly asking Joe how he would discuss future treatment ineffectiveness. Joe responded with a common "I don't know" statement. Unwilling to accept this passive, external locus of control statement, which suggested it was the counselor's responsibility to insure treatment progression without Joe's collaborative efforts (e.g., you "fix" me, or you "do counseling to me"), the counselor listed three different means that Joe could use (e.g., verbal statements, letter, or voice mail).

Joe also was given the option of other methods which were not identified by the counselor, "which of these or other methods will you use?" Again, Joe's response suggested little commitment. Therefore, the counselor confronted Joe's seeming lack of commitment. This time Joe indicated he would inform the counselor if treatment was perceived as ineffective. Yet the counselor did not stop here. He then asked what new behaviors Joe would initiate within the upcoming week that would demonstrate his progression and the treatment's efficacy. Joe balked at the request. However, the counselor continued until Joe identified two behaviors (a negative urine screen and AA attendance) that would demonstrate Joe's commitment. Again the counselor didn't stop. The counselor then asked when these new, healthy behaviors would be demonstrated. The counselor concluded by reestablishing rapport and thanking Joe for his investment in treatment.

Other AOD-related questions within the clinical interview are important as well. Has the client received detoxification in the past or been hospitalized for AOD abuse? Has the client ever been arrested or charged with AOD violations (e.g., DUI's, AOD-related assaults, drunk and disorderly conduct) or is the client facing current AOD-related charges? Additionally, most clinical interviews will ask about: (a) previous psychiatric hospitalizations, (b) previous mental health counseling (e.g., when, where, positive outcomes, and prescribed antipsychotic, antidepressant, and antianxiety medications that were helpful), (c) past and current medical traumas or disease (e.g., head injuries, birth complications, diabetes) and prescribed medications (including those currently prescribed), (d) current family environment (e.g., names and ages of partner and children, number of times divorced), (e) family of origin experiences (e.g., names, ages, occupations, perceptions of parents and siblings, AOD abuse by parents and siblings), (f) educational experience (e.g., last grade completed, degree areas, favorite subject areas), and (g) work experiences (e.g., is the client employed, what does the client do, does the client view work as a job or a career?). These questions are typically included within Tier One of the clinical interview.

A basic Clinical Interview Assessment Form is shown in Fig. 3.1. This form can be completed by the client prior to the clinical interview or be completed by the counselor during the Tier One clinical interview itself. Should the form be completed by the client before the clinical interview, the counselor can review the form and identify clinically remarkable responses (e.g., previous substance abuse hospitalizations) that warrant additional information and discussion. These discussions can then occur within the Tier One clinical interview.

FOUR STANDARDIZED INDIVIDUAL CLINICAL INTERVIEWS

Four standardized clinical interviews are described next. Each can be used in conjunction with the previously described clinical and historical perspective interview techniques. All are specific to substance-abusing persons and provide risk-related AOD abuse criteria. Counselors use one or more of the four clinical interviews described here within the first CLISD-PA Model tier. Information gathered

Please take a few moments to complete this form. Accurate information will assist your counselor in providing the most appropriate treatment. Thank you!

Last Name _____ First Name _____ Middle Initial _____

Date of Birth_____ Age _____ Telephone Number _____

Address _____

_____

_____

Please Describe What You Wish To Accomplish By The Conclusion Of Your Treatment

_____

_____

_____

_____

Household Information (Circle the Response Which Best Describe You).

I am: Single

          Married (How Long?_____) (Number of Marriages_____)

          Separated (How Long?_____)

          Divorced (How Long?_____)

          Spouse deceased (Year?_____)

          Have a Significant Relationship (How Long?_____)

How would you relate your current relationship?

          Excellent   Good   Fair   Poor

How many persons live in your home?_____

          Number of persons who are your dependents?_____

How would you rate the quality of your home life?

          Excellent   Good   Fair   Poor

Religious/Spiritual preferences_____

Children

Name   Age   Gender   Any Problems? Please Explain

_____ _____ _____ _____

_____ _____ _____ _____

_____ _____ _____ _____

_____ _____ _____ _____

Others Living in Your Home

Name   Age   Gender   Relationship (Mother, Roommate, etc.)   Any Problems

_____ _____ _____ _____

_____ _____ _____ _____

_____ _____ _____ _____

FIGURE 3.1. Clinical Interview Assessment Form

Please List All Drugs, Substances (e.g., Tobacco, Marijuana, Cocaine, etc.) and Alcohol You Have Taken or Used Today and Each of the Previous Seven Days. Include the Amount of Drugs, Substances or Alcohol Used Each Day (e.g., one ounce, two joints, three cigarettes, 12 beers).

Drugs, Substances, and Alcohol Used Today   Amounts
(Day One)

_____   _____
_____   _____
_____   _____

Drugs, Substance, and Alcohol Used Yesterday   Amounts
(Day Two)

_____   _____
_____   _____

Drugs, Substances, and Alcohol Used Day Three   Amounts

_____   _____
_____   _____

Drugs, Substances, and Alcohol Used Day Four   Amounts

_____   _____
_____   _____

Drugs, Substance, and Alcohol Used Day Five   Amounts

_____   _____
_____   _____

Drugs, Substance, and Alcohol Used Day Six   Amounts

_____   _____
_____   _____

Drugs, Substances, and Alcohol Used Day Seven   Amounts

_____   _____
_____   _____

Drugs, Substances, and Alcohol Used in the   Amounts
Past Month

_____   _____
_____   _____
_____   _____

(*Continued*)

Drugs, Substances, and Alcohol Used Within the Past Year	Amounts
_____	_____
_____	_____
_____	_____

How Many Packs of Cigarettes Do You Smoke per Day   _____

How Many Alcoholic Drinks Do You Consume in a
  Typical Day?   _____

How Many Illegal Drugs to You Use in a Typical
  Day?   _____

Have You Ever Been Arrested For Possession of an
  Illegal Substance or for Using an Illegal Substance?   _____

Have You Ever Been Arrested For Driving under the
  Influence or Similar Charges?   _____

Do One or More of Your Close Friends Use Illegal Drugs?_____

Have You Ever Been Treated for Alcohol or Substance
  Abuse Concerns?   _____

Have You Ever Been Hospitalized Because of Your
  Drinking and Drugging, or Psychiatric Concerns
  (e.g., Suicidal Thoughts, Depression, etc.)?   _____

Please List All Medications You Are Currently Taking or Which Are Prescribed by Your Physician:

_____

_____

Family Background:
Please list the names and ages of your parents, step-parents, or those that raised you. Please include deceased persons' names and the approximate dates of their deaths.

_____

_____

Relationship With Father Growing Up: Great   Good   Fair   Poor
Relationship With Mother Growing Up: Great   Good   Fair   Poor
Please list the names and ages of your siblings, step-siblings, and foster-siblings. Please include deceased persons' names and the approximate dates of their deaths.

_____

_____

Overall Relationships With Siblings and Step-Siblings When Growing Up"
                                              Great   Good   Fair   Poor

Current Job:
Please Indicate the Following Information Regarding Your Current Job:
Job Title (e.g., Waitress, Accountant, Student, etc.): _____
Name of Employer: _____
Years at This Job: _____
Hours Worked Per Week:_____
Describe Your Level of Work Satisfaction: _____

Past Three Jobs:
Last Job Title: _____
Name of Employer: _____
Years At This Job: _____
Hours Worked per Week: _____
Describe The Reason for Employment Ending:

_____

Previous Job Title: _____
Name of Employer: _____
Years at This Job: _____
Hours Worked per Week: _____
Describe The Reason for Employment Ending:

_____

Previous Job Title. _____
Name of Employer: _____
Years at This Job: _____
Hours Worked per Week: _____
Describe The Reason for Employment Ending:

_____

Educational Background:
Circle Highest Grade Completed: 1 2 3 4 5 6 7 8 9 10 11 12   College: 1 2 3 4 5 6
Please provide graduation year for High School: _____ GPA: _____
Please provide graduation year for your Associate's Degree: _____ GPA: _____
Please provide graduation year for your Bachelor's Degree: _____ GPA: _____
Please provide graduation year for your Master's Degree: _____ GPA: _____

Health and Fitness:
Do you have any physical complaints (Describe)?

_____

Are you under a physician's care for any diseases, chronic illnesses, or physical conditions?

_____

Describe your current health and fitness levels:

_____

FIGURE 3.1. Continued

from these clinical interviews is used to determine whether specific *DSM–IV–TR* Substance-Related criteria are met. Should further information be required, counselors may either ask relevant follow-up questions within the clinical interview or seek clients' releases, allowing counselors permission to conduct Tier Two, the significant other clinical interviews.

CAGE

The CAGE was developed by Ewing and Rouse in 1970 and is one of the most widely used clinical interviews within the addictions speciality (O'Hare & Tran, 1997). The original purpose for developing the CAGE was to assess alcohol abusing persons and determine whether or not they were alcoholics. Considerable research has been conducted on the CAGE, and it has been suggested as being both accurate and useful in assessing clients who may be alcohol abusing or dependent (Allen, Eckardt, & Wallen, 1988; Bush, Shaw, Cleary, Delbanco, & Aronson, 1987; Ewing, 1984; Heck & Williams, 1994; Smith, Collins, Kreisberg, Volpicelli, & Alterman, 1987). The CAGE interview can be utilized by counselors assessing clients ages 16 and older and is noted as having both internal reliability and criterion validity (National Institute on Alcohol Abuse and Alcoholism, 1995). Each letter of the interview's name corresponds to one of four clinically relevant items posed via counselor engendered questions. These questions are:

1. Have you ever felt as though you should **C**ut down on your drinking?
2. Have you ever felt **A**nnoyed by someone who was criticizing your drinking?
3. Do you ever feel **G**uilty about your drinking?
4. Do you ever take a drink in the morning to steady your nerves or to get rid of a hangover (**E**ye opener)?

One point is given for each question affirmatively answered. Thus, clinical interview scores can range between 0 and four. One affirmative response suggests a strong possibility of alcohol dependence; two or more affirmative responses suggest alcohol dependence is highly likely.

Form 90: Drinking Assessment Interview-Intake

This face-to-face, clinical interview was developed for use in Project MATCH. The project was an alcohol abuse and dependence investigation funded by the NIAAA and included investigations conducted by nine separate clinical research units (NIAAA, 1996). The purpose of Form 90: Drinking Assessment Interview-Intake is to "provide primary dependent measures of alcohol consumption and related variables" during a 90-day assessment period (NIAAA, 1996, p. 1).[11] Form

---

11. Although there exists a nearly identical, posttreatment clinical interview version of the Form 90, as well as telephone follow-up and collateral clinical interview versions, only the Drinking Assessment Interview-Intake Form is described here.

90's test-retest reliability was noted as "excellent" (NIAAA, 1996, p. 5). Especially noteworthy are the instrument's sound psychometric properties related to: (a) total alcohol consumption, (b) drinks per drinking day, (c) percentage of abstinent days, and (d) percentage of heavy drinking days (Del Boca & Brown, 1996; NIAAA, 1996; Tonigan, Miller, & Brown, 1997).

This clinical interview begins with 37 open-ended questions (e.g., "During this period, how many days did you spend in a hospital or treatment program where you stayed overnight?") (NIAAA, 1996, p. 54). Questions relate to four domains: (a) demographics (gender, weight, etc.), (b) living experiences (number of days hospitalized for detoxification, number of days incarcerated, etc.), (c) current medication use (types of prescribed medications for medical problems, types of prescribed medications for emotional problems, etc.), and (d) periods of abstinence (e.g., date of first drink during a period, date of last drink during a period).

Clients review and plot their drinking behaviors along a printed 1-week grid (Fig. 3.2). This grid begins with the last day they consumed alcohol (day 1) and sequentially represents each day of that week (i.e., days 1 through 7). Reporting includes both drinking and abstaining days. Days are divided into three periods (i.e., morning, afternoon, and evening). Thus, the entire grid contains 21 separate time periods (e.g., 7 days by 3 periods). Specifically, it is important to denote whether or not clients were abstinent during each period. If clients consumed alcohol during a period, the alcohol type (e.g., beer, wine, liquor), amount (e.g., 6 ounces), and proof or percentage strength (e.g., 20 proof or 12% alcohol) are noted within the corresponding time period. Clients also document the beginning

	Morning	Afternoon	Evening	Total SECs
Monday	Time:	Time:	Time:	____.__
Tuesday	Time:	Time:	Time:	____.__
Wednesday	Time:	Time:	Time:	____.__
Thursday	Time:	Time:	Time:	____.__
Friday	Time:	Time:	Time:	____.__
Saturday	Time:	Time:	Time:	____.__
Sunday	Time:	Time:	Time:	____.__

Total number of standard drinks (SECs) per week   38.   ____.__

Estimated BAC Peak for steady pattern week (mg%)   39.   ____.__

[Enter all days of this pattern on calendar]

[If the above pattern does not describe all drinking weeks, ask:] "Now on the other weeks when you were drinking, was your drinking at all the same from week to week?"

FIGURE 3.2. Modified Form 90: Client Intake Interview Weekly Drinking Grid. Source: National Institute on Alcohol Abuse and Alcoholism (1996, p. 84).

and ending time of their drinking behaviors within each of the 21 periods (e.g., Monday, afternoon from 1 to 3 p.m.).

Upon grid assessment completion, apparent AOD-abusing patterns are identified and discussed. For example, did clients report they typically began consuming large quantities of beer immediately after leaving work or did they note abusing alcohol before beginning their first class at school? Precipitators to these AOD-abusing behaviors are noted. For example, did the clients indicate they consumed alcohol upon the invitations of coworkers who jointly used alcohol after work, or did clients report they consumed alcohol immediately before classes to lessen their anxious feelings? Further information is then sought regarding these precipitators.

A second-week grid is completed next (e.g., days 8 through 14). The alcohol consumption process is repeated for this week in the same manner as the first week. Again, drinking and drugging behaviors during the week are analyzed. Similarly, alcohol consumption patterns and drinking precipitators are noted. The 2 weeks of alcohol consumption are compared and contrasted, and the process is repeated for each week during the entire 90-day period (i.e., days 15 through 90).

Next clients identify and analyze drinking patterns different from those typically noted on the weekly grids. Specifically, clients identify times within the last 90 days in which they consumed more or less than their usual alcohol amounts. For example, should an atypical binge drinking episode be noted on a Monday evening, it may be learned that the client was attending a colleague's birthday celebration and that the client typically consumed greater than usual alcohol amounts at such birthday celebrations. Concomitantly, it might be noted that the client consumed less than usual alcohol amounts on mornings prior to potential employment interviews. Clients then report similar times during the 90-day period in which their greater or lesser drinking behaviors matched this newly identified pattern of "episodic" drinking (NIAAA, 1996, p. 60).

Finally, clients complete a card-sort technique (NIAAA, 1996, p. 62). Here, clients are given a stack of 14 cards (Fig. 3.2). Ten of the cards name a specific drug type commonly abused. These cards include: (a) nicotine, (b) cannabis, (c) sedatives, (d) hypnotics, (e) steroids, (f) amphetamines, (g) cocaine, (h) hallucinogens, (i) inhaled toxicants, (j) opiates, and (k) other drugs. Other names for substances within the corresponding psychoactive substance abuse classification are also included on the cards. For example, the Cannabis Card (card number 2) cites marijuana, pot, and hashish. Giving clients the drug cards in numerical order with card number 1, "Nicotine" on top of the deck and number 11, "Other Drugs," on the bottom, counselors ask clients to sort the drug cards into two piles. Drugs that clients have used at least once are placed atop the card that states, "Yes. Drugs I have used at least once." Drugs never used are placed on the opposite card, which states, "No. Drugs I have not used." Clients then note the frequency in which these corresponding substances were used during their lifetime, as well as the 90-day period under review (Fig. 3.4).

Form 90	OTHER DRUGS
Drug Card Sort	Designer drugs such as Amyl/Butyl Nitrates (poppers), Nitrous Oxide (laughing gas), Over-the-counter remedies like Dextromethorphan (DM), etc. 11
Yes	No
Drugs I have used at least once	Drugs I have not used
NICOTINE	CANNABIS
Tobacco cigarettes, snuff (dip), Chewing tobacco, Nicotine patch or gum	Marijuana (pot), Hashish
1	2
SEDATIVES	HYPNOTICS (Downers)
Librium, Valium, Ativan, Xanax, etc.	Quaalude (ludes), Barbiturates, Seconal (reds), Amytal (blues), Nembutal (yellow jackets), etc.
3	4
STEROIDS	AMPHETAMINES (Uppers)
	Amphetamine (Speed), Methamphetamine, Dexedrine, Benzedrine, Ritalin, Ice, etc.
5	6
COCAINE	HALLUCINOGENS
Freebase, Crack, Powder, Paste, etc.	LSD (ACID), Mescaline (Peyote), PCP (Angel Dust), Morning Glory Seeds, MCMA (Ecstasy), Mushrooms, etc.
7	8
INHALED TOXICANTS	OPIATES
Aerosol Sprays, Glue, Paint, Gasoline, etc	Heroin, Morphine, Opium, Methadone, Percodan, Demerol, Codeine, etc.
9	10

FIGURE 3.3. Modified Form 90 Drug Card Sort. Source: NIAAA (1996, pp. 117–118).

	Lifetime Use?	Weekly Use Year = 52 Month = 4	Current Period
Nicotine Specify:	__(0) NO __(1) YES	Lifetime Weeks: _____	_____Days
Cannabis Specify:	__(0) NO __(1) YES	Lifetime Weeks: _____	_____Days
Sedatives Specify:	__(0) NO __(1) YES	Lifetime Weeks: _____	_____Days
Hypnotics Specify:	__(0) NO __(1) YES	Lifetime Weeks: _____	_____Days
Steroids Specify:	__(0) NO __(1) YES	Lifetime Weeks: _____	_____Days
Amphetamines Specify:	__(0) NO __(1) YES	Lifetime Weeks: _____	_____Days
Cocaine Specify:	__(0) NO __(1) YES	Lifetime Weeks: _____	_____Days
Hallucinogens Specify:	__(0) NO __(1) YES	Lifetime Weeks: _____	_____Days
Inhaled Toxicants: Specify:	__(0) NO __(1) YES	Lifetime Weeks: _____	_____Days
Opiates Specify:	__(0) NO __(1) YES	Lifetime Weeks: _____	_____Days
Other Drugs Specify:			

FIGURE 4.4. Modified Form 90 Other Drug Use Chart.
Source: NIAAA (1996, pp. 117–118).

The Michigan Alcoholism Screening Test (MAST) and the Short Michigan Alcoholism Screening Test (SMAST)

The Michigan Alcoholism Screening Test (MAST) can be used as a clinical interview and consists of 25 alcohol-specific questions (Selzer, 1971) (Fig. 3.5). Clients respond either "yes" or "no" to each question. Questions are assigned to one of three distinct alcohol-related domains: (a) drinking patterns, (b) drinking effects upon social, occupational, and medical areas, and (c) previous treatment. MAST scores can range from 0 to 53 and are derived from summing the total number of alcohol-weighted responses. Each question response is given between 0 and 5 points. For example, question 4 states, "Do you ever try to limit your drinking to certain times of the day or to certain places?" Either a "yes" or "no"

The Michigan Alcoholism Screening Test (MAST)

		Yes	No
1.	Do you feel you are a normal drinker?	___	___
2.	Have you awakened in the morning after some drinking the night before and found that you could not remember a part of the evening before?	___	___
3.	Does your wife (or parents) ever worry or complain about your drinking?		
4.	Can you stop drinking without a struggle after one or two drinks?	___	___
5.	Do you ever feel bad about your drinking?	___	___
6.	Do your friends or relatives think you are a normal drinker?	___	___
7.	Do you ever try to limit your drinking to certain times of the day or to certain places?	___	___
8.	Are you always able to stop drinking when you want to?	___	___
9.	Have you ever attended a meeting for Alcoholics Anonymous (AA)?	___	___
10.	Have you ever gotten into fights when drinking?	___	___
11.	Has drinking ever created problems with you and your wife?	___	___
12.	Has your wife (or other family member) ever gone to anyone for help about your drinking?	___	___
13.	Have you ever lost friends or girlfriends/boyfriends because of your drinking?	___	___
14.	Have you ever gotten into trouble at work because of drinking?	___	___
15.	Have you ever lost a job because of drinking?	___	___
16.	Have you ever neglected your obligations, your family, or your work for two or more days in a row because you were drinking?	___	___
17.	Do you ever drink before noon?	___	___
18.	Have you ever been told you have liver trouble? Cirrhosis?	___	___
19.	Have you had delirium tremens (DTs), severe shaking, heard voices, or seen things that weren't there after heavy drinking?	___	___
20.	Have you ever gone to anyone for help about your drinking?	___	___
21.	Have you ever been in a hospital because of drinking?	___	___
22.	Have you ever been a patient in a psychiatric hospital or on a psychiatric ward of a general hospital where drinking was part of the problem?	___	___
23.	Have you ever been seen at a psychiatric or mental health clinic, or gone to a doctor, social worker, or clergyman for help with an emotional problem in which drinking had played a part?	___	___
24.	Have you ever been arrested, even for a few hours, because of drunk behaviors?	___	___
25.	Have you ever been arrested for drunk driving after drinking?	___	___

FIGURE 3.5. The Michigan Alcoholism Screening Test (MAST).
Source: Selzer (1971).

response to this question receives the same 0 score. Thus, no matter how clients respond to this question, no points are assigned. However, a "yes" response to question 9, which states, "Have you ever attended a meeting for Alcoholics Anonymous [AA]?" results in an immediate 5 points. Most questions, however, receive either 1 or 2 points depending on the specific question. A cumulative score of 5 points or greater is generally considered clinically significant and suggests alco-

The Short Michigan Alcoholism Screening Test (SMAST)

		Yes	No
1.	Do you feel you are a normal drinker?	___	___
2.	Does your wife, husband, a parent, or other near relative ever worry or complain about your drinking?	___	___
3.	Do you ever feel guilty about your drinking?	___	___
4.	Do friends or relatives think you are a normal drinker?	___	___
5.	Are you able to stop drinking when you want to?	___	___
6.	Have you ever attended a meeting of Alcoholics Anonymous?	___	___
7.	Has drinking ever created problems between you and your wife, husband, a parent or other near relative?	___	___
8.	Have you ever gotten into trouble at work because of your drinking?	___	___
9.	Have you ever neglected your obligations, your family, or your work for 2 or more days in a row because you were drinking?	___	___
10.	Have you ever gone to anyone for help about your drinking?	___	___
11.	Have you ever been in a hospital because of drinking?	___	___
12.	Have you ever been arrested for drunken driving, driving while intoxicated, or driving under the influence of alcoholic beverages?	___	___
13.	Have you ever been arrested, even for a few hours, because of other drunken behaviors?	___	___

FIGURE 3.6. The Short Michigan Alcoholism Screening Test (SMAST).
Source: Selzer, Vinokur, & van Rooijen, 1975).

hol abuse. Scores between 10 to 19 are indicative of moderate alcoholism, and scores above 20 are considered severe alcoholism.

Three years after the original MAST was published, the Short Michigan Alcoholism Test (SMAST) was developed by Selzer, Vinokur, and Van Rooijen (1974) (Fig. 3.6). These researchers used a statistical procedure called stepwise multiple regression and determined that the use of just 13 of the original MAST questions was sufficient to assess alcoholism. Unlike the original MAST, where 0 to 5 points were awarded per question, depending on the specific question, each SMAST question response is simply awarded a single point when it reflects past or present alcohol use pathology. Here, for example, if a client answered "yes" to the question "Have you ever been in a hospital because of drinking?" she would receive 1 point. Thus, for many, the SMAST scoring is somewhat simpler and less confusing. A total SMAST score of 3 or greater suggests significant probability for alcoholism. Scores of 2 or below typically suggest normal drinking.

SUBSTANCE-Q Addictions Scale

The SUBSTANCE-Q Addictions Scale is an atheoretical assessment scale designed to be used as a clinical interview with potentially AOD-abusing persons (Juhnke & Scholl, 1997) (Fig. 3.7). The scale is founded on a clustering effect of 10 risk factors identified within the literature. These cluster-specific responses commonly occur among AOD-abusing clients. When risk factors are assessed in

Substance-Abusing Family Member/Significant Other
Undersocialized
Behavioral Problems
Stressful Life Events
Tobacco Use
Academic or Work Problems
Negative Affect
Cohort Substance Abuse
Endorses Substance Abuse
Quit in the Past or Previously Attempted Quits

FIGURE 3.7. The SUBSTANCE-Q Addictions Scale.

sequence, the first letter of each risk factor corresponds with the acronym SUB-STANCE-Q. Thus, the acronym serves as a reminder for each of the 10 risk factors that warrant assessment. Following the established "S" through "Q" sequence insures a thorough assessment. Each high-risk factor is indicated next with a brief summary suggesting the reason for its inclusion.

SUBSTANCE-ABUSING FAMILY MEMBERS
Persons whose parents and siblings are AOD abusing are at greater risk for abusing AOD themselves. This seems especially true when AOD-abusing parents and older siblings are respected and revered, and when these AOD-abusing family members are noted as being important role models. Additionally, when clients are living with AOD-abusing family members, psychoactive substances are often readily available within the home and there appears to be less concern about persons using AODs or becoming addicted. This may occur because AOD-abusing family members don't perceive they have experienced significant negative consequences related to their AOD abuse and don't perceive themselves as being addicted.

UNDERSOCIALIZED
This factor refers to persons who report few significant friends or limited interactions with significant others. Often these persons will present with poor interpersonal skills or reported alienation feelings. Here, it is unknown whether or not their AOD-abusing behaviors have stunted their social development or interpersonal skills, whether these individuals initially had limited desire to interact socially, or whether a combination of these factors influences their undersocialization.

BEHAVIORAL PROBLEMS
There exists a high correlation between deviant and AOD-abusing behaviors. For example, some clients may have been formally charged with criminal behaviors related to charges such as prostitution, driving while under the influence (DUI), selling AODs, or shoplifting. Still others may present as highly impulsive and sensation seeking. In either case, this correlation is noteworthy and warrants appropriate investigation.

STRESSFUL LIFE EVENTS

Reported stressful life events and AOD abuse are also correlated. Specifically, many AOD-abusing persons report using psychoactive substances to reduce anxiety related to stressful life events. Some of these persons may be predisposed to anxiety and therefore experience stressful events as being more acute than do nonabusing persons. However, it is also possible that AOD abuse brings about stressful life events as well. For example, AOD-abusing persons may experience stressful life events resulting from their failure to maintain employment due to absenteeism or may experience stressful life events related to dysfunctional interpersonal relationship dynamics. Thus, these stressful life events may be exacerbated by AOD-abusing behaviors.

TOBACCO USE

There exists another correlation between tobacco use and AOD abuse. Here it is noted that a sizeable percentage of persons who present with AOD abuse concerns also use tobacco.

ACADEMIC OR WORK PROBLEMS

Although there is a misperception by some that all AOD-abusing persons experience academic or work problems, this simply is not true. Many AOD-abusing persons are intelligent and do well scholastically and at work. However, there are indicators suggesting that a significant percentage of AOD-abusing persons do experience such noted problems. Academic and work problems may result from significant absenteeism or interpersonal difficulties with peers, coworkers, and authority figures (professors, supervisors, etc.). Additionally, it may be that those finding academics or work difficult may turn to AODs to reduce stressors resulting from same.

NEGATIVE AFFECT

For this scale, negative affect indicates two or more of the following: (a) lethargy, (b) lack of ambition, (c) pessimism, (d) low self-esteem, or (e) a low need for achievement. When combined with other risk factors, negative affect may signal increased probability for AOD abuse.

COHORT SUBSTANCE ABUSE

Data suggests that there exists increased probability that individuals will abuse AODs when their close friends and peers are abusing these same substances. Whenever clients note that their close friends and peers are AOD abusing, further inquiry is warranted.

ENDORSES SUBSTANCE ABUSE

This risk factor is especially noteworthy. Here, persons are indicating that they are AOD abusing. Thus, they automatically warrant treatment. Many times persons initially coming into treatment or being mandated into treatment will indicate they abuse AODs. Their statements should be believed and appropriate treatment interventions should be established.

QUIT IN THE PAST OR PREVIOUS ATTEMPTS TO QUIT
This risk factor is related to persons who indicate that they have quit or attempted to quit AOD abuse in the past. Often these persons will indicate numerous attempts to discontinue AOD abuse all together or will indicate they have attempted to decrease their AOD abuse.

Substance-Abusing Family Member/Significant Other
   0   No substance-abusing family members
   5   At least one respected family member abusing substances on a regular basis
  10   At least one respected family member abusing substances who has had substance-related negative effects (e.g., job termination, DUI charges) resulting from frequent and regular substance abuse

Undersocialized
   0   Good social skills and significant support from others
   5   Limited social skills or limited support
  10   Poor social skills or very limited support

Behavioral Problems
   0   No deviant, criminal, or antisocial behaviors noted
   5   Unconventional attitudes or minor rebellion toward authority figures or minor law infractions
  10   Recent or recurrent criminal behaviors or high sensation seeking or animosity toward authority figure.

Stressful Life Events
   0   Stressful life events denied and client appears to be experiencing a life free from major stressors
   5   Some noteworthy stressful life events are noted. These stressors are reported at times as being difficult but are neither insurmountable nor thoroughly overwhelming
  10   Noteworthy stressful life events are noted and the client reports that the stressors are often perceived as overwhelming

Tobacco Use
   0   Client denies smoking tobacco
   5   Client reports occasionally smoking tobacco cigarettes or cigars, but reports smoking less than one pack of tobacco cigarettes each week and less than three tobacco cigars per week.
  10   Client reports smoking at least one pack of tobacco cigarettes or one tobacco cigar per day

Academic or Work Problems
   0   No academic or work problems noted
   5   Decline in academic work relations or performance or attendance resulting from substance abuse or substance-related behaviors, or in jeopardy of being dismissed, suspended, or failed due to substance abuse or substance-related behaviors
  10   Academic course or work failure resulting from substance abuse or substance-related behaviors, or significant decline in academic work relations or performance or attendance resulting from substance abuse or substance-related behaviors

(Continued)

FIGURE 3.8. SUBSTANCE-Q Addictions Scale Behavioral Scoring Anchors.

Negative Affect
   0   No lethargy or lack of ambition or pessimism or low self-esteem or low need for
       achievement noted.
   5   Moderate amounts of any of the aforementioned noted
   10 Significant amounts of any of the aforementioned noted
Cohort Substance Abuse
   0   No close friends or peers are reported as abusing AODs
   5   Infrequent AOD abuse by close friend(s)
   10 Frequent AOD abuse by close friend(s)
Endorses Substance Abuse
   0   Client denies AOD abuse
   5   Client reports infrequent AOD abuse
   10 Client reports frequent AOD abuse
Quit in the Past or Previously Attempted Quits
   0   No previous attempts or thoughts of discontinuing alcohol use
   5   No previous attempts or thoughts of discontinuing drug use other than alcohol
       which costs less than $10 per week, or one or fewer attempts to discontinue AOD
       use
   10 Does not perceive a need to discontinue drug use of more than $10 per week, or
       more than one attempt to discontinue AOD use.

FIGURE 3.8. Continued

SUBSTANCE-Q ADDICTIONS SCALE SCORING AND INTERVENTION GUIDELINES
Each of the listed risk factors can receive a score between 0 (complete absence of
a risk factor) and 10 (significant manifestation of risk factors). Proposed intervention guidelines are based on the total number of points received (Fig. 3.8 and 3.9).
This number can range between 0 and 100. The intended purpose of this clinical
interview scale is to insure a thorough addictions assessment and augment counselors' clinical judgment when it is perceived that clients may be AOD abusing.
Therefore, the instrument is used only when clients are perceived as possibly
having an AOD abuse-related concern. In addition to noting AOD-related risk
factors, the scale's numerical score is correlated to general clinical guidelines that
suggest minimal intervention standards. These general guidelines should be ad-
justed according to the client's specific needs and voiced concerns.

LOW SUBSTANCE-Q SCORES
Persons perceived as AOD abusing and having scores between 0 and 15 may very
well have suspect responses. Such low scores may indicate clients are attempting
to present themselves in a most favorable manner and are not admitting their AOD
abuse concerns or related experiences. Such low scores suggest clients are indicating a relative absence of AOD-abusing behaviors and experiences commonly endorsed by AOD-addicted persons. The primary issue with such low scores is the
incongruence between the counselor's initial perceptions related to the client's
suspected AOD abuse, which originally incited the AOD assessment, and the

Scores	General Clinical Guidelines
0 to 15	Consult clinical supervisor to clarify whether initial AOD concerns regarding the client were likely unfounded. If concerns were unfounded and no basis for questioning the veracity of the client's responses exists, disseminate information indicating how client can access counselors if needed in the future and provide a single follow-up telephone call in 10 to 14 days to reassess possible needs. Oppositely, should the client's responses be suspect, additional assessment via significant other clinical interviews and AOD specialty assessments (e.g., the Substance Abuse Subtle Screening Inventory–III) is warranted.
16 to 39	If responses do not appear suspect, participation in counseling should be encouraged to address AOD abuse or other voiced concerns. If responses appear suspect, additional assessment via significant other clinical interviews and AOD speciality assessments (e.g., the Substance Abuse Subtle Screening Inventory–III) is warranted.
40 to 59	Counseling and 12-step participation should be advocated. The local 24 hour helpline and relevant support group (e.g., AA, NA) telephone numbers should be provided. Client must agree to a "no suicide" and a "no harm" contract. Additional assessment is necessary to determine types, frequency, and amounts of AODs used—especially AODs used within the current year. Rule out the need for detoxification.
60 to 100	Counseling and 12-step participation are required. In addition to providing local helpline and 12-step support group numbers, and requiring the client to agree to a no suicide and no harm contract, detoxification and a restricted environment must be ruled out. Additionally, further assessment is required. Specifically such assessment should note types of AODs used, as well as the frequency of use and amounts typically taken.

FIGURE 3.9. SUBSTANCE-Q Addictions Scale Scores
with General Clinical Guidelines.

client's current low score. Consulting with one's clinical supervisor and professional peers can help clarify whether the counselor's original concerns were likely unfounded or whether such concerns suggest that the client's SUBSTANCE-Q responses are likely suspect.

Should the counselor's original concerns seem unfounded, clients should be provided information specifically indicating how to contact counselors in the future should help be needed. A single follow-up telephone call within the next 10 to 14 days to reassess the situation and remind persons of available services is suggested. On the other hand should a client's responses appear suspect, additional assessment is clearly warranted, and depending on the outcome of these assessments, relevant interventions should be conducted to ensure clinically appropriate treatment. Thus, within the CLISD-PA model, counselors progress to significant other clinical interview to obtain others' input regarding a client's AOD-related behaviors.

Additionally, it should be noted that the presence of certain risk factors, even by themselves, warrant further assessment and intervention. For example, persons endorsing AOD abuse receive addictions treatment recommendations. Those who report stressful life events, academic or work problems, or negative affect are also referred for counseling.

LOW TO MODERATE SUBSTANCE-Q SCORES

Scores between 16 and 39 suggest persons who may be abusing substances. Additional assessment is warranted if it appears responses are suspect or if counselors are uncertain whether *DSM–IV–TR* abuse or dependence criteria are fulfilled. Recommendations for follow-up counseling are made as a means to address presenting AOD abuse or other voiced concerns. Follow-up visits are used to monitor the clients' immediate conditions and insure that appropriate services are made available should a change in their conditions warrant more intense interventions. Giving clients a business-size card indicating both the local 24-hour crisis and local support group telephone numbers printed on the front and 35 cents taped to the back can provide clients with the means to obtain help should they need it.

MODERATE TO HIGH SUBSTANCE-Q SCORES

Those scoring between 40 and 59 points are endorsing a moderate to high number of AOD abuse risk factors and likely warrant addictions treatment. Based on the number of endorsements made, these clients may well be accurately endorsing their AOD abusing behaviors. Further assessment related to the types of AODs used, onset of AOD, frequency of use, and money typically spent each week on AOD-abusing behaviors will likely be helpful. Willingness to participate in a relevant 12-step support group might also be investigated with these clients and strongly encouraged. Additionally, given the frequency of suicide and violence among AOD persons, both a "no suicide" and a "no harm" contract are utilized. Here, clients promise counselors and significant others (e.g., spouse, friend, family member) that they will call the 24-hour crisis hotline should they feel overwhelmed, depressed, or like hurting themselves or others.

Certainly, such contracts hold no legal merit, and they can't inhibit someone from dangerous behaviors. However, they do provide counselors with robust information and delineate a well-prepared plan that clients and their families and friends can follow. For example, should a client refuse to enter into a no suicide contract, it is clinically appropriate to assess the client for immediate danger and to hospitalize if necessary. In other words, if the client refuses to agree to a no suicide contract, it suggests that she has suicidal ideation and may have a plan to harm herself. Thus, further assessment is warranted and protective measures must be enacted to protect the client from self-harm.

HIGH TO SEVERE SUBSTANCE-Q SCORES

Scores of 60 or greater suggest the endorsement of significant AOD abuse, as well as possible environmental and emotional stressors. These persons are at significant risk for qualifying for substance abuse or dependence and likely warrant the most direct intervention. Depending on the amount and frequency of noted AOD abuse, persons whose scores exist at the extreme end of this AOD risk continuum warrant possible referral for detoxification. Concomitant to addictions counseling, 12-step support group participation should be required. As indicated for moderate to high responses, a no suicide and no harm contract should also be agreed on and the 24-hour crisis hotline number should be provided.

Clearly, counselors should recognize that the presence of any single 10-point factor does not mean persons are substance abusing or dependent. However, a clustering of high risk factors, as noted earlier, suggests increased substance abuse or dependence risk. Again, high scores with single factors such as academic or work problems, behavioral problems, or stressful life events may not by themselves qualify a person for substance abuse or dependence criteria. However, they may suggest the need for general counseling services.

POTENTIAL CLINICAL INTERVIEW DISADVANTAGES

Although many potential clinical interview advantages are noted, there exist some potential disadvantages which warrant acknowledgment. The most noteworthy potential disadvantage of the clinical interview as compared with paper-and-pencil or computer-generated assessment instruments is its source of error. As "live instruments," counselors can be fallible. Certain cues such as facial expressions, voice inflection, and eye contact may be unintentionally given by the counselor. Such behaviors could then inadvertently maneuver the client to answer in a particular manner. Additionally, facial expressions, voice inflections, and other behaviors may be misperceived or misinterpreted by counselors. Thus, counselors could erroneously pursue irrelevant questioning. Also, some counselors may appear uncomfortable with certain topics of concern, causing the possibility of losing valuable information (Lanyon & Goodstein, 1982). However, these biases are reduced when clinical interviews are structured (Bruss, Gruenberg, Goldstein, & Barber, 1994; Flynn et al., 1995; Mannuzza, Fyer, & Klein, 1993; Spitzer, Williams, Gibbon, & First, 1992). Structured assessments can serve both clients and counselors well when counselors understand that all assessments need to be matched to client needs and that error possibilities always exist.

TIER ONE CONCLUSION: DETERMINING THE NEXT STEP AND ESTABLISHING A CONTEXT FOR LATER ASSESSMENT

By the individual clinical interview's conclusion a thorough face-to-face clinical assessment has been completed and counselors have sufficient information to determine whether or not additional assessment is warranted. Should further assessment be necessary, the counselor begins Tier Two and meets with the client's significant others. However, the extreme importance of the individual clinical interview should not be taken lightly.

The individual clinical interview establishes the foundation for all further assessments and provides a context for understanding information gathered in later tiers. For example, more traditional assessment instruments may suggest a client is angry, depressed, experiencing familial stressors, and AOD abusing. Yet such information needs to be placed within the context of the client's immediate circumstances and stressors. Tier One of the CLISD-PA model does exactly this. Thus, in the case of a 30-year-old alcohol dependent mother of two adolescents who was terminated from her employment as a direct result of her alcohol use and mandated into counseling by Child Protective Services, the individual clinical interview helps the counselor learn that the client's angry feelings stem from a number of perceived injustices at work and home. More importantly, the counselor learns what these specific perceived injustices are (i.e., interpersonal struggles within her marriage, and parenting issues that arise with her two adolescent sons during extended absence by their father). Such information is vital to accurate diagnosis and treatment. Furthermore, such contextual information cannot be adequately gained via traditional paper-and-pencil or computer-generated assessment instruments.

SUMMARY

A general overview of the CLISD-PA model and a detailed outline of Tier One have been described. Readers were provided general CLISD-PA model assumptions, as well as potential clinical interview benefits and disadvantages. Additionally, readers gained information concerning specific clinical interview techniques such as projective, circular, and directive questioning and ways in which to clarify the clinical interview's purpose. Suggestions related to the management of noncompliant, court-mandated clients were given, and four standardized clinical interviews were also described. Readers should now have a greater understanding of the model and the types of questions necessary to evaluate clients within this first tier.

TIER ONE CLINICAL INTERVIEW SKILL BUILDER

The primary intent of this chapter has been to familiarize readers with the general CLISD-PA model and describe the first tier of this Model. Readers will find three clinical vignettes related to Tier One. Readers can use the vignettes to practice their individual clinical interview skills. Readers can then compare their individual clinical interview responses to the answers that immediately follow.

CLISD-PA Tier One Skill Builder Vignette 1: Alesha

Alesha presents as a 23-year-old, Euro-American female with average intelligence. She was referred to your agency by her probation officer and Child Protective Services. Alesha was arrested for selling a controlled substance. She has two additional charges pending related to criminal trespassing and prostitution. Alesha agreed to a "volunteer substance abuse assessment" in lieu of a 90-day jail sentence with a $2,000 fine. Alesha has a 5-year-old daughter and a 3-year-old step-son who reside with her. During her assessment, Alesha reports "being addicted to heroin," "living in an abuse relationship with my current partner," and "feelings of grief, because I didn't live up to my mother's dreams for me before she died."

Question 1

Given the significant information gained via projective, circular and directive questioning within clinical interviews, please compose two queries that could be used with each of the three noted techniques within Alesha's Tier One individual clinical interview.

    (A) Please compose two projective questioning queries:

        1. _____

        2. _____

    (B) Please compose two circular questioning queries:

        1. _____

        2. _____

    (C) Please compose two directive questioning queries:

        1. _____

        2. _____

Question 2

The clinical vignette notes that Alesha has been referred by both her parole officer and Child Protective Services.

    (A) What potentially negative consequences resulting from the clinical interview might you wish to describe to Alesha?

        _____

        _____

        _____

    (B) Indicate how you would state these potentially negative consequences to Alesha.

        _____

        _____

        _____

    (C) Please indicate how you might refer or encourage Alesha to speak with her legal counsel.

        _____

        _____

*Possible Projective, Circular, and Directive Questioning Queries for
CLISD-PA Tier One Skill Builder Vignette 1: Alesha*

QUESTION 1 POTENTIAL PROJECTIVE QUESTIONING RESPONSES

1. Alesha, if a woman very similar to you, with two young children living at home, court charges pending, and an abusive partner came here today, what three words do you believe she would use to describe her feelings about being here?
2. Given that you have both a 5-year-old and a 3-year-old living with you, I wonder if at times things aren't challenging at home. What words might you use to describe your home life?
3. I've heard people describe their parents in many ways. What words would you use to describe your parents?
4. What word would you use to describe what it is like to be referred from both your probation officer and Child Protective Services to be here today?
5. You state that you are in an abusive relationship with your partner. What words would you use to describe your partner?
6. A lot of people with whom I speak are addicted to heroin and report what it is like for them. What four words come to mind for you when you hear the words "heroin" and "addiction"?
7. What words best describe your children?
8. You say you are addicted to heroin, Alesha. What words might you use to describe your experiences with this drug?
9. If heroin were a person who would listen to you, what four things would you say to heroin?
10. Sometimes people have some pretty strong feelings about being here. What words would you use to describe what it is like for you today?

QUESTION 1 POTENTIAL CIRCULAR QUESTIONING RESPONSES

1. Alesha, you say you are addicted to heroin. If heroin could talk, how would it describe you?
2. What three words do you believe your partner would use to describe you?
3. You indicate that your mother had some pretty high expectations for you and the accomplishments she expected you to attain. Would you be so kind as to describe just a couple of the personal attributes and skills she knew you have.
4. If your children were sitting on your lap, how would they describe you?
5. It sounds as though you love your children very much and want to enter into treatment for both you and them. When you children are old enough to understand that you voluntarily entered into addictions treatment partially for them, what strengths do you believe they will say you demonstrated?
6. If your best friend, Angela, were here right now, what would she say were your best characteristics?
7. What behaviors do you think your probation officer would have to see for her to think you were making progress toward your abstinence goals?

8. Based on your report, it seems as though you had a long interview with Ms. Clora at Child Protective Services. What strengths do you believe she sees in you?
9. Sometimes it seems that parents just don't understand what children are trying to do. It sounds like this is the way things are with your father. You indicate that you want him to respect and appreciate you, but that he thinks that you are doing some things that you shouldn't. If he were here right now, what things do you think he would tell you to do differently in your life?
10. It sounds as though your sister has been with you during good and bad times. What things could she tell me about you that would really help me more fully understand who you really are?

QUESTION 1 POTENTIAL DIRECTIVE QUESTIONING RESPONSES

1. Alesha, you state you are addicted to heroin. Help me understand why you believe that.
2. Is the reason you are here for today's assessment because you want to avoid going to jail and paying a $2,000 fine, or are you really committed to beating your addiction?
3. Help me understand the things that you do that make you a good mother to your children.
4. You say your partner is abusive to you. What do you want to do about that?
5. What new behaviors are you willing to initiate today which will help you stop using heroin?
6. Do you believe that Child Protective Services is likely to place your children in foster care due to your addiction?
7. Has your partner ever harmed or threatened the children's safety?
8. Tell me exactly what you wish to accomplish by being here today.
9. Are your criminal trespassing and prostitution charges related to your addiction?
10. How old were you when you began using heroin?

Question 2 Responses

(A) Given that Alesha was referred by her probation officer and Child Protective Services, and that Alesha agreed to voluntarily participate in a substance abuse assessment in lieu of a jail sentence and a fine, it is important to inform Alesha that there may exist potential negative consequences for her participation. Specifically, the counselor will want to indicate the possibility that Alesha's substance abuse assessment may have an impact on the custody of her children. In other words, despite recent laws enacted to protect clients from possible sanctions related to their AOD treatment, should a judge determine that Alesha's AOD abuse poses an immediate and probable danger to her children, she may lose custody. Alesha should be encouraged to speak with her legal counsel before participating in the assessment.

Should Alesha report that she already has spoken to her legal counsel related to potential assessment negative effects and feels comfortable participating in the assessment, it should be determined whether or not Alesha wishes to have the assessment forwarded to specific persons or a specific agency. If she does, appropriate releases of confidentiality must be completed and signed. Once the releases have been signed, it is helpful to speak with whoever is requesting the assessments. Often these persons or agencies will want specific factors to be assessed. In other words, if Alesha signed a release of confidentiality for the addictions assessment to be forwarded to Child Protective Services and Judge Jones, it would be important to understand what specifically they wish assessed. This should be done before the assessment. For example, the counselor may learn that the assessment is to determine whether or not Alesha was under the influence at the time she was arrested for criminal trespassing and prostitution. It is unlikely a general addictions assessment would have specifically investigated this single incident in great detail. Therefore, the counselor would probably be required to reinterview Alesha to make an informed response related to this question. Given the cost and inconvenience of reinterviewing, it is best to make certain one knows exactly what assessment questions are being sought by the requesting court or agency before the clinical interview is conducted.

Additionally, it may be that the counselor either cannot adequately respond to a specific question or may feel uncomfortable doing so. In the example noted, the counselor may believe it is beyond her professional expertise to adequately assess whether or not Alesha was under the influence at the time of Alesha's arrest. Should this be the case, the counselor would inform Alesha of her inability to adequately respond to the specificity of the posed question and ask whether Alesha wished the counselor to address this issue with Child Protective Services and Judge Jones. Should Alesha wish the counselor to contact Child Protective Services and Judge Jones, the counselor can learn exactly what they wanted via the assessment and suggest assessment questions that seem professionally appropriate. Thus, if the counselor believes she cannot make an adequate assessment of whether or not Alesha was under the influence at the moment of her arrest, the counselor may feel she can adequately assess whether Alesha appears to have a history of addiction-related behaviors that match those noted during the arrest.

(B) A number of statements related to potentially negative consequences of assessment participation are possible. Statements similar to these are appropriate:

"Alesha, although Child Protective Services and Judge Jones are requesting an addictions assessment and you have signed a release of information form asking me to forward assessment findings to them, I am wondering if participation in the assessment may have some potential negative effects on you or your children related to custody."

Or:

"Despite the fact that you want to provide Child Protective Services and Judge Jones the assessment information related to your heroin use, the behaviors commonly associated with heroin use and being under the influence may be perceived by Child Protective Services and Judge Jones as dangerous to your children. Thus, the appropriateness of your custody of the children may be questioned."

(C) Direct statements encouraging Alesha to speak with her attorney would be best. Two such statements are:

"Given the possible negative consequences related to your children's custody and the proposed assessment, I would believe it would be in your best interest to discuss the possibility of potentially negative effects resulting from an addictions assessment with your attorney."

Or:

"Alesha, I certainly am not an attorney and don't know much about the law. Despite the fact you want to participate in the assessment, I am concerned that things you say may have potentially negative effects upon you and your children. If you haven't spoken to your attorney related to such possible negative effects of assessment participation, I would strongly encourage you to speak to her and learn whether or not such participation may have the potential to impact your custody situation or your sentencing. Let's call your attorney and get a consult over the telephone. That way you can determine what's in your best interests and how I can be most helpful."

CLISD-PA Tier One Skill Builder Vignette 2: Ming

A Practice CAGE Assessment

Ming is a 47-year-old male who voluntarily seeks an addictions assessment. He began using alcohol in his late teens. Although he has attempted to discontinue his alcohol use on three separate occasions, he has not been successful. Ming consumes "three to six beers a day" and becomes "combative" at times—especially when his wife criticizes his drinking behaviors. Ming feels guilty about his drinking and notes that when he is under the influence, he often is mean to his wife and friends. He denies ever using alcohol or other drugs in the morning or on first awakening.

(A) Please identify the four CAGE factors.
1. _____
2. _____
3. _____
4. _____

(B) Please describe how you would use the CAGE with Ming.

_____

_____

_____

_____

_____

(C) Based on Ming's clinical vignette, please, score and provide an analysis of his results.
Total Score: _____
Ming's CAGE Score Suggests:

_____

_____

CAGE Assessment Answers

(A) CAGE Factors Include:
1. **C**utting down on drinking.
2. Feeling **A**nnoyed by those who criticize your drinking.
3. **G**uilt feelings related to drinking.
4. Using alcohol as an **E**ye Opener.

(B) Using the CAGE with Ming: Given that Ming is a volunteer client, it would be suggested that the counselor begin by establishing some parameters regarding the assessment and describe how the information gained via the assessment would be used. Thus, the counselor might state something like:

Counselor: Ming, it is my understanding that you are possibly concerned about your alcohol use and perceive you may have an alcohol problem.

Client: Yes, I wouldn't be here if this were not true.

Counselor: Well, I am glad that you are here and wish to be helpful to you. Would be willing to participate in a clinical interview? I would likely begin the clinical interview with a straightforward and brief assessment interview called the CAGE. This particular interview demonstrates a high degree of reliability and validity, meaning that we can feel fairly confident that your truthful responses will provide an accurate assessment which would help determine if an alcohol problem is present. The interview is structured, so I will ask four questions and seek your responses. As I understand your assessment request, the information derived by the CAGE and our clinical interview would be provided only to you or those whom you wish for me to forward the assessment to. However, should I perceive you are a danger to yourself or others, I would be required by law to break confidentiality and intervene as necessary to protect you or others.

Client: I'm not a danger to anyone. I merely wish to learn whether or not I have a drinking problem. Can we begin?

Counselor: O.K., Ming. Have you ever felt as though you should cut down on your drinking?

Client: Actually, I have attempted on three occasions to discontinue my alcohol use. I've not been successful. The first time I tried to stop using alcohol was when I was in college. It lasted about a week before I fell off the wagon. Then, about a year ago, I became aware that nearly every time I drank, I would either verbally abuse my wife or embarrass her or my children. Often I would drink until I blacked out. Anyway, I tried to stop drinking. But within a month I was consuming more alcohol than ever. The last time I stopped was last week. I'm embarrassed to admit it, but I couldn't even make it a day without my alcohol.

Counselor: I appreciate your honesty and your willingness to be truthful, Ming. Let's move forward to the second CAGE question. Have you ever felt annoyed by someone who was criticizing your drinking?

Client: All the time. My wife and children constantly complain about my drinking. Even my boss has been on my case. He was angry the other day that I ordered two beers during lunch. I wasn't even drunk.

Counselor: So, I'm hearing you say that you have felt annoyed by others who criticized your drinking.

Client: Yes.

Counselor: Have you ever felt guilty about your drinking?

Client. Yes. I spend money that could be going toward the kids' college education, and I often feel guilty about the things I say when I drink. The alcohol just helps me relax, and I say things and behave in ways that accidentally hurt the people I love the most.

Counselor: Finally, Ming, do you ever take a drink in the morning to steady your nerves or to get rid of a hangover?

Client. I can't remember the last time I've had a hangover. Frankly, I don't use alcohol in the mornings or when I awaken. I never have and likely never will. To me, I don't start drinking until around noon. Then, look out. I'm drinking and working. I don't really believe alcohol affects me like other people.

(C) Based upon Ming's clinical vignette his total score is 3. He has: (a) attempted to cut down his drinking, (b) felt annoyed toward those he perceived as criticizing his drinking, and (c) felt guilty related to his drinking. One point is given per affirmative answer. Given that two or more affirmative responses suggest alcohol dependence is likely high, Ming's score suggests he likely has an alcohol problem and treatment is warranted.

CLISD-PA Tier One Skill Builder Vignette 3: Tony

A Practice SUBSTANCE-Q Assessment

Tony is a quiet, 21-year-old, Hispanic-American who frequently disengages himself from others and demonstrates little interest in social interactions. He claims "no friends" and says, "I do better by myself." He reports that he typically spends his free time watching "science fiction" movies. Tony believes others perceive him as "quiet," "shy," and "nice." Despite ongoing speech therapy, he has a pronounced lisp and stutters when he is nervous. Both as a youngster and as an adult, Tony was often the target of peer-engendered pranks and jokes. He indicates that these experiences led him to begin "experimenting" with alcohol, marijuana, and later cocaine. "It was my way of escaping." He states, "I started using just to get free of all the hassles people were putting on me." Tony reports that his father has abused alcohol "for as long as I can remember." He indicates that father often would use alcohol to "drown his feelings of anger and resentment." Tony's oldest brother, Arthur, frequently abuses both alcohol and cocaine, as well. Tony states, "Arthur is always using." According to Tony, Arthur is well liked by nearly everyone and is identified as the "successful one" within the family. Tony denies behavioral problems and indicates he has never been arrested or charged with any criminal offenses. He also denies major stressful events in his life. "Frankly, life is going pretty good." When asked about tobacco use, Tony laughs, noting, "That stuff causes cancer. I would never use it." Tony works in the mobile tool crib of a local construction company. His job consists of distributing construction materials and tools to others. He denies work-related difficulties: "I just show up for work and do my thing." When asked about high school, Tony reports he graduated 3 years ago with a 3.90 grade point average. Although Tony acknowledges an inhibited desire for traditional, middle socioeconomic status achievement markers (e.g., a college degree, a new car), he does not display lethargy, lack of ambition, pessimism, or low self-esteem. Given his lack of acknowledged peer relationships, peers are not noted as using substances. Tony does report previous attempts to quit using alcohol and cocaine, "It was just getting too very expensive. I kept telling myself, 'You don't need that stuff.' But each time, I went back to using."

As a counselor in an employee assistance program, you have been asked to use the SUBSTANCE-Q Addictions Scale to assess Tony's AOD risk. Tony came to you as a result of failing a randomized drug screen. Based on this vignette, please indicate the score you would give Tony (Fig. 3.7 provides behavioral anchor scores) on each factor and the total score. Then, provide the corresponding clinical interventions as noted in Fig. 3.8 and any further clinical recommendations that you would encourage.

TONY'S CLINICAL VIGNETTE SCORING
    Substance Abusing Family Member/Significant Other   ___ points
    Undersocialized   ___ points
    Behavioral Problems   ___ points
    Stressful Life Events   ___ points
    Tobacco Use   ___ points
    Academic or Work Problems   ___ points
    Negative Affect   ___ points
    Cohort Substance Abuse   ___ points
    Endorses Substance Abuse   ___ points

Quit in the Past or Previously Attempted Quits   __ points
TOTAL POINTS: _____
Recommended Clinical Intervention:

_____

_____

TONY'S CLINICAL VIGNETTE SCORING

Substance Abusing Family Member/Significant Other	10 points
Undersocialized	10 points
Behavioral Problems	0 points
Stressful Life Events	0 points
Tobacco Use	0 points
Academic or Work Problems	0 points
Negative Affect	0 points
Cohort Substance Abuse	0 points
Endorses Substance Abuse	10 points
Quit in the Past or Previously Attempted Quits	10 points

TOTAL POINTS: 40
Recommended Clinical Intervention:

Based on the clinical vignette, Tony's SUBSTANCE-Q Addictions Scale score of 40 indicates a moderate to high risk for substance dependence. Counseling and 12-step participation are warranted. Tony should also be given the 24-hour helpline and local support group telephone number. Given that Tony reports using alcohol, marijuana, and cocaine, numbers for each of these groups should be provided. Additionally, a "no harm" contract should be agreed to by Tony. Here, Tony would promise not to harm himself or others and would agree to contact the helpline number should he feel like harming himself or others.

REFERENCES

Allen, J. P., Eckardt, M. J., & Wallen, J. (1988). Screening for alcoholism: Techniques and issues. *Public Health Report, 103*, 586–592.

Bruss, G. S., Gruenberg, A. M., Goldstein, R. D., & Barber, J. P. (1994). Hamilton Anxiety Rating Scale interview guide: Joint interview and test–retest methods for interrater reliability. *Psychiatry Research, 53*, 191–202.

Bush, B., Shaw, S., Clearly, P., Delbanco, T. L., & Aronson, M. D. (1987). Screening for alcohol abuse using the CAGE questionnaire. *American Journal of Medicine, 82*, 231–235.

Del Boca, F. K., & Brown, J. M. (1996). Issues in the development of reliable measures in addiction research: Introduction to Project Match assessment strategies. *Psychology of Addictive Behaviors, 10*, 67–74.

Edelbrock, C., & Costello, A. J. (1990). Structured interviews for children and adolescents. In G. Goldstein & M Hersen (Eds.), *Handbook of psychological assessment* (2nd ed., pp. 308–323). Elmsford, NY: Pergamon.

Ewing, J. A. (1984). Detecting alcoholism: The CAGE Questionnaire. *Journal of American Medical Association, 252*, 1905–1907.

Ewing, J. A., & Rouse, B. A. (March 1970). *Identifying the hidden alcoholic.* Paper presented at the 29th International Congress on Alcoholism and Drug Dependence, Sidney, Australia.

Flynn, P. M., Hubbard, R. L., Luckey, J. W. Forsyth, B. H., Smith, T. K., Phillips, C. D., Fountain, D. L., Hoffman, J. A., & Koman, J. J. (1995). Individual Assessment Profile (IAP) standardizing the assessment of substance abusers. *Journal of Substance Abuse Treatment, 12*, 213–221.

Gutterman, E. M., O'Brien, J. D., & Young, J. G. (1987). Structured diagnostic interviews for children and adolescents: Current status and future directions. *Journal of the American Academy of Child and Adolescent Psychiatry, 26*, 621–630.

Heck, E. J., & Williams, M. D. (1994). Using the CAGE to screen for driving-related problems in students. *Journal of Studies on Alcohol, 56*, 282–286.

Hodges, K. (1993). Structured interviews for assessing children. *Journal of Child Psychology and Psychiatry, 34*, 49–68.

Hodges, K., & Cools, J. N. (1990). Structured diagnostic interviews. In A. M. LaGreca (Ed.), *Handbook of child and adolescent assessment* (pp. 65–81). Needham Heights, MA: Allyn & Bacon.

Juhnke, G. A. (1996). The adapted SAD PERSONS: A suicide assessment scale designed for use with children. *Elementary School Guidance and Counseling, 30*, 252–28.

Juhnke, G. A., & Scholl, M. B. (1997, April 5). *SUBSTANCE-Q: A substance abuse assessment scale*. Presented at the 1997 American Counseling Association World Conference, Orlando, FL.

Kadushin, A. (1983). The social work interview (2nd ed.). New York: Columbia University Press.

Lanyon, R. I., & Goodstein, L. D. (1982). *Personality assessment* (2nd ed.). New York: Wiley.

Mannuzza, S., Fyer, A. J., & Klein, D. F. (1993). Assessing psychopathology. *International Journal of Methods in Psychiatric Research, 3*, 157–165.

National Institute on Alcohol Abuse and Alcoholism, U.S. Department of Health and Human Services. (1995). *Assessing alcohol problems: A guide for clinicians and researchers* (National Institute of Health Publication No. 95-3745). Bethesda, MD: Author.

National Institute on Alcohol Abuse and Alcoholism, U.S. Department of Health and Human Services. (1996). *Form 90: A structured assessment interview for drinking and related behaviors* (National Institute of Health Publication No. 96-4004). Bethesda, MD: Author.

O'Hanlon, W. H., & Weiner-Davis, M. (1989). *In search of solutions: A new direction in psychotherapy*. New York: Norton.

O'Hare, T. M., & Tran. T. V. (1997). Predicting problem drinking in college students: Gender differences and the CAGE questionnaire. *Addictive Behaviors, 22*, 13–21.

Sabnani, H. B., & Ponterotto, J. G. (1992). Racial/ethnic minority-specific instrumentation in counseling research: A review, critique, and recommendation. *Measurement and Evaluation in Counseling and Development, 24*, 161–187.

Sattler, J. M. (1988). *Assessment of children* (3rd ed.). San Diego, CA: Jerome M. Sattler.

Selzer, M. (1971). The Michigan Alcoholism Screening Test: The quest for a new diagnostic instrument. *American Journal of Psychiatry, 127*, 1653–1658.

Selzer, M. L., Vinokur, A., & Van Rooijen, L. A. (1974). A Self-Administered Short Michigan Alcoholism Screening Test (SMART). *Journal of Studies on Alcohol, 36*, 1653–1658.

Smith, D. S., Collins, M., Kreisberg, J. P., Volpicelli, J. R., & Alterman, A. I. (1987). Screening for problem drinking in college freshman. *Journal of American College Health, 36*, 89–94.

Spitzer, R. L., Williams, J. B., Gibbon, M., & First, M. B. (1992). The Structured Clinical Interview for *DSM–III–R* (SCID): I. History, rationale, and description. *Archives of General Psychiatry, 49*, 624–629.

Tonigan, J. S., Miller, W. R., & Brown, J. M. (1997). The reliability of Form 90: An instrument for assessing alcohol treatment outcome. *Journal of Studies on Alcohol, 58*, 358–364.

Vacc, N. A., & Juhnke, G. A. (1997). The use of structured clinical interviews for assessment in counseling. *Journal of Counseling and Development, 75*, 470–480.

Chapter 4

Significant Other Interviews: Understanding and Promoting Change through Others

Chapter 4 Outline

Chapter 4 Learning Objectives:

You will:

- Learn to build on previously described individual interview techniques.
- Attain a greater understanding of the uses of projective, circular, and directive questioning with clients and their significant others.
- Learn how to use information provided via "an intervention" to confront clients' drinking and drugging behaviors and to use a joint client–significant other strengths analysis session to promote symbiotic change via strength-based assessment and goals.

- Describe potential benefits resulting from the systems oriented assessment process, which includes concurrent querying of clients and their significant others.
- Learn how to use systems assessment to demonstrate significant other solidarity and promote significant others' preidentified responses to future client AOD abuse.
- Describe six specific phases of the significant other interviews.

ASSESSING AND PROMOTING POSITIVE, SYSTEMIC CHANGE

Although some may subscribe to the notion that assessment is strictly a history-gathering, evaluation, and diagnostic process between an individual client and a counselor, I disagree. Counselors espousing such a view fail to understand the assessment process's significance and its inherent potential for promoting insight and creating positive change—especially change between clients and their significant others. Certainly, assessment's primary purpose is to understand our clients and their presenting symptomatology. Yet no part of the CLISD-PA assessment process holds greater potential for (a) formulating the most accurate assessment based on external observers, (b) confronting client AOD-abusing behavior, (c) engendering insight related to self and others' interactions, and (d) promoting healthy, systems-oriented change, than the significant other interview. Clearly, the significant other interview process can be used to evaluate and diagnose via individual and significant other inquiry.

More importantly, though, the significant other interview initiates actual treatment. Because the clients' significant others are present during this assessment process, counselors can concurrently query clients and significant others. Thus, counselors can gently confront incongruence between clients' and significant others' perceptions and beliefs. Furthermore, counselors can cultivate systemic change opportunities in which clients and significant others discuss presenting symptomatology and possible correlates to their AOD-abusing behaviors.

Some readers may be thinking, "How is it helpful to concurrently query clients and significant others, and why would I want to assess persons other than my client?" The previous chapter briefly suggests the answers. Clients' responses to Tier One individual clinical interview questions are based on a mixture of client perceptions and beliefs. This mixture is important, because clients' perceptions and beliefs can range from completely accurate to completely inaccurate. Despite potential clinical benefits of understanding even completely inaccurate perceptions and beliefs, it is vitally important to gain a thorough and accurate understanding of the facts about the client's presenting concerns (Doweiko, 1996). Such understanding is central to treatment planning and effective treatment outcomes (Doweiko, 1996). Significant other interviews provide balance to individual clinical assessments and often help compensate for clients' inaccurately stated perceptions and beliefs (Juhnke, 2000). Therefore, significant other interviews are crucial to effective treatment. Specifically, significant others' perceptions of clients, the presenting clients' symptomatology, and social, environmental, and physical factors that influence the symptomatology help counselors best address pressing concerns.

An example of this is illustrated in the following case vignette. A client reports that she drinks to intoxication only one time per week and denies any correlation between her alcohol abuse and other factors. However, during the significant other interview, her roommate notes that within the last 6 months the client has been intoxicated most evenings and typically consumes a fifth of vodka every 2 days. The roommate further reports that the client's alcohol consumption escalates whenever the client perceives her boyfriend is spending greater amounts of time with his friends than with the client. Thus, the roommate within the significant other interview presents a mixture of perceptions and beliefs that are different from the client's. This new information clearly warrants further attention and discussion within the significant other interview process.

Additionally, the roommate lends important information indicating possible social stressors that promote the client's increased dysfunctional alcohol consumption, something that the client either was unaware of or chose not to share. Had the counselor not gained this key assessment information before treatment initiation, valuable time and energy could have been spent addressing the client's inaccurate beliefs and perceptions mixture.

In other words, without the roommate-provided information, the client and counselor likely would have implemented less efficient, non-symptom-directed treatment goals. Such goals would probably be designed to identify precipitators and social stressors correlating to times of client increased alcohol consumption. These goals would likely be directed at identifying times when the client's symptomatology is more robust or problematic. Based on the roommate's statements and the ensuing discussion between client and roommate within the significant other interview related to these beliefs and perceptions, it is likely that immediate treatment goals can move beyond merely identifying potential precipitators and social stressors. Hence, the goals can now be directed toward eliminating or diluting the strength of these precipitators and stressors and implementing new coping behaviors.

Additionally, significant other interviews have the potential to engender client insight related to the presenting concern and therefore may promote more effective client behaviors. Significant others can respectfully confront clients regarding inaccurately presented or omitted behaviors. Given that clients identify and invite trusted significant others to participate in the interview process, conflicting statements are not easily dismissed or ignored. This is especially true when beliefs and perceptions are corroborated by more than one significant other during the interview process.

Using the previous case vignette as an example, if the first roommate's statements were further corroborated by a second roommate and the client's boyfriend, their collectively presented beliefs and perceptions would be difficult to deny or ignore. Additionally, the client may gain significant insight as to the gravity of her drinking behaviors. Based on my experience, this is especially true when beliefs and perceptions are respectfully presented and noted as a sincere concern by each significant other. For example each significant other may indicate something like:

> "Diane, you are very important to me. I believe you have a drinking problem, because you were drunk nearly every weeknight for the past six months. There has not been an evening this past week when you haven't been drunk. You are drinking a fifth of vodka every other day. You asked each of us to come here tonight to help you help yourself. So, don't tell the counselor you're only getting drunk 'one night a week' and don't tell her you only drink a 'little bit,' when these statements are not true. Let's be honest and help get the best counseling for you. This means you've got to be fully honest when you tell the counselor how often you're drunk, and when you tell her how much you drink. We won't accept anything less than your full honesty, because if you can't be truthful about your drinking, you are wasting your and my time."

Clients with whom I've counseled frequently don't fully understand the severity of their AOD-abusing behaviors until they are cogently and collectively confronted within the significant other interview. Until this point, they often don't believe they are AOD dependent or abusing, or they deny such dependence or abuse. However, when loved and respected family members and friends provide corroborative beliefs and perceptions, insight related to the severity of the client's AOD-abusing behaviors is often gained or admitted.

Some readers might now be thinking, "O.K., I guess it makes sense to interview the clients' significant others, but what does systems-oriented change have to do with my clients' assessments? Why is this important?" Well, the truth is, most AOD-abusing clients with whom I've counseled during the last 15 years experience their addictions linearly. They believe that their pathological AOD use is a direct result of an experience or combination of experiences that "cause" their AOD abuse or some naturally occurring proclivity to AOD abuse. Examples of such cause-and-effect thinking include, "I use marijuana because my father abused me," "You'd drink too if you were married to him," "Memories of Vietnam make me use," and "I've got a chemical imbalance that forces me to shoot up."

More importantly, it is not just clients who believe the clients' drinking and drugging behaviors are due to some experience combination or proclivity. Significant others frequently believe this, too (e.g., "My son wouldn't get drunk and beat her if she just acted like his wife and attended to his needs"). Often when significant others view clients' AOD-abusing behaviors as stemming from a sequella of traumatic experiences or genetic proclivity, significant others respond by both excusing the client's AOD-abusing behaviors (e.g., "It's not his fault for getting drunk and beating his wife. He's got his father's alcoholic genes") and repeating the same inappropriate rewarding behaviors that encourage the client's continued dysfunctional responses (e.g., "You know, I think getting drunk and walking out on her was the best thing you could have done, son. Why don't you sleep it off in your old bedroom, and I'll make your breakfast in the morning. You know you are always welcome here."). Thus, it is imperative that counselors via the significant other interview assess how significant others view the client's AOD-abusing behaviors. Concomitantly, counselors need to learn if significant others excuse or encourage the client's continued AOD abuse. Enlightening significant others related to their behaviors' effects on clients enhances effective treatment.

Therefore, this interview process provides significant others greater opportunity to gain a larger picture of the presenting issues and learn how both their independent and joint systemic behaviors encourage the client's continued symbiotic substance abuse. Concomitantly, the process can challenge significant others to independently and systemically orchestrate new, helpful behaviors to address the client's presenting concerns. Stated differently, this interview process teaches significant others that they are more than a collection of separate individuals who behave independently within a void. Via the significant other interview, those present learn that their independently occurring behaviors are interconnected, and their interactive behaviors create a system that has the capacity to promote new, healthy behaviors both among each other and within the client. Thus, if during the significant other interview one person is noted as continually rescuing the client from responsibilities when the client is intoxicated, the others can encourage new, nonrescuing behaviors.

For example, in this case, the client's boyfriend might be confronted regarding the manner in which he completes the client's homework and calls her professors when the client is intoxicated and unable to attend classes:

> "John, sometimes it seems as though you want to protect Diane when she is drunk. For example, this week you completed her calculus homework and told her professors that she was too ill to attend class. It may seem as though this is protecting Diane, but actually it keeps her from shouldering the responsibilities of her behaviors. Given that we all want Diane to get better, would you be willing to stop doing her homework and calling her professors when she is unable to attend classes because she is drunk?"

Therefore, encouraging John to change his typical rescuing behaviors has multiple treatment implications. First, given that John has been confronted by Diane's system's members—valued persons very important to Diane—and has been informed that his previous rewarding behaviors are damaging to Diane, John will likely attempt to demonstrate his changed behaviors. The logic of this statement is that John will change his behaviors because he will truly want to help Diane. Concomitantly, he will want to demonstrate to persons valued by Diane that he is committed to helping. Thus, he will likely eliminate behaviors identified by the system as being harmful to Diane and replace these negative, rewarding behaviors with more helpful behaviors.

However, John may not understand what new behaviors he could initiate. Therefore, the counselor can help via the significant other interview process by helping John better understand new, helpful behaviors that John can enact.

Counselor: John, it sounds like you really want to be helpful to Diane. You certainly have invested a great deal of time and effort in attempting to protect Diane from failing her courses. Now I'm hearing from Diane's friends that these protecting behaviors may not be best. I wonder what new behaviors you might begin that would be more helpful to Diane?

John: Gee, I don't know what I could do. I was only trying to help, but it seems that my efforts weren't as helpful as I intended.

Counselor: I think Diane is very fortunate to have friends as committed to her as you and the others here today are. Sometimes we don't know what would be helpful to those facing something as scary as addictions, and we need to ask them. I wonder if Diane would have any ideas.

Diane: I haven't got a clue. I thought his doing my homework was really helpful.

Counselor: I think your friends have brought up a good point, Diane. Should John continue to do your homework, it is of no benefit to you and robs you of your chance to learn. I'm hearing John say that he would like to be helpful, but that he doesn't really know what to do. You and I have discussed the possibility of attending Alcoholics Anonymous, yet you were reluctant to go by yourself. I am wondering, would it be helpful for John to go with you to those meetings?

Diane: Yes, I'm pretty scared of going alone.

Counselor: John, would you be willing to attend daily AA meetings with Diane this month?

John: I sure would. I'd do anything to help.

Counselor: What do the rest of you think? Do you think it would be a positive thing for John to attend AA meetings with Diane?

Carol: I think it would be a great thing and want to thank John for being so willing to help.

Counselor: O.K., so what I'm hearing folks say is this. John's completing Diane's homework and calling her professors is harmful to Diane and unacceptable. I also hear that Diane and John are going to jointly attend AA meetings and that each of you believe this would be helpful. Now, what if John refuses to do Diane's homework, and Diane asks one of her two roommates to do it for her. . .?

Roommate: We simply won't do it.

This vignette demonstrates how the counselor via the significant other interview can help an individual within the system implement new behaviors and concomitantly strengthen the client's system's support of healthy behaviors.

Furthermore, the vignette demonstrates a second treatment implication occurring as a result of the significant other interview—an informed system. Here, the system members learn that John will discontinue his rescuing behaviors and that both Diane and John will be attending AA meetings. Additionally, Diane has learned that her roommate will not complete her homework. Thus, the system has announced its intent to change. Diane now understands that she can no longer expect the system to tolerate her asking John to complete her homework or call her instructors. She also knows that her roommates will not complete her homework. Furthermore, Diane has made a commitment to the people she values by indicating that she will attend AA meetings with John. Therefore, a new expectation is placed on Diane. Given that Diane values the people in the system, it would be difficult to dismiss their expectations.

Conversely, these significant others might tell the client how each of them will collectively respond the next time Diane becomes intoxicated,

Roommate One: O.K., Diane, we want you to understand that we have jointly agreed that the next time you become drunk, John, Carol, and I are going to contact the residence hall director and have her remove you from the dorm room. Additionally, Carol will not work your cafeteria job, and John will not complete your homework. Is this agreed to by everyone?

Carol: Yes, this is what we have agreed. Diane, you need to know that I will not work your job when you are drunk. I've been trying to help you by doing this, but now understand that I have been encouraging your getting drunk by not allowing you to take responsibility for your behaviors.

John: I also agree with your roommates, Diane. Your drinking is causing real problems in your life and mine. I will no longer complete your calculus homework or call your instructors when you are drunk. You need to face your addiction, Diane, and you need to do it now.

Thus, these significant others have described the client's newly unified support system, which will no longer tolerate Diane's pathological drinking.

THE SIGNIFICANT OTHER INTERVIEW

General Overview and Confidentiality Issues

The significant other interview is comprised of six separate phases. Each phase has its own assessment goals, which can be adapted according to the specific treatment milieu in which clients are participating (e.g., inpatient hospitalization, intensive outpatient). The phases are sequenced in a developmental manner designed to: (a) empower clients, (b) orient clients and their significant others to the significant other assessment process, (c) jointly identify the client's strengths and attributes, (d) gather pertinent data related to the client's AOD-related behaviors and confront inaccurate or nonreported AOD-related behaviors, (e) secure significant others' commitment to the client's recovery, and (f) respond to the client's postinterview needs.

During the significant other interview, counselors and clients work without significant others in the first and last phases (i.e., Phases 1 and 6). However, a group assessment format is used in Phases 2 through 5. Here, clients, their significant others, and counselors systemically interact. It is especially important within Phases 2 through 5 to remember that significant others are guests invited by clients to participate in the assessment process. In other words, significant others are neither patients being counseled nor mental health professionals providing counseling. Rather, significant others are charged with participating as consultants.

Thus, significant others provide historical data (e.g., "The first night Diane ever came home intoxicated was December 11, 2000"), report beliefs and perceptions different than the clients' (e.g., "Although you say you have never driven while under the influence, I know you were arrested two months ago on a DUI charge"), and identify the clients' strengths (e.g., "Diane is an excellent writer"). Additionally, they may be called on to describe their past or current feelings (e.g., "John, what was it like for you when Diane told you that you must complete her course assignments for her?"), cognitions (e.g., "Carol, what was your first thought yesterday when Diane came home intoxicated again?"), intentions (e.g., "John, I hear Diane claim that you are threatening to discontinue doing her homework because you no longer love her. Can you tell Diane and me why you no longer will complete her homework for her when she is intoxicated?"), or intended behavioral changes (e.g., "Carol, would you be kind enough to tell Diane how you intend to change your behaviors the next time she becomes intoxicated and threatens to hurt you?").

As client-invited guests, significant others are not bound by professional ethics or confidentiality. Therefore, clients and the significant others should be informed of these issues before the significant other interview process is initiated. For example, counselors should inform clients that although counselors will encourage significant others to keep everything said within the interview confidential, significant others may still tell nonparticipants of potentially embarrassing or hurtful facts or occurrences. Additionally, before any significant others are contacted regarding possible interview participation, clients must sign release of confidential information forms. Minimally, these releases allow counselors to speak with significant others. Furthermore, individual releases should be signed by all participants (e.g., client, counselor, and all participating significant others), thereby providing participants permission to communicate with one another during the course of treatment. Counselors may also require participants to sign a pretreatment contract. This pretreatment contract, although not necessarily legally binding, relinquishes participants' rights to seek case records or to attempt to compel the counselor or other participants to divulge communications or occurrences that took place within the course of the assessment or during treatment.

The six significant other interview phases are described next. The intent of this description is to familiarize readers with the phases and succinctly outline the distinct differences between them.

IDENTIFICATION PHASE

The first goal of this phase is to help clients identify one to three persons who can provide historical and current data regarding clients, the clients' AOD-related behaviors, and presenting clinical symptomatology. Most often, clients will identify a spouse or partner as someone they believe can be helpful in providing such information. Family members are often identified as well. And, depending on the specific client, school or work friends, clergy, neighbors, teachers, and work supervisors are likely candidates.

Given that some clients are initially reluctant to ask significant others to participate in the interview, it is typically best to begin this identification process by reminding clients of persons previously identified as important during the individual clinical interview. As described in the preceding chapter, counselors within the individual clinical interview help their clients identify persons considered most important (e.g., "Jane, who are the three persons who mean the most to you?"). Depending on clients' needs, counselors will remind clients of the previously identified important persons and ask who would be able to describe clients and their symptomatology best.

Counselor: Diane, four persons you previously indicated as being very important to you were your mother, your two roommates, and your boyfriend. Is that correct?

Diane: Yes, they are the most important people in my life.

Counselor: I bet they know you quite well.

Diane: Nobody knows me better than them.

Counselor: If you were to make a list and indicate the persons most able to accurately describe you and the struggles you have had with alcohol, who would be contained in this list?

Diane: It would be my mom, my one roommate, Carol, and my boyfriend, John.

The next goals of the identification phase are to have the client rank these identified persons according to their ability to describe the client and her alcohol struggles, and to encourage the client to consider the importance of having these significant others participate in the assessment process. Here, the counselor might say something like, "Which of these three most important people, your mom, Carol, or John, could most accurately tell me about you and your struggles with the alcohol?" Once the person considered most able to describe Diane and her alcohol struggles is identified, the counselor repeats the process until a rank between 1 and 3 has been completed. Later, this ranking will be used to contact these persons.

Next, the counselor describes the importance of having valued and trusted persons, knowledgeable about the client and her symptomatology, help the counselor better understand both the client and her presenting concerns. Thus, the counselor might state something like,

Counselor: Diane, I am wondering, have you ever closed both eyes so that you could see something better?

Diane: I can't say that I have.

Counselor: Me either . . . as a matter of fact, I like to have both my eyes open when I am trying to see something better, don't you?

Diane: Yeah, sure.

Counselor: Last summer when I was driving through Atlanta and looking for a specific exit, I asked all three people in my car to look for the airport exit. I did this because I wanted to make certain I didn't make a wrong turn, lose valuable time, or get lost. As a matter of fact, sometimes I get so busy driving my car and staying on the road that I don't even know all the things occurring around me. This is why I asked my passengers to help me find the Atlanta Airport exit. I know that three sets of eyes are better than one.

Diane: That makes sense, but I guess I don't understand how this is relevant to my counseling.

Counselor: Well, one of the things I have found so helpful in providing effective counseling is having persons truly valued and trusted by my clients help me better understand clients and the struggles that they so valiantly face. Often these significant others can provide vital information that can help clarify what things are really like for the clients, the problems and stressors they face, and the issues that impact their addictions. Sometimes they even see things that our clients don't, because clients are so focused on everyday events and countless factors related to surviving each day with their addiction. Based on what you've said here today, it seems that you have three trusted family members and friends who know you very well. And it sounds as though you believe your mother knows you best, and that John and Carol know your struggles with alcohol best. Is that correct?

Diane: True.

Counselor: Given that these people know so very much about you and understand the many struggles which you have faced, and given that you value your mom and friends so much, it would be helpful for me to talk with them to learn more about you. I know you want the most effective treatment with the quickest positive results. In my professional opinion, I believe they could be very helpful to providing the end results which you have told me you want.

Diane: You mean asking my mom and friends to come here?

Counselor: Yes. You've told me how important they are to you, and how well they understand you and your addiction-related struggles. I think they could help me better understand you and your struggles through their eyes. Doesn't it make sense to invite the people who know you best, and who you most value, to help you fight your addiction?

Diane: It does make sense, but I'm scared they wouldn't understand and might get mad at me for asking them to talk with you.

Counselor: I'm confused. You say these people are important to you and that you value them. Oftentimes, people who are important to me and value me also think I'm important and they value me too. Do you think that your mother, Carol, and John value you and think you're important?

Diane: Yes.

Counselor: Then, if someone you valued asked you to speak to their counselor, would you do it?

Diane: Of course I would.

Counselor: Then, are you telling me that you won't allow them to be the mother and friends that they likely want to be?

Diane: I guess you're right. I know my mom, Carol, and John love me. If I am to beat this addiction, I need their support.

This vignette demonstrates how counselors can help clients understand the importance of having valued persons who know clients and have knowledge of the clients' AOD-related behaviors participate in the significant other interview. The vignette begins with a metaphor that suggests that others, unencumbered by the client's daily challenges and her addiction, may provide information of which she is unaware. Next, the counselor indicates that her clinical experiences suggest that valued and trusted others are often helpful in providing information important to the assessment and treatment process.[12] When the client negatively reacts to the counselor's first suggestion of inviting the client's significant others, the counselor responds by reiterating the positive things which the client has said about her significant others: "You've told me how important they are to you and how well they understand you and your struggles with addiction." She follows this response with a direct question, "Doesn't it make sense to invite the people who know you best and who you most value to help you fight your addiction?" Thus, the counselor uses the client's own statements to establish the position that these people should be invited to participate in the assessment. Although the client then concedes, stating that the significant others' attendance does make sense, the client states that the significant others might become "mad" at her for asking them to talk with the counselor. The counselor then reverses the situation and asks if the client wouldn't attend a requested interview by someone she valued. Given that the client states she would attend such an interview if asked, she has little

---

12. Counselors should not indicate this if they have not found it to be true.

choice except to acknowledge that her significant others likely would attend as well.

Before actually having the clients invite significant others to participate in the significant other interview, I typically describe the types of questions that will be asked of the client and her significant others. Furthermore, I thoroughly describe the six-phase significant other interview process. Additionally, I attempt to reassure clients that the intent of the interview is to provide information of which they may or may not be aware. Most importantly, I remind clients of the potential benefits of this upcoming interview and tell them of the positive experiences my previous clients have noted as a result of such interviews.

Although I have had as many as five significant others participate in the interview, larger numbers can be challenging, so I typically limit the number of significant others to no more than three. Often one or two significant others are sufficient. In most cases, clients contact their significant others and report the time and location of the requested interview. However, in certain instances with very dependent, ashamed, or depressed clients, I will place the call at their request and jointly the client and I will speak to the significant others.[13]

Clients are instructed not to tell significant others that they will be attending a counseling session or that the client's counselor is "making me call." Instead, I encourage clients to contact significant others and begin by indicating that the significant other is valued, appreciated, and able to provide important information to her counselor that no one else can. Clients are then to "ask" the significant other to help and "invite" the significant other to an "informational interview" with the counselor and one or two other persons. Given that most invited significant others are concerned about the client and usually have heard of the others who have been invited to attend or already know the others prior to the interview, most are willing to participate.

Reticent Significant Others

In my experience, the overwhelming majority of significant others invited to participate readily agree. Most are truly concerned for the client's well-being, and are less concerned about the interview's preappointment details than the client's immediate needs. Often these folks will make themselves available despite their demanding schedules. For example, during one recent assessment, my client contacted his mother at work and requested she participate in the significant other interview later in the week. Instead, the mother pleaded that the client and I not leave the clinic until she arrived. She immediately canceled her work-related appointments, left her office, and arrived at the clinic within 30 minutes. Upon my meeting this mother, she stated that she had known of her son's alcohol and substance abuse for years, but this was the first time he had initiated treatment himself. The impact of this mother's immediate and complete support for her son was

---

13. This is done in my clinic office with two extension telephones.

quite moving for the client and demonstrated the support he would likely garner from his family system.

Less common are those who are reticent to participate. Typically, these significant others: (a) have previously experienced the client's chronic history of unsuccessful treatment attempts, (b) are struggling with their personal addiction-related concerns, or (c) are less familiar with the client than the client perceives. Hence, these significant others are often less invested in the clients' successful recovery than the client.

Because we often need only one or two significant others to participate in the interview, I encourage clients to contact the next person on their rank order list when someone flatly refuses or establishes unrealistic parameters regarding their interview attendance. However, when it becomes apparent that all previously identified significant others are reluctant to attend the interview, I encourage clients to role-play their telephone calls with me.

Suggestions are made regarding the clients' verbal communications during these role-plays. Once clients have created what I consider to be a fairly sincere and cogent request, I ask the client to call to a newly identified significant other, and I will listen to the client's presentation. Rarely a client is refused at this point. However, on occasions when this has happened, we have reviewed the relationships the client had with the identified others. On one such occasion, it became apparent that each of the significant others contacted by the client was related to his ex-live-in partner, whom he had physically abused. On another occasion, a review of the contacted significant others revealed persons with whom the client had been incarcerated. Clients were then asked to rank-order parents, siblings, grandparents, and other family members related to significant other interview participation. In both cases, siblings attended and actively participated in the significant other interview.

Denials That Significant Others Exist

It makes sense that clients fulfilling severe *Diagnostic and Statistical Manual of Mental Disorders* (4th edition)–Text Revision (*DSM–IV–TR*) disorders such as schizophrenia, paranoid type, and paranoid personality disorder, where there exists pervasive distrust of others, may not identify significant others. Clearly, I would not be surprised if persons with these diagnoses denied the existence of significant others. Yet I have found that the majority of my clients with such acute diagnoses will, over time, identify family members such as a parents or siblings or case managers who can provide a relevant and helpful AOD history. In nearly every case, my clients fulfilling these *DSM–IV–TR* criteria have independently solicited persons to participate in the interview process. Therefore, I am especially suspect of relatively well-functioning clients who deny significant other relationships. Most often I interpret these clients as either exceedingly guarded or uninvested in treatment. An example of responding to a client who originally reports no significant others is presented next. The counselor might state:

Counselor: I'm confused. You seem to be an intelligent and articulate person, who clearly has the ability to form significant and rewarding relationships. Yet you indicate that you have no significant relationships and that no one knows you or can provide viable information related to your addicted behaviors. Are you telling me that you are completely unaware of anyone who could provide information about you and your presenting concerns, or are you telling me that you don't want anyone who can provide this information to do so?

This vignette demonstrates how the counselor first begins with a sincere compliment. Specifically, the client is told that the counselor perceives the client as intelligent and articulate. The same sentence concludes by gently challenging the client's statement that she has no significant others. Here, the counselor implies that not only does the client have an ability to establish modest relationships, but based on her demonstrated intelligence and articulate communications, she has an ability to create "rewarding" relationships. The incongruence between the counselor's complementary perceptions and the client's statement is then made. Hence, the client must deny the counselor's compliments regarding her intelligence and her ability to communicate, if she is to espouse the position that she has no relationships. Finally, the counselor asks an "either–or" dichotomous question.

This dichotomous question forces the client's response. Given that the significant other interview follows the individual clinical interview in which the client likely discussed significant others, it would now be difficult for the client to deny significant others' existence. Therefore, should the client claim the first option, that no significant others exist, she is likely recanting her previous statements from the individual clinical interview and expressing the belief that no one can provide information about her. It has been my experience that even the most resistant clients will not endorse this first option, as it is relatively indefensible and most clients realize that there exists at least a handful of people who can provide the requested information. Should the client endorse the second dichotomous option, she indicates that significant others exist, but that she doesn't want them to disclose information about her. Thus, she is declining to fully participate in treatment. The result is a type of therapeutic double bind that challenges the client to abandon her position that others will not be invited to participate. The following clinical vignette demonstrates how to address clients who first deny the existence of significant others and later resist contact with these persons.

Diane: Listen to what I am saying. There is no one who knows me or who can tell you about my drinking and drugging.

Counselor: So you've not interacted with anyone since your birth and no one has ever been with you when you've used?

Diane: I'm not saying that.

Counselor: What are you saying?

Diane: I'm just saying that all my friends think they know me, but they really don't. Besides, none of them would be able to tell you any more than I've already told you.

Counselor: So what you are really telling me is that friends and family have observed you, but they would be unable to provide accurate information about you. And you don't want me to speak with them because you believe they cannot provide anymore information than what you've told me.

Diane: Yeah.

Counselor: So, of your friends and family members, who have you spent the most time with in the last month?

Diane: I don't know, probably, Sondra.

Counselor: How about asking Sondra if she would be willing to come in and tell us a little bit about the "you" that she knows.

Diane: No way!

Counselor: Based on my clinical experiences, I have found that friends and family members can often provide very useful information that can help speed the treatment and recovery process. Isn't that what you want?

Diane: Yes.

Counselor: Additionally, friends and family often can provide a very helpful support system for those in recovery. Would you be willing to call Sondra and have her meet with us, so I can learn her perceptions of you and your alcohol and drug use?

Diane: Are you thick or something? I said no.

Counselor: Whom would you be willing to have come in and provide information?

Diane: Like I said, no one.

Counselor: No one at all?

Diane: No one.

Counselor: If there was one person who you could feel comfortable asking, who would that be?

Diane: I don't know. Maybe my brother.

Counselor: It sounds as though you believe your brother would come in if you asked.

Diane: He is the only one besides Sondra who has ever appreciated me.

Counselor: I'll tell you what, let me tell you more about the kinds of things that typically happen during these important interviews. Then let's see if we can't contact your brother and find out what time he would be willing to come talk with us.

The intent of this exchange is not to badger the client, but rather to help identify at least one external observer who can provide vital information about the client and hopefully the client's AOD abuse. Instead of indicating that the client is lying when she indicates there is no one who can tell about her AOD abuse, the counselor merely questions if she has ever interacted with anyone since her birth. This clearly opens the doors for the identification of someone with whom the client has interacted.

When the client clarifies that she has "friends" but that they neither know the "real" client nor can provide further information, the counselor responds by restating what the client said. Specifically, the counselor does not argue with the client by attempting to persuade her that the client's significant others would be able to accurately describe the client's behaviors or provide more information than the client has already given. Instead, the counselor simply asks who she has spent the most time with during the last month. Again, this is a gentle way of identifying persons the client has interacted with without debating the client-presented concern that no one truly knows her.

When the client finally does identify someone, the counselor merely asks if the client would be willing to have the person participate in the interview. When this is declined, the counselor again attempts to reiterate the reason for inviting significant others to participate and the importance of the significant other interview. The counselor asks a second time whether or not the client would be willing to ask Sondra to participate. Once again the client declines a willingness to contact the person she has identified. Thus, the counselor places the responsibility of identifying an external observer back to the client by asking whom the client would be willing to ask to attend the interview. Again, the client refuses to identify a significant other. The counselor then asks who the client would feel comfortable asking to participate in the significant other interview. The client finally identifies her brother. Instead of immediately having the client contact her brother, the counselor indicates that she will further discuss the typical interview process, and jointly the client and counselor can make the decision to schedule the brother's interview.

Ultimately, should the client be unwilling or unable to identify at least one significant other to participate in the interview, the counselor has at least three distinct options. First, should the counselor believe that sufficient data has been attained via the Tier One clinical interview, the counselor may choose to entirely forgo the significant other clinical interview. Of course, this decision is questionable, because the counselor should only have initiated the significant other interview if sufficient information was not obtained during the Tier One clinical interview. Thus, one of two things has occurred. Either the counselor initially had sufficient information to treat the client and inappropriately decided to gather unnecessary information. Or the counselor did not have sufficient information for treatment, suggested the significant other interview as a means to gain the needed information, and then relinquished therapeutic and administrative control to the client by not gathering the still needed treatment-relevant information.

On the other hand, if the counselor believes the client is truly committed to treatment and, despite the client's refusal or ability to identify someone to participate in the significant other interview, further treatment-relevant information is necessary, the counselor could move directly to Tier Three, speciality and personality assessments. Stated differently, here, the counselor believes the client has legitimate concerns related to the significant other interview. Examples of such clinically appropriate concerns would include clients who have: (a) a severe *DSM–IV–TR* diagnosis such as paranoid personality disorder, (b) recently experienced the deaths or debilitating chronic illnesses (e.g., Alzheimer's, ALS) of the clients' most significant others, (c) recently immigrated to the region and are isolated from significant others, or (d) experienced extreme emotional or physical trauma from significant others. In such cases, it makes sense to bypass the significant other interview and move to the third tier.

Bernice[14] was such a client. Although highly committed to treatment, she had an extreme history of significant other disappointments and was unable to identify significant others with whom she felt comfortable. Thus, it was clinically appropriate to bypass the significant other interview. Bernice qualified for multiple *DSM–IV–TR* diagnoses including bipolar disorder, dependent personality disorder, and alcohol dependence. Her biological father had sexually abused Bernice between the ages of 9 and 12. He later abandoned Bernice and her mother when Bernice was 14. Her mother died later that same year in an automobile accident, and for nearly a year she moved between multiple foster care homes. She was finally adopted by a very dysfunctional family system in which she was repeatedly abused by the male family members. When Bernice's stepmother died, her step-siblings refused to allow her to enter the funeral home or attend the funeral service. The evening of the funeral her stepbrother came to Bernice's trailer, apologized for the family's inappropriate behaviors, and left a bag indicating that the siblings had identified "some things Mom would have wanted you to have." Bernice told me that the bag contained Bernice's mother's soiled undergarments.

Finally, should the counselor believe that additional information is needed and the client continues to be resistant and unwilling to participate, a third distinct option is to confront the client and apprise her of other available options. This third option is demonstrated here:

Counselor: Diane, would you help me understand what is happening?

Diane: Sure, what . . .

Counselor: Well, it is my understanding that you have come here, because you really want to get better and control your addiction, is that correct?

Diane: Uhmm.

Counselor: And you've invested considerable time answering some pretty challenging questions. Would you say that is correct?

---

14. Not the client's real name.

Diane: Yeah, so what's the point?

Counselor: For the last ten minutes or so, you've indicated that no one truly knows you. Additionally, you have been unwilling to identify even one person who could be helpful to my better understanding the problems you have discussed or the strategy which we can use to help you.

Diane: You've got that right. You're not going to speak with anyone.

Counselor: Help me understand what you think I'm going to say to them?

Diane: You're not going to say anything, because you're not going to talk with anyone about me. Truthfully, I don't think I've got an alcohol problem. Let's face it, I'm really here because my attorney said it would look good to the judge if I was in counseling, not because I think I need to get better. So you can ask all you want, but I'm not going to let you speak to anyone. And I'm not going to take those tests you talked about.

Counselor: So what I hear you saying is that you are only here because your attorney sent you?

Diane: Yes, that's the only reason.

Counselor: You're not here because you want help?

Diane: I want help getting my license back. I don't want to stop my drinking and drugging, because I don't do drugs enough to have a drug problem.

Counselor: I thank you for being so honest, Diane. I am here for another reason. I want to help people beat their addictions and have the lives they want. Regretfully, this doesn't seem to match what I hear you saying. Although you deny an alcohol or drug problem, you have been arrested for multiple DUIs and you continue to use. Additionally, during the first part of our interview you indicated that you often consumed more alcohol than you intended, that you haven't been able to stop your alcohol use despite numerous efforts to do so, and that you experienced a number of interpersonal problems linked to your alcohol use. It is my professional opinion that you need help and that underneath the bravado which you exhibit, you know you need help.

Diane: Well, you're wrong. Like I said, I am here only because of my attorney. I don't have an alcohol or drug problem.

Counselor: So help me understand what you thought we would be doing in session?

Diane: I don't know . . . talking about why I keep losing my license I guess.

Counselor: Based upon what you've told me, it sounds as though you keep losing your license because you have been driving while you were under the influence of alcohol. Is it possible that we could initiate counseling designed to address your alcohol use as it relates to your driving?

Diane: Stop it already. I'm not going to really counsel, I just want you to say I'm in counseling so I can get my license back.

Counselor: Diane, I think you know you have an alcohol and drug problem. But, until you are willing to truly participate in the assessment and treatment process, I cannot work with you. That wouldn't be fair to you. When you get tired of the problems related to your drinking and drugging, and become committed to addressing your alcohol and drug problems, let me know.

Diane: You have to let me stay in counseling so I can get my license back. That's your job.

Counselor: Diane, I want to help. But until you are ready to fully participate in the counseling process we would just be wasting your time and mine. Let me know when you really mean business.

Diane: Screw you. All you want is my money anyway.

Counselor: I wish I could introduce you to some of the intelligent and capable people I have counseled who experienced situations very similar to yours. Many of them originally just wanted their licenses back. As we counseled, they realized the same drinking and drugging issues which kept getting them in trouble with the police stopped them from having the relationships, jobs, and lives they so desperately wanted. Diane, intelligent and capable persons like you can have very high success rates and can make their lives what they want. How about we work on the goal of both getting your license back and reducing your drinking and drugging?

Diane: No.

Counselor: I think someday you will make the decision to quit your drinking and drugging, Diane. And when you do, I will be looking forward to working with you.

Here, we note the counselor gently confronts the client. She does this by first asking for the client's help and next reminding the client of reasons the client stated for being in counseling and the time the client has already invested in the assessment process. Next, the counselor reports the demonstrated resistant behaviors, specifically, the client's unwillingness to identify anyone to participate in the significant other interview. Next, the counselor carefully presents the need for input from the significant other. These are noted as helping the counselor better understand the client and her presenting problems and develop a successful treatment strategy. When the client states that she will not allow the counselor to speak with anyone, the counselor seeks to determine possible underlying anxieties about the process and what will be said to significant others. The client indicates that she does not perceive she has an AOD-related problem and that she is present at her attorney's urging. Additionally, she flatly refuses to participate in further assessment. The counselor thanks the client for her honesty, states the clear difference between the client's reason for attending counseling vis-à-vis the counselor's, confronts the client's denial of AOD-related problems with facts previously presented by the client as problematic, reiterates her professional opinion that the client warrants treatment, and finally suggests that unconsciously the client is aware of her treatment need. Again, the client denies any need and reports that her attendance is a result of her attorney's direction. The counselor again attempts to connect with the client by asking what the client expected during the counseling process. This is done to see if the counselor can capitalize on such expectations and minimally provide AOD-related counseling that might be facilitated under the guise of something else. Again, this is unacceptable to the client. Finding a continued unwillingness to counsel, the counselor finally indicates that the session, and further treatment, is concluded. The counselor encourages the client to return "when" she becomes tired of the problems resulting from her AOD abuse and when she becomes committed to resolving these problems. This statement is important. It implies the client ultimately will find the problems tiring and that sooner or later she will commit herself to extinguishing these AOD-related problems. In other words, the client is not being judged as incapable of successfully experiencing counseling nor abandoned for her unwillingness to seek immediate treatment. Merely, the counselor is saying, come back when you are ready to fully participate.

When the client demands that the counselor get the client's license back, the counselor again places boundaries on the counseling process, noting that when the client is committed to participate in counseling, the counselor will help. When the client becomes verbally insulting, the counselor ignores the insult and attempts to instill a desire for the client to participate in counseling. This is accomplished by reporting how others successfully completed counseling and found the process helpful, despite merely initiating counseling in an effort to retain their licenses. Again, the counselor compliments the client by indicating she has the necessary intelligence and skills to successfully change her life. The counselor closes by making one last invitation. When the client again refuses, the counselor reports that she believes the client will at some time make the decision to discontinue her AOD abuse and that the counselor looks forward to working when her when this decision is finally made.

The final decision to dismiss clients from the assessment process ultimately rests on the counselor and her clinical judgment. When it becomes apparent that, despite the counselor's best attempts, a client is uninvested and unwilling to cooperate, it is incumbent on the counselor to dismiss the client. However, the key to this decision must be that it is in the client's best interest to be dismissed. In other words, should the counselor believe that counseling will be ineffective or highly diluted due to the client's lack of investment or unwillingness to cooperate, then the counselor should dismiss the client and encourage the client's return when the client becomes an invested and engaged participant. This, however, does not mean that counselors should dismiss clients because clients are nonenthusiastic or ill-mannered.

Dr. William Purkey eloquently illustrates this point via an anecdotal story about a Japanese samurai. The samurai was employed by an emperor to behead persons who continually failed to pay their debts and taxes. As a professional, the samurai merely was fulfilling the charge assigned to him by the emperor. Thus, he had no malice toward those he was paid to behead. One day the samurai encountered a debtor he was assigned to behead. As the samurai drew his sword and prepared to behead the debtor, the debtor spit in the samurai's face and insulted the samurai's mother, wife, and children. Enraged, the samurai, resheathed his sword and walked away. Later, when asked by the emperor why the samurai failed to behead the obnoxious and insulting debtor, the samurai simply explained it would be unprofessional to behead someone out of anger or malice.

This story contains a parallel meaning for addictions counselors, who frequently encounter angry, obnoxious, and ill-mannered court-mandated clients— especially during the initial assessment process. Often these clients do not seek treatment; rather, they are required to participate by some external agency or source. As professionals, counselors must never dismiss clients in response to the clients' caustic behaviors. Instead, dismissal is a means to promote future commitment to the counseling process. This is accomplished by: (a) allowing external forces such as judges and probation officers demonstrate nonparticipation consequences, (b) allowing intrapsychic forces to escalate feelings of discomfort, and (c) instilling hope that counseling will be successful when clients dedicate themselves to the treatment process.

INTRODUCTION PHASE

The first introduction phase goal is to reduce both client and significant others' anxiety. In most cases, whatever anxiety exists quickly dissipates as the counselor introduces herself, welcomes the client's significant others, and succinctly outlines the purpose of the information meeting. Both the self-introduction and welcome should be brief. Significant others are present to help the client and typically are indifferent to the counselor's educational background, credentials, and training.

I have also found it helpful to compliment significant others for their attendance and to characterize their role as that of being "knowledgeable consultants." Therefore, I indicate that the purpose of the informational meeting is for them to help me understand the client and learn how I can be helpful. Additionally, I encourage significant others to make a verbal commitment to the client and to each other. Therefore, a typical introduction will likely begin similarly to this:

Counselor: Hello, my name is Jerry Juhnke. I am a counselor here at New Horizons and on Diane's behalf, I'd like to welcome and thank you for coming. Your being here today demonstrates your commitment to helping Diane and your willingness to support one another as Diane enters a new era of her life as a drug-free person. The purpose of today's informational meeting is for me to better understand who Diane is and learn how I can best help her. Diane has identified each of you as someone very important to her. You are the people who know her best. So, today, Diane and I are asking you to be her consultants. Is anyone opposed to helping Diane today or participating as a consultant to her recovery?

John, is this acceptable to you? Are you willing to help Diane today and participate as a consultant to her recovery?

John: Sure, whatever I can do to help.

Counselor: Mother, how about for you? Are you willing to help Diane and participate as a consultant to her recovery?

Mother: Of course I am.

Asking significant others to forthrightly comment on the interview process's acceptability and to verbalize their willingness to help the client is crucial, because it provides significant others an opportunity to present and address legitimate concerns that may hinder their full cooperation. Additionally, it is a means to demonstrate to the client the commitment she can anticipate from her significant other support system. Such verbalized commitment further promotes a united spirit among participants, thereby reducing the probability of someone intentionally or unintentionally sabotaging successful assessment and treatment.

The second goal of this phase is multifaceted. Here, the counselor reexplains releases of information and the limits of confidentiality in greater detail, establishes meeting rules, responds to voiced concerns, and insures that participants unknown to all significant others participating in the assessment interview are introduced. The initial release form must be signed by the client prior to the initial significant other informational meeting. This release clearly indicates that the client gives her consent for the counselor to speak to each invited significant other and to gather treatment-relevant information for the purposes of treatment planning, diagnoses, and intervention. Additionally, it would be wise to secure correlating releases from each significant other, consenting to the privilege to communicate with each participant including the client and the counselor. I typically want the releases signed, notarized, and returned to me prior to the informational meeting. However, if this cannot happen or if a significant other has forgotten to complete the form, I make certain all releases are completed, witnessed or notarized, and dated at this time.

Related to the limits of confidentiality and informational meeting rules, I typically begin by indicating that although I as the counselor am the only one bound by professional confidentiality ethics and laws, it would be important to promise to the client and one another that everything that is stated during the informational meeting stays confidential and that significant others not discuss the occurrences or communications outside the information interview. I then seek verbal confirmation of this request from each person present. For example, the counselor might say:

Counselor: Before we go any further, I need to bring up the topic of confidentiality. It is important for you to know that I cannot guarantee that everything you say in this meeting will be confidential. I am unaware of any law that states that you cannot share information or report to others what is said or what happens in this informational meeting to persons who are not present. In other words, you should be cautious about sharing sensitive information or information that could be potentially embarrassing or harmful. The law clearly states that I am the only one here who is bound by confidentiality. Therefore, I cannot discuss what happens here outside of this room unless I either have your permission to do so or I believe that you or someone else is in danger. However, knowing the importance of confidentiality and the need to have faith in each other, I am wondering if each of you would be willing to make a confidentiality pledge to one another. Although this pledge may not provide legal recourse for breaking confidentiality and understanding that it may not be legally binding, the pledge would be made by each of us, stating that whatever is said in today's meeting stays in the room and is not shared outside this room to anyone unless someone is being a danger herself or in danger of being injured. Would this be acceptable to you?

Diane: I'd like that.

John: Yes, this makes sense.

Mother: Certainly.

Counselor: O.K., Diane, John, and Mother, I am hearing that each of is pledging not to report anything which is said or done in this room to someone other than yourselves or me, is that correct?

Diane, John, & Mother: Yes.

Next, the counselor establishes the informational meeting rules. Although these rules can vary from counselor to counselor and are at the complete discretion of the counselor, I have found that seven basic rules are important for the meeting. These include:

EACH PERSON SHOULD BE TREATED WITH RESPECT
Participants should respect each other by treating each other as they wish to be treated. No one should swear at another, call another derogatory names, or be caustically sarcastic. Threats of violence or implied threats will not be tolerated.

EACH PERSON AGREES TO SPEAK TRUTHFULLY
Participants promise to speak the truth at all times. No one should be accused of lying.

EACH PERSON AGREES TO SPEAK FOR HERSELF
Participants may describe behaviors that they observed in others (e.g., "I saw Diane consume a fifth of Vodka at 8 p.m. last night"), but participants will not speak for others (e.g., "Diane is too scared to tell her mother what she really thinks about her father") or attempt to interpret observed behaviors (e.g., "I think Diane was scared that John was going to break up with her").

EACH PERSON AGREES TO PARTICIPATE
Participants will contribute via their active participation. Nonparticipation suggests an unwillingness to support the client or an inability to provide necessary support. Thus, it is vital that participants invest themselves in the interview process.

EACH PERSON AGREES TO ASK QUESTIONS
Participants will ask questions and have the right to expect honest and thorough responses.

EACH PERSON AGREES TO REMAIN FOR THE ENTIRE INFORMATIONAL MEETING
Participants can leave the informational meeting for a personal break, but must agree to return to the meeting.

EACH PERSON AGREES TO SUPPORT THE CLIENT AND PARTICIPATING
SIGNIFICANT OTHERS
Participants verbally agree to demonstrate their support of the client and others present by encouraging one another and helping in whatever ways deemed appropriate and helpful.

After the rules are discussed, clarified, and agreed to, the counselor asks participants if there exist any concerns or questions related to the informational meeting process or about anything said to this point. Finally, the counselor invites the client to introduce any participants who may not know one another.

STRENGTHS ASSESSMENT PHASE

The primary goal within this phase is to have significant others: (a) describe healthy ways in which the client is meeting her current needs, (b) identify ways in which the counselor as well as other nonprofessionals can help the client secure the client's goal of being substance free, and (c) encourage continued significant other positive behaviors toward the client (VanDenBerg & Grealish, 1996). This is done by providing clients and their significant others feedback regarding what they are already doing well, reinforcing these healthy behaviors, and advancing clients' and significant others' understanding of even healthier, new behaviors that could be adopted (VanDenBerg & Grealish, 1996). The result is a collaborative assessment and data-providing venture in which significant others, counselor, and client jointly learn what is working and helpful, and what is perceived as helpful in the future. Such a collaborative and positively framed experience is foreign to most AOD abusing clients. Many become emotive and are heartened to hear others say positive things about them.

Recently, one client with whom I counseled reported that he thought he was "a failure and a disappointment to everyone." However, during the strengths assessment phase he heard his mother and wife report a number of noteworthy accomplishments he had achieved, their continued love for him despite his addiction and associated addicted behaviors, and healthy and appropriate ways in which he was sharing marital and parenting responsibilities and achieving career success. The client openly wept during the strengths assessment phase as these significant others meticulously described the healthy manner in which he was working to achieve his sobriety and become the AOD-abstinent spouse and parent that he so desperately wished to become. By the conclusion of this phase it was evident that both the client and the client's support system had galvanized in a manner in which they previously had not. The client described the experience as being "the single most important day of my life" and noted that he could not have progressed in his sustained sobriety without learning that his significant others found him "worthy to be loved."

Despite the support occurring within this phase, the intent of the strengths assessment is not to "gloss over" or minimize client-presented concerns or difficulties. This would clearly be a harmful injustice to the client. Instead, the intent is to learn what is going well and identify how the client, counselor, and significant others contribute to this process. Thus, the strengths assessment phase encircles the client within a powerful, systems-oriented treatment milieu that continues support opportunities for the client and his or her significant others.

Finally, the strengths assessment phase provides an opportunity to establish rapport and trust among participants before moving to the next assessment phase. Such opportunities are critical to the assessment process, because significant others disclose information regarding their observations and interactions with the client during this upcoming phase. Often significant others will need to respectfully confront incongruent perceptions related to the client and his or her AOD-related behaviors. In other words, this phase establishes the foundation on which clients can be challenged. Therefore, it is imperative that the counselor help the client and the significant others affirm and support one another in the strengths assessment phase. This can be accomplished by asking clients to respond to supportive statements made by significant others during the strengths assessment phase. For example, the counselor may say something like:

Counselor: Diane, what was it like to have your mother tell you that she loves you?

Diane: [Weeping] I can't fully describe what it was like, because it was so unbelievable. After all the mean things which I did to her and Daddy, to learn that she loves me means so much.

Mother: Oh Baby, you know I love you and always will.

Diane: I know that now, Momma, but I didn't know that you still loved me until you told me. I had thought you hated me, because I was a drunk and wasn't living up to your expectations of me.

Counselor: Sometimes when people love us, they don't know how to respond when we are addicted or tell us that we need help. Mother, if you could say just one thing to your daughter about her committing herself to her sobriety, what would you say?

Mother: Honey, I'd tell you that I know you can beat this thing. You are strong just like your grandma and smart just like your daddy. I know you can be sober and stay sober. More importantly, though, Diane, I'll do everything I can to support you in your counseling. But I won't lie to you. If you begin drinking again, I'll get right in your face and call you a drunk again and tell you that you need counseling.

Counselor: What do you hear your mom saying, Diane?

Diane: I hear her saying that she believes I can beat my addiction.

Counselor: I hear her saying that, but I also hear her saying something else too.

Diane: What's that?

Counselor: I hear your mother saying that she loves you, that you can successfully address your addiction, and that she will support you in every way possible. But I also hear her saying that she is going to be truthful with you and call things the way she sees it. Do you hear her saying that?

Diane: Yes, I do. That's the way my mom does things.

Counselor: Does that mean she doesn't love you or that she is not trying to be helpful when she tells the truth?

Diane: Of course not. It merely means that she is trying to be helpful and knows telling the truth will help me face my addiction.

This vignette demonstrates two elements central to the latter half of this phase. First, it promotes an opportunity for daughter and mother to further build rapport and establish trust. This is done by emphasizing the mother's statement that she "loves" Diane and encourages Diane to report what hearing this means to her. Second, it inoculates Diane from responding inappropriately to truthful statements in the upcoming phase. Thus, not only is her mother indicating that she will make truthful statements, but the daughter encourages such statements and indicates the purpose in the mother's statements is to help Diane successful combat her addiction.

DRINKING AND DRUGGING HISTORY PHASE

In this phase, the chief goal is to promote the counselor's understanding of the client via others' external observations. Thus, the counselor will seek information from those who know the client well. Specifically, the counselor will solicit information related to the client's past and current AOD abuse, as well as the client's cognitive functioning, mood and affect, insight and judgment, interpersonal skills and social interactions, vocational history and marketable work skills, and environment. Therefore, this phase might begin with the counselor first lauding the client and her significant others and then asking AOD-related questions. An example is presented next.

Counselor: It is readily apparent that Diane is invested in this assessment process and the treatment which she has initiated. Furthermore, it seems that Diane is most fortunate to have family members and friends such as yourselves who are so supportive and committed to her recovery. One thing that we've heard today, is that Diane wants each of you to be truthful and help provide information to the best of your recollection. Is that right, Diane?

Diane: Yes. Please be truthful.

Counselor: Now speaking truthfully doesn't mean disrespectfully or mean-spiritedly. However, it does mean providing accurate information about what you know. So I would like to ask some general questions about your relationship with Diane and then move to some questions about things which you have possibly observed or experienced with Diane. Is that all right with you, Diane?

Diane: Certainly.

Counselor: O.K., John, would you mind if we start with you?

John: By all means.

Counselor: John, how long have you known Diane?

John: Well, I've known Diane since our freshman year in college. We started at State in 2000. And we began dating about a year ago.

Counselor: Can you tell me about the first time you saw Diane drink alcohol?

John: Like I said, it was freshman year and everybody drank. We were at our dorm floor party and Diane had a keg in her room. Everybody was drinking and getting plowed. Diane drank more than anyone, but it never seemed like she was drunk. She was the life of the party. Playing quarters and drinking everyone under the table.

Counselor: When did you realize that Diane had a drinking problem?

John: About six months ago, when we began seriously dating, it was quite apparent to me that she was an alcoholic. She couldn't sleep without drinking at least half a bottle of vodka a night. She would black out once or twice a week and not remember what we had done the night before, and she was so intoxicated most days that she couldn't attend daytime classes.

Counselor: Did you ever see or suspect that she was using other substances like marijuana, cocaine, hash, or LSD?

John: No, I'm quite sure she doesn't use any of those things. However, when she is semi-sober, she does smoke a lot of cigarettes.

Other relevant questions are noted in Table 4.1. Questioning continues related to these eight drinking and drugging history areas until the counselor believes sufficient information has been provided to ensure effective treatment.

TABLE 4.1. Other Drinking and Drugging History Phase Questions
for Diane's Significant Others

Current Alcohol and Other Drug Use

1. What substances have you observed Diane using within the last 30 days?
2. Within the last month, how many times have you seen Diane under the influence of alcohol or another drug? Please describe these instances for me.
3. Tell me about the last time you saw Diane using, purchasing, or possessing alcohol, another drug, or drug paraphernalia like a bong, roach clip, rolling papers, or syringes.
4. Within the last 30 days, tell me about the times when you suspected that Diane used alcohol or another drug.
5. Approximately how much money have you seen Diane spend on alcohol or other drugs in the last few weeks? And describe the ways in which she would get or purchase these drugs.

Past Alcohol and Other Drug Use

1. Tell me about the first time you saw Diane use alcohol or another drug. Please tell me when this was, what substances and how much Diane used of each, and to what degree she seemed under the influence.
2. Please describe how Diane's alcohol and other drug use has developed or discontinued since you originally met her.
3. Which drugs and substances have you seen Diane use since you became acquainted with her and which drug does she use the most?
4. In what ways have you observed Diane influenced by her use of alcohol or other drugs?
5. During the time you have known Diane, when did she use alcohol and other drugs the most, and when did she use alcohol and other drugs the least?

Cognitive Functioning

1. Some people are good at math, some people are good at writing, others are good at problem solving, and still others demonstrate their intellectual and "brain" abilities in other ways. Help me understand how you have observed Diane demonstrate her intellectual and "brain" abilities.
2. Each of us faces numerous mathematical problems that require our attention every day. These can range from paying bills at restaurants, gas stations, or stores, to balancing our checkbook. Please tell me how you have seen Diane solve some of these or other daily math problems and how skilled she is at completing math-related tasks.
3. I have found that some people remember just about anything which they have heard, seen, or experienced, and others struggle to remember. Please provide me with some examples of Diane's ability to remember names, appointments, people, events, and experiences.
4. When I was in school, some people would learn things very quickly whereas others had a more difficult time learning and completing tasks. Tell me about some times when Diane needed to learn something new, maybe for work, a game, or a hobby, and how easily such learning came for her.
5. Certain people love to read, are good writers and spellers, and have very sophisticated vocabularies. For others, reading, writing and spelling are difficult. Please describe Diane's reading, writing, spelling, and vocabulary skills to me.

Mood/Affect

1. Sometimes people who are depressed: (a) lose interest in doing the things they used to enjoy, (b) just don't feel like eating and unintentionally lose weight or sometimes they just can't stop eating and gain weight, (c) don't have any energy, feel worthless, or can't concentrate, or (d) think about suicide or talk about disappearing. Tell me about any times that you might be aware when Diane was depressed, really down, or blue.

2. Help me understand the times when Diane was excessively anxious or worried, maybe had an inability to control her anxiety or worry, or had difficulty concentrating or sleeping because of anxiety or worry.
3. Certain people seem to need hardly any sleep and have times when they are loud, very talkative, distractible, and/or believe they have special relationships with other people or God. Give me some examples of times you may have experienced any of these things with Diane.
4. Please describe any times when Diane may have been exceedingly irritable or when she had unusual mood swings between either being very happy and then becoming very depressed or being very irritable and angry and becoming very happy.
5. Tell me about times when Diane has suggested or said something that indicated to you that she was thinking of hurting herself or committing suicide, or when she was hospitalized.

Insight and Judgment

1. Some people know themselves quite well but others have a difficult time understanding who they are or what they want out of life. Please give me some examples of how you have known Diane has a good understanding of herself.
2. Tell me about Diane's personal understanding of the reasons and motives behind her behaviors?
3. Certain people have excellent judgment related to others, experiences, and situations. These people often know when they should say certain things or behave in specific manners. I also know people who lack judgment and often say or do things that get them into trouble. For example, I know of a man who tried to make people laugh during a funeral. Please describe how your have seen Diane use her judgment skills.
4. How have you seen Diane use her common sense?
5. Please tell me about the last time you were aware of when Diane did not use good judgment.

Interpersonal Skills and Social Interactions

1. Describe Diane's interpersonal skills and her ability to interact with others.
2. Please provide some descriptions of how Diane interacts with people she knows well.
3. How are Diane's behaviors different when she interacts with those she doesn't know well?
4. How does Diane get along with people in authority—you know, people like her college professors, the police, her supervisor at work?
5. Tell me how Diane gets along with other people.

Vocational History and Marketable Work Skills

1. How does Diane get money to pay her bills?
2. Tell me a little bit about Diane's job, the type of work she does, the money she makes at that job, and her enjoyment of work.
3. Describe the things Diane dislikes and likes most about her work.
4. What do you believe are the three most important qualities or skills employers see Diane possessing?
5. Give me some examples of things Diane does well and the types of jobs which would utilize these skills.

Environment

1. Tell me a little bit about where Diane lives.
2. Who lives with Diane and how close does she live to friends and family?
3. How physically and emotionally safe is the environment in which Diane lives?
4. Who or what in Diane's immediate environment is the greatest danger to her?
5. If you could, what three changes would you make to Diane's living environment that would make it emotionally, physically, and spiritually better for Diane?

Incongruence is a prominent feature in this phase and needs to be thoroughly addressed. For example, during the previous Tier Two individual clinical interview the client may describe mild dysfunctional alcohol abuse and deny the use of other drugs or substances. However, during the Tier Three significant other interview, it may be reported by the client's significant others that the client's alcohol use is quite severe. Additionally, it may be learned that the client frequently abuses other substances such as inhalants (e.g., propellents found in aerosol cans) and often becomes suicidal afterward. Thus, this phase allows the counselor an opportunity to confront the incongruence. For example, the counselor might say:

Counselor: Diane, help me understand. During our individual clinical interview, you indicated "occasional" alcohol problems and reported drinking to intoxication approximately one time a week. Yet, today, if I understand correctly, your boyfriend, John, and your roommate, Carol, report that you are intoxicated most days and that you are experiencing blackouts at least three times a week. Can you help me understand the incongruence between what you told me and what I'm hearing today from John and Carol?

Diane: John just doesn't want me to drink and is making my drinking sound worse than it is. My drinking isn't as big of a problem as they make it out to be.

Counselor: I don't know, it sounds like a pretty big problem to me. John, did I correctly misunderstand that Diane is intoxicated most days and that her blackouts are occurring at least three times a week?

John: Yes.

Counselor: John, would you be willing to turn toward Diane and tell her that's why you think her drinking is out of control?

John: Listen, Diane, two nights ago you were so drunk that you fell asleep on the sofa while you were smoking. You didn't even know that your cigarette burned a hole in the sofa. The whole place could have caught fire. Your drinking has gotten out of control.

Diane: O.K., I had a little bit to drink and fell asleep. I don't know why you're getting all upset. I flipped the sofa cushion over and no one will ever see the hole.

Counselor: Diane, I think you're missing the point. John, are you telling Diane that you're concerned she is going to burn another hole in the sofa or are you telling her that her drinking behaviors have gotten to a point that they are a danger to her and to others?

John: I'm saying that your drinking is killing you, Diane, and you've got to stop before it's too late.

Counselor: Diane, what do you hear John telling you?

Diane: That I'm drinking too much and that he doesn't like it.

Counselor: John, is that what you're saying?

John: Kinda. I guess I want you to know that I love you, Diane, and that I don't want you to die from your drinking.

Counselor: It sounds as though John and Carol are concerned and want to help. Neither wants you to die from your drinking, Diane. Based upon what they are telling me related to the amount of alcohol you consume daily and the symptoms that you are exhibiting, I think they are correct. You may very well be in danger of dying from your alcoholism or from alcohol poisoning. Now can you help me understand how many times a week that you are intoxicated? You said once a week; John and Carol have indicated most days. Which is it?

Diane: O.K., O.K., I'm usually drunk just twice a week. There, are you satisfied?

Counselor: John and Carol, Diane indicates that she is drunk just twice a week. Yet I heard both of you say that she is drunk most days. Which is it?

Carol: Last week she was drunk every day.

John: Yes, I'd say she was drunk at least six out of the seven days last week.

Counselor: Diane, they say you were intoxicated six or seven days last week. You say once or twice. Which is correct?

Diane: I guess maybe I didn't think I was getting drunk that often. They are probably right. I just don't remember.

Counselor: Diane, you also told me that you weren't using any other substances except alcohol, is that correct?

Diane: Yes.

Counselor: But today both John and Carol have indicated that you are huffing aerosol can vapors. Can you help me understand?

Diane: Yes, I am. I didn't think anyone knew.

Counselor: How many times a day are you huffing?

Diane: About once or twice a day.

Counselor: John and Carol, does that seem to match your perceptions?

John and Carol: Yes. That seems about right.

Counselor: What other drugs are you using?

Diane: None.

Counselor: John and Carol, are you aware of any other drugs which Diane is using or has used?

John and Carol: No.

Counselor: Additionally, Diane, John and Carol tell me that after you've huffed you frequently report feelings of hopelessness and depression.

Diane: Yeah, so what?

Counselor: Well, I'm wondering if you would be able and willing to promise John and Carol that you won't kill yourself and if you have feelings or thoughts about killing yourself that you will call this help line telephone number?

Carol: If you killed yourself, Diane, we would feel terrible.

Diane: I never thought you really cared.

Counselor: Let's discuss how we can mutually agree to respond should you, Diane, have such feelings in the future.

This vignette demonstrates how the counselor gently confronts the client using both client and significant other statements related to her AOD abuse. The vignette ends, however, by initiating a discussion regarding a unified and collaborative suicide intervention plan among counselor, client, and significant others. Thus, this phase quite naturally unfolds into the reestablishing phase.

REESTABLISHING PHASE

Insuring Sufficient Data Gathering

The three primary goals within the reestablishing phase are to: (a) insure that the client, as well as the significant others, believe that sufficient data gathering has occurred to generate a thorough and accurate understanding of the client and the client's substance abuse and establish effective treatment goals, (b) teach clients how to ask significant others for help, (c) communicate and reestablish significant others' commitment to the client and her life independent from drugs, and (d) conclude significant other reestablishing phase participation. Therefore, this phase begins with a scaling question (Cade & O'Hanlon, 1993; O'Hanlon & Weiner-Davis, 1989). Scaling questions allow the client and significant others to assign numerical values to the assessment process and the final appraisal picture. These numerical values reflect the participants' perceptions related to the client and the client's substance abuse. Thus, the counselor might ask:

Counselor: On a scale of one to ten, with one indicating not at all accurate and ten indicating a perfect reflection of Diane and her substance abuse, what score would you assign related to our new, joint understanding of Diane and her current degree of substance abuse?

Each participant would provide a score. Should all participants indicate a fairly high score, such as 8 and above, the counselor might respond by saying something like:

Counselor: So it sounds as though we all agree that we have a pretty good understanding of who Diane is and her current degree of substance abuse?

Should all participants agree that this statement is true, the counselor would likely ask Diane if she believed the participants truly understood who she was and her current substance abuse. If Diane affirmed the participants' perceptions, the counselor would merely ask Diane if there was anything further the participants needed to know. If nothing was identified by Diane, the counselor would move to the next scaling question.

Counselor: Diane, everyone here believes we have a pretty good understanding of who you are and your current degree of substance abuse. Do you believe this is true?

Diane: Yes, this has been a very thorough and complete process. I think all of you have a very accurate picture of who I am and what substance I use.

However, should Diane report that there was further key information that her significant others needed to understand, she would be asked to provide the information at this time. If further information was provided by the client, the original scaling question would be restated and the process would be repeated until all participants and Diane believed an accurate assessment picture reflecting Diane and her substance abuse was provided.

Contrastingly, should one or more participants indicate low scaling question scores, the counselor might ask what further information would be required to move the participants' scores higher.

Counselor: I'm hearing Carol say that she would assign a score of three. Therefore, Carol is indicating a concern that we may have a relatively inaccurate understanding of Diane and the addictive substances she uses. Carol, help us understand what things we need to learn about Diane and the addictive substance she uses before we conclude today's informational meeting.

Once Carol identifies the specific information she needs to perceive she accurately understands Diane and the substances Diane uses, Carol will be instructed to query Diane until she feels relatively comfortable.

Asking for Help

When all participants acknowledge a satisfactory understanding of the client and her substance abuse, the counselor will ask the client to behaviorally describe how her significant others can be helpful to her as she begins her recovery process. It is incumbent upon the counselor to help the client request behaviorally anchored descriptions that are small, realistic, and completely attainable. This can be challenging as clients often don't know what to ask or are unaccustomed to making requests understandable. Requests should be made to one specific participant at a time and clients as well as significant others need to understand that requests may be denied. An example is provided:

Counselor: Diane, both Carol and John have demonstrated their desire to help by being here today. What they need to know now is how to help. Two things you need to understand before you ask for help. First, Carol and John have the right to consider or turn your requests down. In other words, they may be unable or unwilling to fulfill your requests. Many times people turn down requests because other obligations exist which inhibit them from being able to help as they want. So, should Carol and John turn down your request it would not necessarily mean that they don't like you or don't want to help. Is that correct, Carol and John.

John: Yes. We want to help.

Carol: Uh hmm.

Counselor: Second, for Carol and John to fully understand your request, it has to be made in a way that is specific. In other words, they need to know exactly what the behavior will look like. For example, instead of saying something like "I want you to communicate with me," it would be important to say, "When I get off work at the cafeteria at 7 p.m. on Tuesday and Thursday nights, I would like you to call me and ask me questions about my day." Given what I have seen you do so far today, I know that you are able to make very specific requests, Diane. Are you ready to ask Carol and John for help?

Diane: Yes. I really need their help.

Counselor: O.K., why don't you turn toward Carol, look her straight in the eyes, and ask for her help.

Diane: Carol, I really need your help.

Counselor: Good, now tell her what you want.

Diane: Carol, I want you to be there for me.

Counselor: O.K., Diane, good job. However, I don't know if we really understand what you fully mean. Look at Carol at tell her what "being there for you" will look like.

Diane: I don't know. I guess it means that she will listen to me when I need to talk.

Counselor: Good, now ask her if she will be willing to listen to you when you need to talk with her.

Diane: Will you listen to me when I really need to talk with you?

Carol: You know I will, Diane.

Counselor: Diane, how will you let Carol know when you really need to talk with her? I know that some clients simply call someone on the telephone and say, 'I need to talk,' others walk to their friends' homes and ask them for help, and still others convey their need to speak in yet other ways. How will you specifically indicate to Carol when you need to talk with her so that she understands beyond a shadow of a doubt that you need to speak with her?

Diane: I would just say, "Carol I need to talk. Will you listen to me?"

Counselor: What if Carol is in the middle of doing something like her taxes or something and just can't speak with you at that time? How will you handle it then?

Diane: I don't know.

Counselor: Could you say, "It sounds like this is a bad time for you to talk. When can we get together, because I really need to talk soon?"

Diane: Sure, I could say that.

Counselor: O.K., let's practice this. Turn to Carol and say, "When can we get together, because I really need to talk soon?"

Diane: So, when can we get together, because I really need to talk soon?

Carol: I can't talk until tomorrow.

Diane: But I can't wait until tomorrow. You said I could talk with you anytime I needed and I need to talk tonight.

Counselor: Good, you are letting her know that you need help right now. Excellent work.

Communicating Commitment

After the client has asked her significant others for help with her most pressing issues and her significant others have responded, the counselor reestablishes verbal commitment between the significant others and the client. Again, scaling questions are used. This time, however, instead of using scaling questions to determine whether or not the significant others understand the client's substance abuse, significant others are asked to identify their levels of commitment to the client and her recovery.

Counselor: Carol, you wouldn't be here unless you were committed to Diane and her recovery. Would you look at Diane and tell her on a scale from one to ten, with one indicating not at all committed and ten indicating completely committed, how committed you are to both Diane and her recovery?

Should the client indicate average to high commitment (e.g., scores between 5 and 10), the counselor might ask the significant other to describe behaviors which the client will see suggesting such commitment. Here, the intent is to encourage new, helpful, significant other behaviors that will promote the client's abstinence. Additionally, responses by the significant other further serve as a means to demonstrate her commitment to the client. Thus, whenever the client observes the noted "commitment behaviors," the client will be reminded of the commitment that the significant other has toward the client and her recovery. It has been my experience that when clients observe such noted commitment behaviors by significant others, clients are heartened and rededicate themselves to the recovery process.

Counselor: You report a score of eight, indicating that you are very committed to both Diane and her recovery. What things will Diane see you doing that will demonstrate your significant commitment to her?

Carol: Frankly, I hadn't thought about it [momentary pause] . . . well, she will see that I contact her at least once a week to learn what I can do to be helpful for her.

Counselor: Do you really mean that? I mean after all, if you don't contact her and ask what you can do to be helpful at least one time per week, Diane may believe that you are abandoning her or that you have forfeited your commitment to her and her recovery.

Carol: I wouldn't say something if I didn't mean it.

Counselor: Diane, what do you hear Carol saying?

Diane: I hear Carol saying that she is committed to me and my recovery, and that she is going to take an active role in my recovery by calling me one time per week to find out how she can be helpful.

Counselor: Is that correct, Carol?

Carol: Yes.

Counselor: Diane, I hear Carol saying that she is very committed. But what happens if Carol catches the flu and has a lot of things going on and accidentally forgets to call you. What would that mean to you?

Diane: I don't think she would forget, but if she did, I might think that she isn't committed to me or my recovery anymore.

Counselor: Carol, given what you've said, it certainly doesn't sound to me as though you are going to forget calling Diane. However, if the worst-case scenario occurred and something came up inhibiting your call to her, should it suggest to Diane that you are no longer committed to her or her recovery?

Carol: Of course it wouldn't . . . but if something did happen and Diane feared that I wasn't committed to her, Diane should call me and say, "Hey, you didn't call. Are you still committed to me?"

Counselor: Diane, what do you hear Carol saying?

Diane: I hear Diane saying that she doesn't plan on forgetting, but if she does forget or if I think she is no longer committed to me or my recovery, I need to call her and ask.

Counselor: Carol, is this correct?

Carol: You've got it exactly correct, Diane. If I don't call or if you have any question related to my commitment to you, call me immediately so we can talk. I love you as a sister and want you to know that I will do everything I possibly can to help you beat your addiction.

If, however, a client indicates low to below-average scaling question responses related to commitment (e.g., scores between 1 and 4), the counselor should seek clarification related to the low scores and identify what new behaviors the significant other will need to observe in the client to increase the significant other's commitment level.

Counselor: Carol, you've indicated that on a scale between one and ten your level of commitment is three. This suggests that you have some commitment, but that your commitment level is not very strong. Can you help me understand your response?

Carol: Sure, we've all been through this at least a dozen times with Diane. She says she is going to stop using, then within a month she is back on the bottle and is worse than ever. I attended Al-A-Non and learned that I don't control other people's behaviors. If Diane wants to quit she will. I can't make her.

Counselor: Agreed, you can't make her, but I don't think that is the question here. The burden for Diane's recovery is on Diane, not you. However, I also know that unless addicted persons have support from their significant others—people such as yourself who are extremely important to Diane— the process is even more challenging and the probability for full recovery is less likely. Diane can recover without anyone's help, but your commitment to her is vital and she is asking for your help. What I'm hearing you say is that Diane has attempted recovery before, and that you have found the process frustrating or difficult when she is unsuccessful. I think what we are doing today is working to ensure the greatest potential for Diane's success. Are you committed to helping Diane attain that highest probability of a successful recovery?

Carol: Yes, but I am not willing to sacrifice myself for Diane and her recovery.

Counselor: Good, because neither Diane nor I wants you to sacrifice yourself for Diane. However, I'm wondering what things would you need to begin seeing Diane doing to increase your commitment from a three to a five?"

Carol: Listen, if I could see Diane really being committed, you know, like attending AA on a daily basis or stopping her alcohol use, I would increase my commitment to a ten.

Counselor: So I'm hearing you say that when you begin seeing Diane attend daily AA meetings and discontinue her alcohol use, you will increase your commitment to her.

Carol: Yeah, that's it.

Counselor: Diane, what are you hearing Carol say?

Diane: Carol's saying that she's been there for me in the past and that she's committed. However, she has to see me start working my program before she will be able to move her commitment from a three to a five.

Counselor: Carol, is that correct.

Carol: Yes, all I've got to do is see her really work her program for the next month and I will become even more committed to her.

These vignettes demonstrate how the counselor can challenge clients and their significant others in constructive ways to encourage their commitment to the client and the recovery process.

Concluding Significant Other Reestablishing Phase Participation

The purpose of this phase is to help participants gain a sense of closure related to the significant others' participation, provide a brief recap of the session's positive highlights and agreements, and discuss any further thoughts or concerns. Additionally, given that all participants have signed releases of confidentiality, the counselor encourages the significant others to apprise each other, the client, and the counselor of any changes, concerns, or progress. Given the high degree of suicidal behaviors among substance-abusing clients (Rogers, 1992), the counselor also describes high-risk factors that may indicate suicidal ideation and appropriate intervention guidelines. In addition to the counselor's business card with telephone number, all participants are given the local 24-hour helpline number and are informed that if they believe the client (or anyone else) is suicidal or a danger to someone else they should immediately contact the helpline number. Furthermore, they are reminded that they may always contact the 911 emergency services dispatcher or take the client to a local hospital emergency room should they perceive she is in imminent danger. Finally, the counselor makes a few last closing comments related to the visible support and caring demonstrated via the participants. An example vignette is provided:

Counselor: We have accomplished much today. We've learned that Diane is committed to her abstinence from alcohol and each of you has echoed your commitment to her via this process. Furthermore, each of you has identified ways in which you are going support Diane and her recovery. For example, John will attend daily AA meetings with Diane, and Carol will call Diane each week to learn how Carol can be helpful. Your being here today clearly demonstrates your support of Diane, as well as Diane's commitment to addressing her addiction. Before we conclude, however, I want to encourage each of you to contact one another related to any progress or concerns that might become apparent to you. So, should you believe that Diane is doing a great job attending her AA meetings, call her and tell her, as well as the rest of us. Too often people only convey the bad things or what is going wrong. Diane, who do you think will be the first to call you and tell you how well you are progressing?

Diane: My mother . . . she always is the first to tell me how well I'm doing.

Counselor: John and Carol, it sounds as though you will need to act quickly to call before Diane's mother does. Mother, who do you think will be the first to call Diane to tell her about the positive things she is doing?

Mother: I strongly suspect it will be John. He is always telling Diane when she is making progress.

Counselor: Good, I'm glad Diane can count on you to provide her with support regarding her progress. Conversely, however, call each other and visit Diane should you believe Diane is beginning to drink again or you have other concerns. We may be able to meet at that time to discuss such potential concerns and insure Diane is making the progress that she wants. Next, let me talk about something which no one likes to discuss, but is very important. This is the issue of suicide and violence. Addicted persons have a high potential for harming themselves and others. If Diane states that she is thinking about killing herself or someone else, or should you believe she is in danger of harming herself or others, ask her. When you say, "Diane, are you thinking about killing yourself?" you are showing you care. Asking the question won't cause Diane to commit suicide. Rather, your question provides Diane an opportunity to let us know if she needs help. Diane, if Carol, John, your mom, or I asked whether you were thinking about killing yourself or not, would you become angry?

Diane: No, I would think you were just trying to help.

Counselor: Even if Diane would get angry, her anger is not the issue. The issue is keeping her alive. If you believe she is thinking about suicide, ask her. It may save her life.

John: What happens if I think she is going to kill herself, but she says she's not?

Counselor: On the back of my business card is the local 24-hour helpline telephone number. Call them. They are very responsive and can help. If they say they can't or if you believe she needs immediate help, call the 911 Emergency Services Dispatcher or take Diane to the hospital emergency room.

Diane: Hey, I don't want people to send me to some psycho hospital. I'm not going to kill myself. I want to live.

Counselor: I don't think you are a danger to yourself, Diane. And I'm sorry if I've misconveyed in anyway that you are a danger. You are not. However, we want you to live and not die. What I'm talking about is "should" someone believe you are seriously thinking about killing yourself. Should this ever happen I want people to know how to intervene to save your life. Each person here has indicated that you are important and they support you.

Diane: O.K., I just don't want you to think that I'm crazy.

Counselor: I don't. As a matter of fact, I think that you are quite healthy and moving forward on your road to recovery. Crazy people don't realize they need help, and they continue drinking and drugging. I sincerely commend you on taking this opportunity to contact each of these important people. Despite potential concerns and fears about how people might respond to the interview, you asked people to help. As I've listened and interacted with each person here, I have truly come to appreciate their clearly visible dedication to you. Each wishes to help. This is something that always doesn't happen, Diane. Additionally, not only have you asked for help, but you have done so in a manner that deserves much credit. Not once did you point a finger at anyone or condemn others for telling the truth or for their attempts to help. I am most impressed and sincerely believe the behaviors I have seen here suggest investment on the part of those who love you and a dedication on your part to successfully live alcohol free. Thank you for allowing me to work with you. Are there any further concerns or issues that need to be discussed?

Carol: No.

John: Not from me. I just want Diane to know that I love her and will help in any way I can.

Mother: Nothing that I can think of.

Diane: I think we are all set.

Counselor: O.K., Diane, once you say good-bye to folks, why don't you come back into the office and we will finish today's meeting.

POSTASSESSMENT PHASE

Unlike the previous four phases, this phase is conducted between the counselor and client without the presence of the client's significant others. The goals of this final phase revolve around debriefing the client related to the significant other clinical interview, clarifying any unanswered questions that the client or counselor might have, and describing the next step in the assessment process. Thus, either the counselor will indicate that sufficient data has been gathered related to the client's presenting concerns to establish a thorough treatment, or the counselor will indicate what speciality instruments will be administered in Tier Three. Thus, this final phase may start like this:

Counselor: From my vantage point, Diane, it seems that the interview went well. Each person indicated what seemed like a sincere commitment to you and your recovery. Each seemed to provide very relevant information, and each indicated specific things that they agreed to do. Were you surprised how well things went?

Diane: I was pretty anxious, especially with my mom and John being together for the first time. Although I was anxious, I had thought they would be willing to help. The only concern I have is whether or not John will really help me attend the AA meetings.

Counselor: I guess the real concern isn't whether or not John attends, but whether or not you will attend the AA meetings if John doesn't go with you.

Diane: You are right. It is about me and my commitment to attend. But I will be angry as heck if he doesn't follow through.

Counselor: Do you have any other thoughts or concerns related to the experience?

Diane: Not really. What happens from here?

Counselor: Actually, based on the information that everyone provided and our initial meeting, I believe I have sufficient information to make an informed clinical diagnosis and help you in the establishment of your chosen treatment goal. Why don't we meet again next Thursday at the same time? Please bring in a short list of the relevant treatment goals that you would like to address, and we can work from there."

SUMMARY

This chapter described the significant other interview and Tier Two of the CLISD-PA model. Potential benefits resulting from this systems-oriented assessment process, which includes concurrent querying of clients and their significant others, were provided. Additionally, readers learned how to use systemic assessment to demonstrate significant other solidarity and promote significant others' preidentified responses to future client AOD abuse. Six specific phases of the significant other interview were described. Corresponding phase goals were noted and clinical vignettes portraying actual assessment interventions reflecting phase goals were given. Readers also learned how to respond to significant others who are reluctant to participate, as well as, clients who may deny the existence of significant others. Informational meeting rules were also described.

CLISD-PA TIER TWO: SIGNIFICANT OTHER INTERVIEWS SKILL BUILDER

This chapter described the significant other clinical interview. Readers will next find a clinical vignette and questions regarding the readings completed thus far. Readers can use the vignette and questions as a means to prepare for the significant other clinical interview process. Additionally, readers are encouraged to compare their responses to the authors' proposed answers on pages 190 through 194.

CLISD-PA Tier Two Skill Builder Vignette 1: Rick

Rick presents as a healthy, 39-year-old, Euro-American male with slightly lower than average intelligence. Rick has worked as a county sanitation employee for the last 2 years. He was hired after completing an 18-month vehicular manslaughter sentence. This sentence was the result of his operating a motor vehicle while under the influence of marijuana and unintentionally killing a pedestrian. Rick resides in a state that revokes the vehicular motor licenses of all persons convicted of such crimes. Two years after completing their sentences, state residents may petition for reinstated driving privileges. Thus, Rick is requesting such an assessment. Assessment results will be forwarded to the local Department of Motor Vehicles hearings officer. Rick has signed all appropriate releases allowing you to forward his assessment results.

Question 1

Based on information provided within the preceding chapter, describe how you would discuss potentially negative assessment consequences prior to engaging in Rick's requested assessment:

_____

_____

After discussing these potentially negative assessment consequences, Rick requests that the assessment begin and the counselor initiates the Tier One clinical interview. During the individual clinical interview, Rick identifies the most important people in his life as his 22-year-old live-in girlfriend, Page, and his 36-year-old brother, Harry. He further reports that he hasn't used "any illegal substances" since his incarceration approximately 4 years ago. However, during the interview the smell of marijuana is noted on and about the client. When you first question Rick regarding the marijuana smell, Rick denies the smell: "I don't smell anything." Then he reports a "vague dope smell" on the coat he is wearing. He states, "It must be the coat. I found it at the dump. Whoever had it before me probably smoked marijuana or something."

Given Rick's guarded and brusque responses related to your questions and the incongruence between his statements that he "no longer uses" and the current cannabis smell on and about the client, you believe further assessment is warranted and recommend to Rick the need to proceed to Tier Two, the significant other interview. You thoroughly describe the significant other interview and ask Rick to identify "one or possibly two" persons he would like to invite for the informational interview process. Rick responds, "I don't know anyone," and denies the existence of any significant others.

Question 2

Please describe five potential responses you might use in response to Rick's statement that he doesn't know anyone.

1. _____
2. _____
3. _____
4. _____
5. _____

Question 3

What four examples were provided by the author as potential reasons to bypass the significant other interview and move to the third tier of the CLISD-PA?

1. _____
2. _____
3 _____
4. _____

Question 4: Six Phases of the Significant Other Interview

Identify the six phases of the significant other interview and list the goals of each phase.

Phase	Goals
_____	_____
_____	_____
_____	_____
_____	_____
_____	_____
_____	_____

Response to Question 1: Discussing Potentially Negative Consequences

Given that Rick is requesting that the assessment finding be forwarded to the local Department of Motor Vehicles hearings officer, the counselor may wish to discuss potentially negative consequences of a less than favorable assessment. For example, the counselor may wish to indicate something similar to what is presented here and have the client sign a document prepared by the counselor's legal counsel in order to ensure protection against potential future litigation brought forward by a disgruntled client.

Counselor: Rick, I believe your request makes a lot of sense. However, you need to be clearly aware of the potential negative consequences of an evaluation that may reflect recent alcohol or other drug [AOD] use. Before you engage in such an evaluation, please be aware that I don't make the determination whether or not you can get your license back. The hearings officer does that. I merely perform an assessment. Based on your responses, the responses of others, and test results, I will indicate to the hearings officer whether I perceive you are currently AOD abusing or dependent. If you are using or if you believe the findings will not support your petition for license reinstatement, I would strongly urge you not to participate in the assessment. Does that make sense?

Rick: Yes.

Counselor: Help me understand what you heard me say.

Rick: I heard you say that you don't make the decision regarding my driver's license, and you said, if I am abusing alcohol or other drugs, that I shouldn't do the assessment.

Counselor: Right. What do you think, should we begin the assessment?

Response to Question 2: Rick's Denial of Significant Others:

1. "I'm confused, Rick. Didn't you tell me a little earlier that your girlfriend, Page, and brother, Harry, were the 'most important people in your life'? Would you be willing to contact one of them and see if they would be willing to participate in an informational meeting?"
2. "Earlier you had indicated that Page was one of the most important people in your life and that you two had been living together since you got out of prison. Wouldn't you think that she would be willing and able to provide some information for the assessment?"
3. "Is it really that you have no friends or family members whom you can ask to participate, or rather is it that you just don't want to have them participate in the informational interview?"
4. "How is it helpful for you not to have someone tell me about the you they know?"
5. "Rick, are you telling me that you don't know anyone in this entire town, not even the guys you work with on the truck, Page, your girlfriend, or your brother, Harry?"

Response to Question 3: Four Reasons to Bypass the Significant Other Interview

1. Severe *DSM–IV–TR* diagnoses.
2. Recently experienced deaths or debilitating chronic illnesses of the client's most significant others.
3. Recent immigration to the region or isolation from significant others.
4. Experienced extreme emotional or physical trauma from significant others.

Response to Question 4: Six Phases of the Significant Other Interview and Their Corresponding Goals

Phase	Phase Goals
Identification phase	Identify trusted significant others who can provide historical and current data regarding the client, the client's AOD-related behaviors, and the client's presenting symptomatology.
Introduction phase	Welcome significant others, reduce potential participants' anxiety, outline the purpose of the informational meeting, compliment participants on their willingness to take an active role in helping each other, explain releases of confidentiality and ensure that all releases are signed, discuss the limitations of confidentiality within the information meeting, and describe the informational meeting rules.
Strengths assessment phase	Encourage significant others to describe the client's healthy behaviors, identify ways in which others can help secure the client's goal of being substance free, encourage continued significant other positive behaviors toward the client, and encourage trust between participants.
Drinking and drugging history phase	Promote the counselor's understanding of the client via others' external and historical observations, and resolve incongruence between client-reported AOD behaviors and significant others' observed AOD behaviors related to the client.
Reestablishing phase	Insure that sufficient data has been obtained to promote an accurate understanding of the client and the client's AOD abuse and establish effective treatment goals, teach clients how to ask significant others for help, secure client and significant other commitment to the client and the client's AOD treatment, inform client and significant others regarding potential suicide risk and available help sources, and conclude significant other participation.
Postassessment phase	Debriefing the client related to the significant other clinical interview, clarify any unanswered questions that the client or counselor might have, and describe the next step in the assessment process.

REFERENCES

Cade, B., & O'Hanlon, W. H. (1993). *A brief guide to brief therapy.* New York: Brunner/Mazel.

Donovan, D. M. (1992). The assessment process in addictive behaviors. *The Behavior Therapist, 15,* 18–20.

Doweiko, H. E. (1996). *Concepts of chemical dependency* (3rd ed.). Pacific Grove, CA: Brooks/Cole.

Evans, W. N. (1998). Assessment and diagnosis of the substance use disorders (SUDs). *Journal of Counseling and Development, 76,* 325–333.

Juhnke, G. A. (1995). *Mental health counseling assessment: Broadening one's understanding of the client and the client's presenting concerns.* Greensboro, NC: ERIC/CASS ERIC Document Reproduction Service No. ED 388 883).

Juhnke, G. A. (2000). *Addressing school violence: Practical strategies and interventions.* Greensboro, NC: Educational Resources Information Center/Counseling and Student Services Clearinghouse (ERIC/CASS).

Lewis, J. A., Dana, R. O., & Blevins, G. A. (1988). *Substance abuse counseling: An individualized approach.* Pacific Grove, CA: Brooks/Cole.

Nelson, M. L., & Neufeldt, S. A. (1996). Building on an empirical foundation: Strategies to enhance good practice. *Journal of Counseling and Development, 74,* 609–615.

O'Hanlon, W. H., & Weiner-Davis, M. (1989). *In search of solutions.* New York: Norton.

Rogers, J. R. (1992). [Current Trends] Suicide and alcohol: Conceptualizing the relationship from a cognitive-social paradigm. *Journal of Counseling and Development, 70,* 540–543.

Selzer, M. L., Vinokur, A., & van Rooijen, L. (1975). A Self-Administered Short Michigan Alcoholism Screening test (SMAST). *Journal of Studies on Alcoholism, 36,* 117–126.

Vacc, N. A. (1982). A conceptual framework for continuous assessment of clients. *Measurement and Evaluation of Education, 15,* 40–47.

Vacc, N. A., & Juhnke, G. A. (1997). The use of structured clinical interviews for assessment in counseling. *Journal of Counseling and Development, 75,* 470–480.

VanDenBerg, J. E., & Grealish, E. M. (1996). Individualized services and support through the wraparound process: Philosophy and procedures. *Journal of Child and Family Studies, 5,* 7–21.

Chapter 5

Standardized Alcohol and Other Drug (AOD) Speciality Assessment Instruments and Drug Detection Testing

Chapter 5 Learning Objectives:
After reading this chapter, you should be able to:

• Describe Tier Three of the CLISD-PA model.
• Describe the fundamental psychometric properties including the different types of reliability coefficients and the primary types of validity.
• Provide a general overview of the five AOD standardized speciality instruments contained within the chapter.
• Identify the four basic drug detection testing types and potential benefits and limitations of each.

INTRODUCTION

Via Tier One and Tier Two clinical interviews, clients and their significant others likely have provided sufficient information related to the clients' most pressing clinical needs and treatment concerns. However, counselors may need further information to either determine presenting concern severity or to help clarify provisional diagnoses. Standardized alcohol and other drug (AOD) speciality assessment instruments such as the Substance Abuse Subtle Screening Inventory–3 (SASSI–3) and the Beck Depression Inventory–II (BDI–II) are invaluable to this process and can help augment the counselor's initial clinical judgment. Thereby, the use of standardized AOD speciality assessment instruments to gather additional client information ensures that relevant treatment goals are established and ranked according to the clients' most pressing clinical needs.

Many standardized AOD speciality assessment instruments can also provide baseline data derived from pretreatment scores. Clinical progress or the lack thereof may then be determined by comparing these pretreatment scores to later scores. For example, some counselors choose to readminister speciality instruments such as the SASSI–3 at specific intervals throughout treatment (e.g., weeks 8 and 16) or at the end of treatment to determine progress. Drug detection testing can also be used in a similar fashion to assess continued abstinence.

Additionally, standardized AOD speciality assessment instruments can be used to support the assessing counselor's diagnoses and treatment recommendations. Many addicted and abusing clients deny their alcohol and other drug (AOD) problems. This is especially common with court-mandated clients or persons petitioning state departments of motor vehicles for the reinstatement of their licenses following driving under the influence charges and/or convictions. Often these clients don't agree with their counselors' assessments and treatment recommendations. Instead, they frequently attempt to dispute the face-to-face clinical interview findings and claim either counselor error or bias. Standardized AOD speciality assessment instruments can provide collaborating evidence. Congruence between speciality instrument results and the assessing counselor's diagnosis and recommendations is difficult to dismiss and further insulates the counselor from potential liability. Thus, for example, should the counselor's initial diagnosis and corresponding treatment recommendations be questioned by the client or the client's attorney, the counselor can demonstrate standardized instrument scores that support the initial diagnosis and treatment recommendations. Concomitantly, should the counselor find no evidence for a substance abuse diagnosis or related addictions treatment, standardized AOD speciality assessment instruments substantiate the counselor's professional judgment and promote liability insulation—especially if the client later is involved in a vehicular accident involving AOD abuse. An example of this situation might be if a counselor finds no substantiating evidence of a substance abuse diagnosis and supports a client's appeal to reinstate the client's driving privileges. Should the client later be involved in a vehicular accident in which someone is killed or severely injured, the counselor may be sued by survivors. Speciality instrument results supporting the counselor's nondiagnosis would champion the counselor's position and, again, potentially provide additional liability insulation.

Finally, many court-mandated or state department of motor vehicles-referred clients attempt to present themselves in the most favorable, non-substance-using manner possible and intentionally attempt to deceive the counselor by either flatly denying continued AOD use (e.g., "I haven't used since I got busted for drinking and driving; I started AA and have truly learned my lesson") or reporting minimal AOD use (e.g., "I use marijuana once or twice a year. Unfortunately, both times I used this year, I got busted"). Many standardized AOD speciality assessment instrument authors have developed scales or other standardized response analyses that alert counselors to such self-promoting behaviors. Thus, even if clients and their significant others somehow manage to deceive their counselors, standardized speciality instruments provide credible evidence that alerts counselors to such deception potential.

In review, then, there are four primary reasons counselors use speciality instruments. These include: (a) gathering additional information regarding clients and their presenting symptoms, (b) providing baseline data and tracking client progress and abstinence, (c) supporting counselors' diagnoses and treatment recommendations, and (d) alerting counselors to clients who may be falsely presenting themselves as non-AOD-abusing. However choosing a speciality instrument requires more than merely understanding why the instrument is to be used. It requires a basic understanding of fundamental psychometric properties.

PSYCHOMETRIC FUNDAMENTALS

Given that most standardized assessment instruments are interpreted according to their ability to be reliable and valid, this section provides a basic review of reliability and validity. This review is paramount to test selection. Counselors who understand these basic constructs have a greater likelihood of selecting speciality instruments that provide useful information about their clients and their clients' treatment needs. Unreliable and invalid instruments do little more than waste the client's available time, resources, and energy.

Reliability

Hypothetically speaking, a perfectly reliable test would provide the exact same score if it were administered to the same client an infinite number of times during the exact same moment. In other words, the score would be consistent and unvaried. The score would have no error whatsoever. An example of such hypothetical reliability might be a substance-dependent client who repeatedly took the same speciality assessment instrument and consistently received an identical substance dependence score on each test administration. In other words, there would be no variation in scores for the same person who took the same instrument at the same moment in time no matter the number of times the instrument was administered.

In reality, however, the situation is quite different. Classic psychometric theory suggests a client's actual test score is composed of two distinct parts: the true score and the error score. (Ghiselli, Campbell, & Zedeck, 1981). Thus, the client's actual score is merely a reflection of the combined true and error scores. Because the client's true score is purely hypothetical, the resulting actual score will likely vary to some degree on each administration. However, with highly reliable assessment instruments, the scores should be relatively consistent or "reliable."

Psychometrists use reliability coefficients to suggest a ratio of true score variance to the observed score variance and commonly depict the reliability coefficient with the letter r. These reliability coefficients can range from 0 (indicating total absence of reliability [all error]) to +1.0 (indicating perfect reliability [no error]). Therefore, when reviewing the psychometric properties of standardized AOD speciality assessment instruments, counselors should attempt to utilize instruments that demonstrate reliability coefficients as close to +1.0 as possible. In most cases, standardized AOD speciality assessment instruments that have reliability coefficients above .75 are acceptable. However, instruments with reliability coefficients below .60 have little useful utility and should in most cases be avoided.

Three Reliability Coefficients

Three reliability coefficients are commonly used with standardized assessment instruments. These include test–retest reliability, alternate-form reliability, and internal consistency reliability. Each has its particular strengths and potential weaknesses.

Test–retest reliability indicates a process in which a group of persons is administered an assessment instrument and readministered the same instrument within a relatively short time period. Often the second administration will occur within a two-week period. The underlying assumption is that the less time which passes between instrument administrations, the greater is the probability that the true score will be assessed. In other words, should a randomly selected group of cannabis-dependent clients who are not participating in treatment be administered the same substance-use instrument on two separate occasions within a relatively short time period, there is less likelihood that the differences in their scores will be related to behavioral change or maturation effects. Instead, if their individual scores were remarkably similar or consistent for both administration one and administration two, we would say that the instrument demonstrated high reliability.

Another type of reliability coefficient is alternate-form reliability—also known as parallel-form reliability. Here psychometrists develop two separate but equivalent tests that are administered to the same group. Because the tests are equivalent there should be no error in the scores. Thus, each individual's scores should be the same on both tests. Typically half the group will be administered one form while the other half is administered the equivalent form. Upon completion, participants are administered the form that they have not yet completed. Thus, if one were creating a speciality instrument regarding cocaine abuse using corresponding *DSM–IV–TR* criteria, two equivalent forms would be used. Each form would examine the same *DSM–IV–TR* cocaine abuse criteria, but would use different questions. Form A would be administered to one half of the group while Form B would be administered to the second half. Upon completion of the first instrument, group members would complete the form that they had not yet been administered. High reliability would be established if individual group members scored the same on the first instrument as they did on the second.

Unlike test–retest reliability, alternate-form reliability does not require participants to return for a second testing. One significant benefit of this reliability form is that only a single testing period is needed. Thus, alternate-form reliability reduces potential memory and practice problems, which can effect test–retest reliability. For example, in test–retest reliability when participants use the same instrument with the very same questions on two occasions, participants may respond based on their memory of the first testing experience (e.g., "I remember answering this question on the last test and will respond the same way again") or may have gained experience in answering their questions, which affects their reliability scores. However, the major difficulty with alternate form reliability is that it is often difficult to create two exactly equivalent instruments.

Internal consistency reliability is typically accomplished by splitting the instrument into two equivalent halves. Commonly psychometrists will pair equivalent questions next to each other and split the instrument into odd (items 1,3,5, etc.) and even (items 2,4,6, etc.) questions. Thus, two separate instruments are created on the same form (e.g., one instrument created from the odd-numbered test questions and another created from the even-numbered test questions). Instruments with high reliability would have identical scores when comparing odd to even test item scores. Potential difficulties with this reliability form are that (a) internal consistency forms of assessing reliability make instrument forms shorter and therefore less reliable, and (b) internal consistency reliability can only be used when the traits or factors being measured are unitary or homogeneous (Drummond, 1996). Table 5.1 summarizes the reliability assessment forms.

TABLE 5.1. Methods of Assessing Reliability

Method	Procedure	Potential Problems
Test–retest reliability (aka, parallel-forms reliability)	Identical instrument administered twice with time between administrations	Practice Memory
Alternate-form reliability	Equivalent instruments administered	Almost impossible to create perfectly equivalent instruments
Internal consistency reliability	Single instrument administered	Uses shortened forms Traits or factors must be unitary or homogeneous

Validity

Validity indicates whether the instrument actually assesses the factor or trait which the instrument's authors claim to measure. In other words, if the standardized speciality instrument is reported as a means to measure a client's alcohol dependence, does it in fact do so? Although there exist different validity types (e.g., face, content, criterion-related, and construct validity) counselors using standardized speciality instruments are typically most interested in criterion-related and construct validity. These validity types specifically either predict future substance use behaviors or suggest the immediate presence of a specific diagnosis (e.g., cannabis dependence).

Face Validity

Face validity is identified by simply reviewing the instrument's questions and noting whether the questions appear to measure what the instrument purports to measure. Thus, standardized speciality instruments that assess whether or not an adolescent client is alcohol abusing would have high face validity if they ask sufficient, relevant questions to determine whether or not clients fulfill *DSM–IV–TR* alcohol abuse and alcohol dependence diagnoses criteria. In other words, addictions counselors knowledgeable in the *DSM–IV–TR* substance use diagnoses determine the presence of face validity, and statistical analysis is not used.

Content Validity

Content validity is often used with educational tests. Here, selected experts typically identify the breadth and depth of items which should be covered regarding a specific area. For example, when the National Board for Certified Counselors (NBCC) was creating the Master Addictions Counselor (MAC) rating, a number of addictions experts identified content areas, goals, and objectives and wrote specific MAC examination test items. Specifically, our charge was to create an overall testing instrument that represented the domains relevant to the necessary

knowledge and practice needed for addictions counselors. Thus, with content validity, experts in the field review the instrument and report that the questions cover
the content area sufficiently.

Criterion-Related Validity

Two types of criterion-related validity exist. Both are important to counselors
selecting standardized addictions speciality instruments.

CONCURRENT VALIDITY

Concurrent validity is important for diagnostic instruments and can be used to
suggest whether there exists a relationship between two different measures. For
example, an addictions counselor may wish to determine if there exists a satisfactory relationship between a well-established and widely accepted addictions instrument such as the Substance Abuse Subtle Screening Inventory–3 (SASSI–3)
and a newly developed, unestablished, and less expensive instrument (e.g., "The
Blue Light, Cheapo Undeveloped Addictions Test") purporting to be "as good as"
the established instrument. In this case the criterion measure would be the established and widely accepted SASSI–3. Thus, the counselor would compare The
Blue Light, Cheapo, Undeveloped Addictions Test to the criterion measure to
determine if a strong relationship existed between the tests. If such a relationship
existed, the counselor might conclude that the instruments demonstrate concurrent validity. In other words, the results of the two instruments suggest they are
measuring the same thing. Similarly, if a director of an addictions research and
training clinic affiliated with an university counseling department uses the Alcohol Use Inventory as the criterion measure, she could compare *DSM–IV–TR* alcohol abuse diagnoses secured by interns at her clinic to determine if concurrent
validity was established. In this case, Alcohol Use Inventory scores would be
compared to *DSM–IV–TR* alcohol abuse diagnoses to determine if the two were
measuring the same thing.

One requirement of concurrent validity is that both the criterion measure and
the correlating measure (e.g., a test score or diagnoses) must be available at approximately the same time. Therefore, the counselor must be able to immediately
compare both measures. If this is not the case, one might be looking at the predictive quality of the measures and not concurrent validity.

PREDICTIVE VALIDITY

Predictive validity is another form of criterion-related validity. Here, the addictions counselor may be using a standardized speciality instrument to predict the
client's risk for future addiction or danger to self related to the client's responses
regarding current alcohol use and related behaviors and beliefs. The criterion in
this example may be future *DSM–IV–TR* substance-related diagnoses based on
the client's immediate test score. In other words, the addictions counselor would
be assessing the instrument's ability to predict future client behaviors.

Construct Validity

A construct typically refers to multiple traits or attributes central to a specific hypothetical term. Addiction, depression, and intelligence are constructs that suggest a clustering of traits or attributes. This form of validity is most important to addictions counselors, as they are typically assessing the presence of multiple traits or attributes that correspond to constructs such as Axis I substance "abuse" or "dependence" disorders or Axis II personality disorders noted within the *DSM–IV–TR*. Table 5.2 succinctly summarizes the four types of validity just described.

STANDARDIZED ALCOHOL AND OTHER DRUG SPECIALITY INSTRUMENTS

Numerous sources within the professional literature indicate both the importance of using assessment instruments and multiple benefits of using assessment instruments to establish pertinent and client-relevant treatment goals (Donovan, 1992; Doweinko, 1996; Evans, 1998; Juhnke, 1995; Lewis, Dana, & Blevins, 1988; Nelson & Neufeldt, 1996; Vacc, 1982; Vacc & Juhnke, 1997). A recent survey of all Master Addictions Counselors (MACs) certified by the National Board of Certified Counselors noted a number of standardized speciality instruments identified as used by and important to addictions professionals (Juhnke, Vacc, Curtis, Coll, & Paredes, in press). Participants in this survey were seasoned addictions professionals who minimally held a master's degree in counseling or a related professional field and had three years of post-master's addictions counseling experience. Three standardized speciality addictions instruments identified within this survey and two other instruments, all of which have convincing clinical utility and match with the CLISD-PA model, are described next. They are listed alphabetically according to adult assessment and, next, adolescent assessment. The adult instruments include the Alcohol Use Inventory, the Adult Substance Use Survey, and the Substance Abuse Subtle Screening Inventory–3. Adolescent standardized speciality addictions instruments include the Adolescent Substance Use Survey and the Substance Abuse Subtle Screening Inventory–Adolescent2.

Alcohol Use Inventory

General AUI Overview

Rychtarik , Koutsky, and Miller (1998) state that the Alcohol Use Inventory (AUI) "is one of the most comprehensive and systematically developed measures of alcohol problems available" (p. 107). The AUI was authored by Horn, Wanberg, and Foster in 1986 and was designed "to measure different features of involvement with the use of alcohol" (Horn, Wanberg, & Foster, 1990, p. 2). The instrument has 228 multiple-choice questions and takes approximately 35 to 60 minutes to administer. It is reported as appropriate for clients ages 16 and older who have at least a sixth-grade reading level (personal communications, S. Nadau, June 22,

TABLE 5.2. Four Validity Types

Type	Goal	Method	Most Commonly Affiliated With Addictions Counselors Use of . . .
Face validity	To determine if the questions appear to measure what the instrument purports to measure.	Experienced counselor reviews test questions to determine if the questions appear appropriate to the domain being tested.	Standardized speciality addictions instruments (e.g., the Alcohol Use Inventory), standardized speciality instruments related to client's voiced concerns.
Content validity	To determine if test questions match content identified as central to the domain being tested.	Experts identify content that should be contained within the domain being tested.	Professional certification examinations (Master Addiction Counselor examination) and state licensing examinations (North Carolina Certified Clinical Addictions Counselor examination).
Criterion-related concurrent validity	To determine if a relationship exists between the criterion measure and another measure (e.g., a similar testing instrument's score purporting to measure the same construct; a diagnosis).	Compare criterion measure scores to another score, diagnosis, or observation.[15]	Standardized speciality addictions instruments (e.g., Substance Abuse Subtle Screening Inventory–3), Diagnostic scores by addictions professionals.
Criterion-related predictive validity	To determine if the instrument predicts future addictive and ancillary behaviors.	Compare instrument scores to future behaviors.	Standardized speciality addictions (e.g., Alcohol Use Inventory), and personality instruments (Minnesota Multiphasic Personality Inventory–II).
Construct validity	To determine if the the instrument measures multiple traits or attributes specific to the hypothetical term or construct.	Compare the immediate addictions instrument scores to the construct being tested (e.g., Alcohol Abuse).	Standardized speciality (e.g., Adult Substance Use Survey) and personality (Minnesota Multiphasic Personality Inventory–2) instruments.

15. Both the criterion measure and the correlating measure (e.g., a test score or diagnoses) must be available at approximately the same time.

2001). The AUI is published by National Computer Systems (NCS) in Minneapolis, MN. The AUI is currently under revision. The AUI authors anticipated the revised AUI would be available in 2002.

AUI Reliability and Validity

Internal consistency reliability was reported between .67 and .93 and test–retest reliability was indicated between .54 and .94 for all scales (Horn et al., 1990; p 24). It should be noted that only one scale score was identified below .60,[16] and that 17 of the 21 scales in which test–retest was used were noted as being higher than .80 (Horn et al., 1990). The instrument authors reported the AUI has content validity, as "it was developed out of a process that ensured that the content would be relevant for making decisions in treatment programs" (p. 30), and support the instrument's construct validity via a number of related research studies. Interestingly, however, the authors suggested that an adequate criterion cannot be defined to support the notion of criterion-related validity:

> There is no agreed-upon operations for specifying alcoholism or any particular undesirable condition associated with alcohol abuse, be it called alcohol dependence or something else. Even if there were consensus agreement that the criterion is, say, an alcohol dependence syndrome . . . there is no consensus agreement about how to measure it. . . . It would be circular in the extreme . . . to validate the AUI against a criterion defined by a subset of AUI measures. (p. 31)

Scales

The AUI has 17 primary scales, which are subdivided into four areas: (a) Drinking Benefits (i.e., drinking to: [1] improve sociability and mental functioning [SOCIALIM], [2] manage moods [MANAGMOOD], and [3] cope with marital problems [MARICOPE]), (b) Drinking Styles (i.e., GREGARUS [social drinking vis-à-vis those who drink alone], COMPULSV [i.e., constantly thinking about alcohol], and SUSTAIND [drinking with no abstinence periods; "somewhat intoxicated every day"; Horn et al., 1990; p. 7], (c) Drinking Consequences (i.e., loss of control over behavior when drinking [LCONTORL], social role maladaption [ROLEMALA], delirium [DELIRIUM], hangover [HANGOVER], and marital problems resulting from drinking [MARIPROB]), and (d) Concerns and Acknowledgments (i.e., acknowledgment of the quantity of consumed alcohol [QUANTITY], guilt associated with drinking [GUILTWOR], prior attempts to deal with the drinking [HELPBEFR], readiness for help [RECEPTIV], and awareness of drinking problems [AWARENES]). Six second-level scales are also provided (Horn

---

16. MARIPROB Scale test-retest scale score was .54. This scale was designed to measure problems such as marital discord resulting from alcohol consumption.

et al., 1990, p. 7). These scales include: (a) Enhanced (those who consume alcohol to enhance their functioning [ENHANCED]), (b) Obsessed (persons who hide bottles, sneak drinks, and drink prior to bed [OBSESSED]), (c) Disrupt1 (those who report alcohol consumption as resulting in life disruptions [lost job, severe hangovers]), and (d) Disrupt2 (persons who experienced uncontrolled life disruption as a result of their drinking and report symptomatology typically associated with heavy drinkers [" . . . has used alcohol substitutes such as shaving lotion," p. 8]), ANXCONCN (anxiety, worry, guilt, shame related to drinking), and ALCINVOL (a client-noted "broad involvement with alcohol" [p. 8]).

Computer-Generated Interpretive Reports versus Hand Scoring

The AUI interpretive report provides a thorough and easily understood narrative interpretation of the client's scores. Furthermore, it provides additional information that helps the counselor differentiate between alcohol abuse and alcohol dependence diagnoses. Templates can be used when hand scoring the AUI. Once the number of endorsed items is summed for each template, the counselor merely needs to mark the profile sheet matching the raw score to its corresponding scale. These scores are easily changed into percentiles by noting the percentile at the bottom of the profile sheet (Table 5.3).

Additionally, unlike for many other standardized instruments, Wanberg (personal communication, June 27, 2001) reported the AUI does not have a scale designed to identify persons misrepresenting themselves in a most favorable manner. Rightly so, Wanberg reported that all information provided by clients is useful. This includes misrepresented information. Wanberg advocated that standardized AOD speciality assessment instruments almost always be used to supplement counselors' clinical judgment and not be used alone to suggest a *DSM–IV–TR* diagnosis. Thus, the Alcohol Use Inventory fits well with the CLISD-PA model, which requires that test results be interpreted within the context of the individual and significant other clinical interviews.

Adult Substance Use Survey (ASUS)

General ASUS Overview

The Adult Substance Use Survey is a standardized speciality instrument developed by Wanberg (1997b). The instrument has 10 self-report clinical scales and one rater scale (personal communication, Wanberg, July 7, 2001). The ASUS was designed to assess AOD use and measure disruption resulting from such use (Wanberg, 1997b). The instrument's authors used normative client samples from those being evaluated for AOD treatment referral in criminal justice, mental health and AOD evaluation centers (personal communication, Wanberg, July 7, 2001). The ASUS requires approximately 10 to 15 minutes to complete. The instrument is appropriate for clients 18 years of age and older who have a seventh- to eighth-

TABLE 5.3. Alcohol Use Inventory: Shawnelle

AUI — ALCOHOL USE INVENTORY
J. L. Horn
K. W. Wanberg
F. M. Foster

Name: Shawnelle   Date: 7-5-02

Gender: F X   M ___   Age: 27   I.D. ___

Agency: ___   Education: College

Hand-Scored Profile

DECILE RANK

		Scale	Raw Score / Decile markers (1–10), X = client score
PRIMARY SCALES			
BENEFITS	1	SOCIALIM	0 · 1 · 2 · 3 · 4 · 5 · 6 · 7 · **X** · 8
	2	MENTALIM	0 · · · 1 · 2 · **X** · 4 5
	3	MANGMOOD	0 · 1 · 2 · 3 · 4 · 5 · 6 · 7 · **X**
	4	MARICOPE	0 · 1 · **X** · 3 · 4 · 5 6 8
STYLES	5	GREGARUS	0 · 1 · 2 · 3 · 4 · 5 · 6 · 7 · 8 10
	6	COMPULSV	0 · 1 · 2 · 3 · 4 · **X** · 5 · 7 8
	7	SUSTAIND	0 1 · 2 · 3 · 4 · 5 · 6 · 7 · **X** · 8 10 11 12
CONSEQUENCES	8	LCONTROL	0 1 · 2 3 4 · 5 · 6 7 · 8 · 9 · **X** 10 · 11 · 12 13 14 18
	9	ROLEMALA	0 · 1 · 2 · 3 · 4 · 5 · 6 · **X** · 8 · 9 10 11 13
	10	DELIRIUM	0 · 1 · 2 · 3 · **X** 5 6 · 7 8 · 9 10 12 13
	11	HANGOVER	0 · 1 · 2 3 · 4 · 5 · **X** 6 · 7 · 8 9 11
	12	MARIPROB	0 · 1 · 2 · 3 · 4 · **X** · 6
CONCERNS AND ACKNOWLEDGMENTS	13	QUANTITY	0 1 2 · 3 · 4 · 5 · 6 · 7 · 8 · 9 **X** 10 11 12
	14	GUILTWOR	0 · 2 3 · 4 5 · 6 · 7 · 8 · **X**
	15	HELPBEFR	0 · 1 · **X** · 2 · 3 · 5 6 9
	16	RECEPTIV	6 12 13 · 14 · 15 · 16 · 17 · 18 · 19 · **X** 20 · 21
	17	AWARENES	2 4 5 6 8 9 10 11 12 13 14 15 16 · **X** 17

		Scale	PERCENTILE markers
SECOND ORDER FACTOR SCALES	A	ENHANCED	1 2 · 3 4 · 5 · 6 · 7 · 8 · 9 · 10 · 11 · **X** · 13 14 17
	B	OBSESSED	1 2 · 3 4 · 5 · 6 7 · 8 9 · 10 11 · 12 · 13 14 · 15 **X** 17 18
	C	DISRUPT 1	2 4 6 7 8 10 1112 13 1415 16 1718 19 2021 22 232425 26 27 **X** 29 30 3234 35 3739 40
	D	DISRUPT 2	0 1 2 · 3 · 4 · 5 · 6 · 7 · 8 · 9 · 10 · **X** · 12 13 14 17
	E	ANXCONCN	0 1 3 4 7 8 9 1011 12 13 14 15 16 17 18 19 **X** 20 21 23
	F	RECPAWAR	10 14 17 18 19 21 22 23 24 25 26 27 28 29 30 31 32 33 **X** 34 3536 38
GENERAL	G	ALCINVOL	1 5 9 10 14 20 21 24 25 27 28 30 32 33 34 36 37 39 40 41 43 44 45 46 48 **X** 52 55 56 58 60 68

PERCENTILE: 1 · 10 · 20 · 30 · 40 · 50 · 60 · 70 · 80 · 90 · 98

Product Number 48014

grade reading level. The Adult Substance Use Survey is comprised of 64 questions. Questions 1 through 31 have five possible response options (i.e., a, b, c, d, or e) with a fill-in-the-blank response asking how many times the client has used the corresponding psychoactive substance within the preceding 6 months. Questions 32 through 64 have four possible response options (i.e., a, b, c, or d) and seek information regarding antisocial behaviors, mental health, and motivation to discontinue AOD use. The Adult Substance Use Survey is published by the Center for Addictions Research and Evaluation, Inc. (CARE), 5460 Ward Road, Suite 140, Arvada, CO 80002. Both hard-copy and computer-scored versions are available.

ASUS Reliability and Validity

Wanberg (1997b) used internal consistency reliability, based on Cronbach's alpha to demonstrate instrument reliability. Wanberg stated, "If the average inter-correlation among these [test] items is high, this indicates that the items together are consistently measuring a single construct" (p. 16). Internal consistency reliability noted within Wanberg's combined study ranged between .75 and .90, with five of the six scales having an internal consistency reliability at or above .80.

The instrument's author cites a number of research investigations which support the instrument's construct validity (Wanberg, 1997b, pp. 16–22). Specifically, the test is purported as having both face and content validity. For example, Wanberg stated, "perusal of the ASUS will indicate that the items are face-valid with respect to the purpose of their measurement" (p.16). Concurrent validity appears supported based upon the significant correlation between multiple raters' and client scores on the instruments scales.

Scales

The Adult Substance Use Survey has eight scales (Table 5.4). The Involvement 1 Scale reports the client's AOD use related to 11 major drug classifications over the client's lifetime (Wanberg, 1997b). Drug classifications include: (a) alcohol, (b) marijuana, (c) cocaine, (d) amphetamines and stimulants, (e) inhalants, (f) heroin, (g) other opiates and painkillers, (h) barbiturates and sedatives, (i) tranquilizers, and (j) tobacco. High scores on the Involvement 1 Scale may suggest the client is reporting low drug use among many drug classifications or robust drug use among only a limited number of drug classifications. Additionally the scale indicates psychoactive substances used within the preceding 6 months. Counselors should be especially attuned to seeking out further information related to such recent use and determine if the client's high scores are a result of broad psychoactive sub-

TABLE 5.4. Adult Substance Use Survey: Krista

SCALE NAME	RAW SCORE	Low				Low-medium DECILE RANK		High-medium		High		NUMBER IN NORM SAMPLE*
		1	2	3	4	5	6	7	8	9	10	
1. INVOLVEMENT1	23										24 43	1,385*
2. DISRUPTION1	55										56 63	1,385*
3. SOCIAL	10					11	13	14	15 16	17 18	19 21 32	1,385*
4. MOOD	9						13	14	13 14 15	16 17 18	20 22 33	1,385*
5. GLOBAL	97									98 166		1385*
6. SIX MONTH	26									30 37	38 51 99	1,385*
7. DEFENSIVE	2	3 4	5	6	7	8	9	10 11	12 13	14 15 21		1,385*
8. MOTIVATION	20									22		1,385*
9. ASUS RATER	16								17		18	1,381*
10. INVOLVEMENT2	23							24 25 26	27 30 32	33 36 40		668**
11. DISRUPTION2	55							56 57	58 63 64	65 68 75		635**
		0	10	20	30	40	50	60	70	80	90 99	
						PERCENTILE		* Adult Criminal Justice		**Public output/input		

stance experimentation or florid substance dependence.

The Disruption Scale denotes negative consequences resulting from psycho-active substance use. Wanberg (1997b) stated, "Persons with high scores on this scale will indicate that drugs cause loss of control over behavior, disruption of psychological and physiological functioning, and causes problems at home, work, and at school" (p. 12). This scale provides the counselor information regarding the client's psychoactive substance abuse and is correlated with the *DSM–IV*'s substance dependence criteria.

The Social Scale provides the counselor information regarding the client's rebelliousness, antisocial behaviors and attitudes (Wanberg, 1997b). The scale produces a historical as well as a current perspective of such antisocial behaviors, but should not be used to establish an *DSM–IV–TR* antisocial personality disorder. Instead, it provides counselors with information regarding how resistant the client may be toward treatment and renders a better understanding of whether or not the client may be subversive within the counseling process.

The Mood Scale alerts counselors to clients who are equodystonic and experiencing intrapersonal discomfort (personal communication, July 7, 2001). Therefore, clients endorsing a significant number of these items may have increased likelihood of "depression, worry, anxiety, irritability, anger, feelings of not wanting to live, and being unable to control emotions and uncontrolled acting out behavior" (Wanberg, 1997b, p. 13). It should also be noted that substance-dependent clients experiencing withdrawal may be experiencing anxiety and depression. Thus, counselors will want to determine if the presence of these items occurred prior to or after substance abstinence.

The Defensive Scale "provides a measure of the degree to which the client is willing to divulge personal and sensitive information on the ASUS" (Wanberg, 1997b, p. 13). Most persons should positively endorse each of these scale items. Unlike the other ASUS Scales, this scale is reverse scored. Thus, items are weighted in the direction of defending. The Motivation Scale provides a measure of change readiness and willingness to enter into counseling.

Involvement 2 and Disruption 2 scales are identical to Involvement 1 and Disruption 1 scales, except that they were normed "against a sample of public hospital patients hospitalized for alcohol and other drug abuse" (Wanberg, 1997b, p. 13). Therefore, counselors have the opportunity of comparing their clients' scores to those of a sample reporting significant AOD disruption. This comparison is of particular value when screening clients in institutional settings where there is considerable variance in the degree of AOD use. Thus, a person who appears extreme when compared to a general outpatient AOD assessment sample may more be more realistically assessed when compared to a clinical inpatient sample. This dual comparison greatly enhances the ASUS's clinical utility. The ASUS also has a rater scale. This scale is completed by those assessing the client and allows counselors to determine the degree of discrepancy between clinical judgment and client self-report.

The final scale is the Global Disruption Scale. This scale "provides a global and overall measure of risk and life-functioning disruption" (Wanberg,1997b, p. 14). Thus, counselors can use this scale to identify AOD-abusing persons who are experiencing debilitating symptomatology levels.

Computer-Generated Interpretive Reports versus Hand Scoring

Raw scores are merely summed for the Adult Substance Use Survey and plotted on the ASUS Profile Summary. Once plotted, decile rank (which includes clearly marked categories titled "Low," "Low-medium," "High-medium," and "High") and percentiles are easily noted on the profile form (Table 5.4). Counselors then compare client raw scores to a suggested referral guideline (Table 5.5).

Substance Abuse Subtle Screening Inventory–3

General SASSI–3 Overview

The standardized substance abuse speciality instruments indicated as most frequently used by and important to addictions professionals were the Substance Abuse Subtle Screening Inventories (i.e., the SASSI–II and SASSI–Adolescent) (Juhnke, Vacc, Curtis, Coll, & Paredes, in press). The current adult version is the SASSI 3. The SASSI 3 was authored by Miller and Lazowski in 1997 and is the newest version of the original SASSI which was published in 1988 (Miller, Roberts, Brooks, & Lazowski, 1997). The SASSI was designed to "identify individuals with a high probability of having a substance dependence disorder, even if those individuals do not acknowledge substance misuse or symptoms associated with it" (Miller et al., 1997, p. 2). The SASSI–3 was developed for persons 18 years of age and older with a minimum of a 4.4 grade reading level (personal communication, F. Miller, July 3, 2001). It takes approximately 15 minutes to complete (personal communication, F. Miller, July 3, 2001) and is composed of 93 questions. The instrument can be ordered directly from the SASSI Institute (1-800-726-0526; e-mail: sassi@sassi.com).

Side one of the instrument contains 26 face-valid items. These items are highly transparent and directly relate to AOD use. They provide information regarding the extent to which the client acknowledges AOD use and define the extent and nature of the client's AOD problem. The second side of the instrument contains 67 question stems which the client endorses either "true" or "false." Unlike side 1 obvious questions, side 2 questions are typically nontransparent and subtle. Thus, clients may not identify their responses as being directly related to their AOD use.

SASSI–3 Reliability and Validity

Test–retest reliability for the Face-Valid Alcohol Scale was 1.0, test–retest for the Face-Valid Other Drug Scale was 1.0, and test–retest for the various subscales ranged between .92 and .97 (personal communication, F. Miller, 3 July, 2001).

TABLE 5.5. Guidelines for the Adult Substance Use Scale

ASUS Involvement Raw Store	ASUS Disruption Raw State	Level	Level of AOD Use Involvement and Problem	These are only screening guidelines and suggestions the Screener needs to use all information available before making decision
0	0	0	Reports no use and no disruption	No referral if corroborated by collateral data
1–3 (Poly)* 1–2 (Mono)**	1– 6	1	Some involvement with minimal disruption, low problem/low needs,	8–10 hour outpatient (OP) AOD education, enhanced assessment. Urine analyses (UAs) if marijuana involved.
2–10 (Poly) 2–3 (Mono)	4–10	2	Low-medium involvement, some disruption, with low-medium problem and needs.	12–18 hour OP AOD education and therapy, in-depth assessment, UAs if marijuana or other drugs are involved.
4–15 (Poly) 4 (Mono)	11–30	3	Medium level AOD involvement and disruption with medium level AOD problem and treatment needs.	4-6 month low-intensity (1–2 hours a week) OP sessions with in-depth assessment. If alcohol only, level problem may be higher; UAs if marijuana or cocaine involved.
9–19 (Poly) 4 (Mono)	26–43	4	Medium-high (AOD) involvement and disruption with medium-high AOD problem and treatment needs,	6–9 month moderate-intensity OP (3–6) sessions a week, in-depth assessment. If alcohol only, problem level may be higher: UAs if marijuana. cocaine or other drugs involved.
> 9 (Poly) 4 (Mono)	40–80	5	High AOD involvement and disruption and high AOD problems with high treatment needs.	6–12 months high-intensity OP (7 or more hours a week): in-depth assessment; may need residential care if unstable AOD) use pattern and abstinence can't be managed outpatient; may need continuing care following high-intensity outpatient for several months; UAs if history of multiple drug use pattern.

Other considerations:
1) If MOOD ADJUST is 9–13, consider further mental health assessment; if MOOD > 13, definite referral to mental health; also look at suicide item 47.
2) If DEFENSIVE raw score > 14, and the profile is flat (e.g., low across all scales), then consider client defensive and needs to be placed in motivational enhancement group, particularly if collateral reports (court, blood alcohol level) indicate drinking problem; if DEFENSIVE > 14, suggest enhance DISRUPTION score by two decile scores.
3) Involvement2 and Disruption2 are based on intensive outpatient and inpatient public hospital patients. A raw score of 30 on Disruption2 indicates that the client is scoring higher than 30 percent of a group of patients in intensive outpatients or hospitalized care for AOD (Alcohol and other Drug) problems.
4) Short or long-term residential care may be needed at any of levels 3 through 5 depending on the acute condition of the client or if AOD abstinence pattern cannot be established.
5) Some clients may have scores at Levels 4 or 5, but do not indicate high levels of life-disruption due to AOD use. This may reduce the level of treatment services that are needed.
6) Use all sources of data for assessment. Use the motivation scale to assist in referral decision making. Clients with high defensive scores and low motivation scores and low scores on INVOLVEMENT and DISRUPTION may benefit from motivational enhancement with retesting at a later date when client feels more comfortable in treatment services.

*Polydrug user   **Monodrug user

163

The alpha coefficient for the entire instrument was .93 (personal communication, F. Miller, July 3, 2001). The SASSI–3 has an overall accuracy of 94% with specificity and sensitivity of 94% as well (Miller et al., 1997). Miller reports the SASSI–3 has a positive predictive power of 98.4% (personal communication, July 3, 2001). Positive predictive power indicates the ratio of true positives to test positives. In other words, 98.4% of the time the SASSI–3 correctly identified persons who actually had an AOD problem. The instrument also demonstrates exceptionally high concurrent validity. For example, the SASSI–3 matched the clients' clinical diagnoses 95% of the time and demonstrated concurrent validity with a number of instruments, including the (a) Michigan Alcohol Screening Test (MAST), (b) Minnesota Multiphasic Personality Inventory–2, and (c) MacAndrew Scale—Revised (MAC–R) (Lazowski, Miller, Boye, & Miller, 1998).

Scales

The SASSI–3 has 10 scales (Table 5.6). Two of these scales are face-valid scales that require clients to describe the extent and nature of their AOD misuse. One of these scales is related to alcohol (Face-Valid Alcohol) and the other is related to all other psychoactive substances (Face-Valid Other Drug). Persons endorsing high Face-Valid Alcohol or Face-Valid Other Drug scores are likely openly acknowledging AOD misuse, consequences resulting from such use, and loss of control related to their AOD use (Miller et al., 1997). High scores on either or both of these two scales may suggest the need for supervised detoxification (Miller et al., 1997).

The Symptoms Scale asks clients to endorse symptoms or problems resulting from their AOD abuse (Miller et al., 1997). Those with high Symptom Scale scores are likely to be heavy users and be part of a social milieu (e.g., family, peers) where AOD use is prevalent. Thus, it may be difficult for these persons to perceive the negative aspects of remarkable AOD use. In other words, given that their friends and family likely use, they may consider AOD abuse normal and abstinence an abnormality.

The Obvious Attribute Scale indicates the degree to which clients acknowledge characteristics typical of AOD-using clients (Miller et al., 1997). Stated differently, persons endorsing a high number of these scale items are indicating a high number of behaviors and characteristics typically indicated by persons who are substance dependent or in recovery from their substance use. High scores suggest clients are receptive to clinical intervention (e.g., group counseling) and able to identify with the experiences of other substance-dependent persons. Conversely, very low Obvious Attribute scores suggest clients who are reluctant to acknowledge characteristics commonly associated with substance-dependent persons and/or personal flaws.

The Subtle Attributes Scale denotes persons who may either be attempting to present themselves in a most favorable light by denying their substance dependence or who may not be recognizing their behaviors as problematic or associated

TABLE 5.6. Substance Abuse Subtle Screening Inventory–3: Patrick

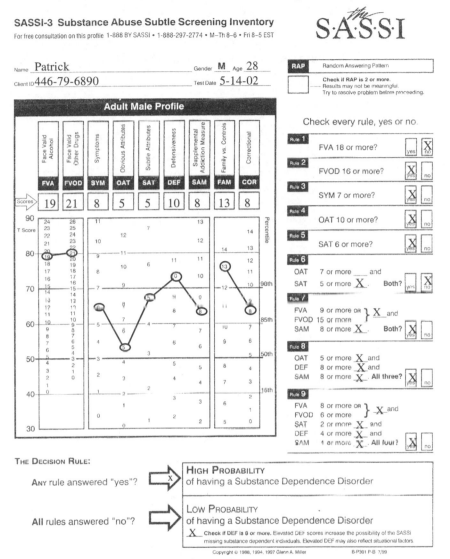

SASSI-3 Substance Abuse Subtle Screening Inventory
For free consultation on this profile 1-888 BY SASSI • 1-888-297-2774 • M–Th 8–6 • Fri 8–5 EST

S·A·S·S·I

Name Patrick   Gender M Age 28
Client ID 446-79-6890   Test Date 5-14-02

with AOD use (Miller et al., 1997). Persons who have endorsed a high number of Subtle Attributes Scale items, especially when the number of these items is higher than their Obvious Attributes Scale items, find it challenging to admit the degree to which AOD is prevalent and problematic within their lives.

Two other scales that directly complement one another and enrich the assessment process are the Defensiveness and Supplemental Addiction Measure scales. As is the case with all assessment instruments, the scores and clinical profiles are used in conjunction with the counselor's clinical judgment to insure appropriate assessment and intervention. The SASSI–3 Defensiveness Scale identifies persons who may be responding defensively. However, the counselor must use her clinical judgment to determine if the defensiveness revolves around AOD abuse issues or other issues (e.g. client personality traits, immediate life circumstances). Clients endorsing a high number of Defensiveness Scale items are attempting to present themselves in a favorable light and minimizing "evidence of personal problems" (Miller et al., 1997, p. 36). When the Defensiveness Scale is used in conjunction with the Supplemental Addiction Measure Scale, counselors can better assess if the client's defensiveness relates to AOD abuse or other areas. Thus, when both the Defensiveness Scale and the Supplemental Addiction Measure Scale scores are elevated, there is increased evidence that the client's defensiveness revolves around personal AOD abuse. However, the counselor must weigh all evidence to make this determination and use her best clinical judgment when making the final clinical diagnosis.

Another important aspect of the Defensiveness Scale is related to low scores at or below the 15th percentile. Such low scores may be indicative of self-abasing or overly self-critical clients. These clients may have problems related to low self-esteem and have "feelings of worthlessness and hopelessness, loss of energy, and suicidal ideation" (Miller et al., 1997). Given the robust correlation between hopeless feelings and suicide, it would be important to assess such clients for suicidal ideation and to provide appropriate intervention.

The Family vs. Control Subjects (Family) Scale identifies persons who may not be AOD abusing themselves, but who likely have family members or significant others who are AOD-abusing and who agreed to participate with their AOD-abusing family members and significant others who entered counseling (Miller et al., 1997). Persons scoring high on this scale are endorsing items similarly to those who are codependent. Therefore, high scores on this scale are a "red flag" to counselors. Such scores indicate the client is endorsing behaviors commonly associated with codependent persons (e.g., sacrificing self to potentially cure an AOD-abusing family member, pathological overinvolvement with an AOD-abusing partner in an attempt to increase the codependent's self-worth feelings Thus, clients with high Family Scale scores may have "potential for codependent behaviors" and should be assessed to determine if they are overly focused upon others and others' needs rather than themselves (personal communication, F. Miller, July 23, 2001). Persons scoring high on this scale may benefit from counseling goals that include establishing appropriate and healthy boundaries.

The Correctional Scale indicates the client's "relative risk for legal problems" (Miller et al., 1997, p. 39). Although the scale was not created to identify specific antisocial psychopathology, it does identify persons who even if they discontinue their AOD abuse may potentially require additional counseling services related to areas such as anger and impulse control. Persons scoring high on this scale may also have a checkered history of difficulties with the legal system.

The final scale is the Random Answering Pattern Scale. This scale suggests the client's scores are likely suspect or invalid should the client have a Random Answering Pattern Scale Score of two or more. Such scores may also be indicative of persons who are unable to read at the required level or who do not speak English as their primary language.

Computer Generated Interpretive Reports versus Hand Scoring

Narrative reports provided by the SASSI Institute are thorough and provide the client's graphed profile (Table 5.7). Hand scoring of the SASSI–3 is quite easy and can be completed within a matter of minutes. Templates are used to identify the number of client positive endorsements for each scale. These raw scores are then circled and plotted on the profile sheet, and the counselor merely checks each of the nine decision rules and the Random Answering Pattern rule on the profile sheet to determine if the client is at high or low probability of having a substance dependence disorder (Table 5.6). The plotted profile can be easily shown to clients, and the percentile markings make it easy for clients to understand how they scored in comparison to others.

The Adolescent Substance Use Survey

General Adolescent SUS Overview

The Adolescent Substance Use Survey was authored by Wanberg (1997a) and is founded on the Adult Substance Use Survey. However, the Adolescent Substance Use Survey was created specifically for use with adolescents and was normed on this specific population. The instrument can be administered verbally as a structured clinical interview within Tier One of the CLISD-PA model, or it can be used as a paper-and-pencil standardized speciality instrument. When used as a paper-and-pencil instrument within Tier Three, it is recommended that clients be ages 15 years and older with a minimum seventh-grade reading level (Wanberg, 1997a). Over all age range for the instrument is "12 to 20 years" (Wanberg, 1997a, p. 12).

The Adolescent Substance Use Survey provides information regarding the client's drug use, current mental health concerns, treatment motivation, and defensiveness toward counseling. It was "designed mainly for screening adolescents for AOD treatment services and can be used in adolescent AOD assessment services, mental health agencies or juvenile justice programs" (Wanberg, 1997a, p.12). Sixty-seven questions comprise the instrument. Administration time is approximately 15 minutes (personal communications, Wanberg, July 7, 2001). Questions 1 through 20 query clients about the types of psychoactive substances used. These questions have six possible response options with an additional fill-in-the-blank response asking the number of times the corresponding psychoactive substance has been used within the preceding 3 months. Questions 21 through 41 ask about substance use symptomatology. These questions have five possible response op-

TABLE 5.7. Substance Abuse Subtle Screening Inventory–3: Monica

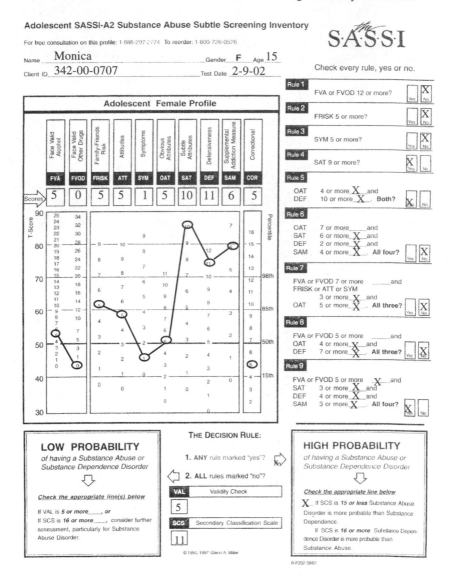

tions and further ask the frequency of the symptomatology within the preceding six months. Questions 42 through 67 ask questions pertaining to emotional and psychological symptomatology, suicidal ideation and parasuicides, drug use, gang involvement, drug selling, and counseling motivation. Each question has four possible response options (i.e., a, b, c, or d). The Adolescent Substance Use Survey is published by the Center for Addictions Research and Evaluation, Inc. (CARE), 5460 Ward Road, Suite 140, Arvada, CO 80002.

Adolescent SUS Reliability and Validity

Once again Wanberg used internal consistency, based on Cronbach's alpha, to demonstrate the reliability of the Adolescent Substance Use Inventory. This time, however, he based his findings on his research with adolescent populations (e.g., juvenile justice clients, school-based referrals and incarcerated juvenile offenders) vis-à-vis adult populations (Wanberg, 1997a). Regarding instrument validity, Wanberg again declared the instrument has concurrent validity based on the strong correlations between the Adolescent SUS scales and clinical rater scales.

Scales

The Adolescent Substance Use Inventory has six self-report scales and one rater scale (Table 5.8). Although some of the scales are identical to the Adult Substance Use Survey, but normed on adolescents rather than adults, there are some noteworthy differences that make this adolescent standardized substance abuse assessment instrument distinct. For example, the Social Scale and the Involvement 2 and the Disruption 2 scales are absent from the Adolescent Substance Use Inventory. Another difference is that the Adolescent Substance Use Inventory Involvement scale, which provides a historical review of psychoactive substances used, reviews a greater number of substances and differentiates between different types of alcohol. The 19 substances reviewed include: (a) beer, (b) wine, (c) liquor, (d) marijuana, (e) cocaine, (f) amphetamines, (g) acid, (h) mushrooms, (i) PCP, (j) glue, (k) gasoline, (l) paint, (m) Wite-Out, (n) rush, (o) heroin, (p) opium, (q) painkillers, (r) barbiturates and sedatives, and (s) tranquilizers. As with the Adult Substance Use Survey, it is important to determine whether persons scoring high on this scale are merely reporting experimentation with a large number of psychoactive substances or if they are frequently using significant amounts of one or two "drugs of choice."

TABLE 5.8. Adolescent Substance Use Inventory: Billy

SCALE NAME	RAW SCORE	Low		Low-medium		High-medium			High			NUMBER IN NORM SAMPLE*
		1	2	3	4	5	6	7	8	9	10	
1. INVOLVEMENT	13										50	1,334
2. DISRUPTION	8						9 10 11	12 14 16	17 20 24	25 31 77		1,334
3. MOOD ADJUST	2			3	4	5	6	7	8...9 10	11 13 28		1,334
4. DEFENSIVE	10										11 12 15	1,138
5. MOTIVATE	6		7...8 9	10	11	12	13	14	15	16 17	18	1,090
6. OADS	25							26 28 29 32 34	35 40 47	48	131	1,334
7. SUSR	14								15	16 17 18		1,334

| 0 | 10 | 2 3 | 0 | 40 | 50 | 60 | 7 | n 8 | 0 | 90 | 99 |

PERCENTILE   Juvenile Justice

The Adolescent Substance Use Inventory Disruption, Mood Adjustment, Motivation, and Defensive Scales are like those previously described for the Adult Substance Use Survey. However, three other scales have been added to the Adolescent Substance Use Inventory. For example, a Motivation Scale has been added. This scale "provide(s) a measure of willingness to discontinue AOD use and to receive help for AOD related problems" (Wanberg, 1997a, p. 23). Clients endorsing a high number of these scale items are likely willing to participate in AOD counseling and are motivated to change their AOD abuse. Another scale added is the Overall Adolescent Disruption Scale (OADS). This scale describes the overall, global features of the client's endorsements related to the psychoactive substances used, problems resulting from such use, and other relevant psychological difficulties or concerns. Finally, the Adolescent-Substance Use Inventory has a Substance Use Rater Scale. These questions are similar to those used in the Adult Substance Use Survey.

Computer-Generated Interpretive Reports Versus Hand Scoring

As with the Adult Substance Use Survey, the raw scores are summed and plotted on the Adolescent Substance Use Inventory. The decile rank and percentiles are easily noted (Table 5.8). And an adolescent referral guideline can be used (Table 5.9).

Substance Abuse Subtle Screening Inventory–A2 (SASSI–A2)

General SASSI–A2 Overview

The SASSI–A2 is the most recently developed standardized addictions speciality instrument created and published at the respected SASSI Institute. It replaces the original SASSI–A, which was first published in 1990. The SASSI–A2 underwent four years of research and development and was normed on 2,326 adolescents between the ages of 12 and 18 (SASSI Institute, 2001). These adolescents came from 48 different treatment and correctional programs and five school systems. The SASSI-A2 was developed to "identify individuals who have a high probability of having a substance use disorder, i.e., substance abuse and substance dependence" and was developed for adolescents ages 12 to 18 years old (SASSI Institute, 2001, p. 1). The instrument is composed of 100 questions, takes approximately 15 minutes to complete, and requires a Grade 4.4 reading level (personal communication, F. Miller, July 3, 2001). The SASSI–A2 can be ordered directly from the SASSI Institute (1-800-726-0526; e-mail: sassi@sassi.com).

Twenty-eight questions comprise the SASSI–A2's side 1. Similar to the SASSI–3 adult version, these items are highly transparent and ask how frequently clients "have had certain experiences that are directly related to alcohol and other drug use" (SASSI Institute, 2001, p. 1). Seventy-two question stems are contained on side 2. Clients can endorse either "true" or "false" for each of the questions. These question stems configure into one of four areas: (a) symptom-related (AOD use acknowledgment), (b) risk (substance misuse degree of risk), (c) attitudinal (attitudes and beliefs regarding AOD use), or (d) subtle items (nontransparent, unremarkable items that identify AOD-abusing clients).

SASSI–A2 Reliability and Validity

The overall SASSI–A2 2-week test–retest coefficient yielded a .89 with six of the instrument's scales having coefficients between .85 and .92. The range for all SASSI–A2 test–retest reliability coefficients was .71 to .92. To demonstrate validity, Miller and Lazowski (2001) again used statistical analyses to demonstrate the SASSI-A2's positive predictive power. Correspondence with the clinical diagnoses of substance use disorders in their studies resulted in a combined sample positive predictive power of 98% (Miller & Lazowski, 2001). Positive predictive power indicates the ratio of true positives to test positives. Thus, in their combined sample of 1,244 subjects, 98% of the time the SASSI–A2 correctly identified persons who actually had a Substance Use Disorder (Miller & Lazowski). The SASSI–2 sensitivity is 95% (Miller & Lazowski, 2001). The instrument also demonstrated a positive predictive power of 99% among participants who had a Defensiveness Scale score of 7 or less (Miller & Lazowski, 2001). Finally, as previously mentioned, the SASSI–A2 has an area of questions noted as subtle items. Rules pertaining to these subtle items demonstrate robust efficacy in correctly identifying adolescents with substance use disorders. Specifically, 10 of these decision rules demonstrated 97% accuracy or better (Miller & Lazowski, 2001). Four of these 10 decision rules accurately identified adolescents presenting with substance use disorders 100% of the time.

Additionally, Miller and Lazowski (2001) reported that the SASSI–A2 has face validity. They state, "As with all prior versions of the SASSI, the SASSI–A2 includes face valid scales that are composed of items that clearly address substance misuse" (p. 5). A brief review of the instrument certainly supports their claim.

Scales

The SASSI–A2 has 12 scales (SASSI Institute, 2001). Similar to the SASSI–3 adult version, the Face-Valid Alcohol, Face-Valid Other Drugs, Symptoms, Obvious Attributes, Subtle Attributes, and Supplemental Addiction Measures scales are used in the SASSI–A2. However, this time the scales are normed on an adolescent population. Interpretation of scores on these items is similar to the information provided on the SASSI–3.

Four new scales have been added to the SASSI–A2. One of these is the Family–Friends Risk Scale. Clients scoring high on the Family–Friends Risk Scale are "likely to be a part of a family and social system that may promote rather than prevent substance misuse" (SASSI Institute, 2001, p. 31). Because they are part

TABLE 5.9 Adolescent Substance Use Survey Suggested Screening Guidelines

SUS Involvement Raw Score	SUS Disruption Raw Score	Severity and Risk Level: Use and Problem Description	These are only screening guidelines and suggestions the screener needs to use all information available before making decision
0–1	0	Level 1: Reports no use and no disruption.	Prevention: No referral if corroborated by collateral data
2–5	0–3	Level 2: Some AOD involvement with minimal use disruption, low problems, low needs.	Intervention level services with enhanced assessment; 8–10 hours of AOD education and UAs if marijuana involved.
4–7*	3–7	Level 3: Low-medium involvement/disruption with low-medium problem/needs; polydrug history of increase risk and severity level.	Marginal treatment level: 10 to 30 hours low intensity (1 hour week) outpatient (OP) AOD education and therapy with enhanced assessment; UAs if cocaine or marijuana involves.
7–10*	4–10	Level 4: Medium AOD involvement/disruption with medium level AOD problem and treatment needs; alcohol only may increase risk level.	Treatment: 3–6 monoth low-moderate intensity (1-3 hours a week) OP with in-depth assessment; if alcohol only, risk level medium-high; UAs if marijuana or cocaine involved.
8–14*	8–16	Level 5: Medium-high AOD involvement and disruption with medium-high AOD problem and treatment needs; determine mono or polydrug.	Treatment: 4–9 month moderate intensity (3–6 hours a week) OP with in-depth assessment. Alcohol only or polydrug may increase risk; UAs if marijuana, cocaine, or other drugs.
> 10	> 16	Level 6: High to very high AOD involvement and disruption and high to very high AOD problems and treatment needs; either monodrug or polydrug pattern increases severity and risk level.	Treatment: 6–12 months high-density (6 or more hours a week) OP; in-depth assessment; may need residential care if unstable AOD use pattern and abstinence can't be managed in OP; continuing care following high-intensity OP; UAs if history of multiple drug use pattern.

Other considerations:
1) If MOOD ADJUST is 7–10, consider further mental health assessment: If MOOD > 10, definite referral to mental health; also examine suicide items 50 and 51.
2) If DEFENSIVE raw score > 10, and the profile is flat (e.g., low across all scale.) then consider client defensive and needs to be placed in motivational enhancement group, particularly if collateral reports (court, school, parents, U≤s) indicate AOD problem; if DEFENSIVE > 14, suggest enhance DIS-RUPTION score by two decile scores.
3) Short or long-term residential care may be needed at any of levels 4 through 5 depending on the acute condition of the client or if AOD abstinence pattern cannot be established.
4) Some clients may have scores at levels 5 or 6, but do not indicate high levels of life-disruption due to AOD use. This may reduce the level of treatment services that are needed.
5) Use all scores of data for assessment. Use the motivation scale to assist in referral decision making. Clients with high defensive scores and low motivation scores and low scores on INVOLVEMENT and DISRUPTION may benefit from motivational enhancement with retesting at a later date when client feels more comfortable in treatment services.

*Determine if monodrug or polydrug uses. Maximum score on one drug increases risk; high score polydrug increases risk.

of a social milieu in which substance use may be promoted or perceived as typical, it is important to insure these clients have sufficient supervision and support
by non-AOD-abusing persons.

Another new scale is the Attitudes Scale. This scale assesses the client's AOD
attitudes and beliefs. Clients who endorse a high number of items on this scale

> are likely to be defensive if they are confronted regarding the consequences of
> their substance use. If the diagnosis and severity of the substance use warrants
> treatment, it is likely that adolescents who have elevated . . . scores will need
> a great deal of structure, supervision, and support to make significant changes
> in their substance use. (SASSI Institute, 2001, p. 32)

The remaining two new scales are the Validity Check and Secondary Classification Scales. The Validity Check Scale is used on the SASSI–A2 instead of the
SASSI–3's Random Answering Pattern Scale. This scale provides further information when the counselor's assessment of the client's diagnosis differs from that
of the instrument's. The Secondary Classification Scale helps differentiate between substance use, substance abuse, and substance dependence disorders.

Computer-Generated Interpretive Reports versus Hand Scoring

Computer-generated interpretive reports and hand scoring for the SASSI–A2 are
similar to those of the SASSI–3.

DRUG DETECTION TESTING

Four primary drug detection tests exist. These include urine, hair, blood, and
Breathalyzer tests. The primary purpose of these tests is to determine the presence
of psychoactive substances. Most purveyors of these drug detection tests, except
those selling Breathalyzers, sell a basic drug detection option that evaluates test
samples for five of the most commonly abused psychoactive substance categories. These categories include cannabinoids (e.g., marijuana), cocaine (e.g., crack),
amphetamines (e.g., speed), opiates (e.g., heroin), and phencyclidine (e.g., PCP).
These substance categories are often referred to as the "NIDA Five." This is because the federal government via recommendation of the National Institute on
Drug Abuse (NIDA) requires employers of commercial class truck drivers to have
substance abuse policies that periodically screen drivers for these five psychoactive substance categories.

Additionally, most purveyors offer expanded drug detection test options and
allow purchasers the option to select additional tests for psychoactive substance
categories such as barbiturates (e.g., phenobarbital), benzodiazepines (e.g., Valium),
and ethanol. Costs can significantly increase when purchasing expanded drug
detection tests. Therefore, the use of expanded detection tests must be carefully
chosen. Since most clients and their significant others will have identified the

client's substances of choice via Tier One and Tier Two clinical interviews, such expanded drug detection tests may be of limited utility unless the addictions counselor needs to continually screen the client for psychoactive substance categories outside the NIDA Five. Here, for example, if the client had previously indicated LSD abuse and the counselor's initial or provisional diagnosis was related to LSD, continual random LSD screenings would be a logical choice. However, if the diagnosis was related to psychoactive substance categories contained within the NIDA Five, there would exist little benefit for the use of expanded detection tests.

No matter which drug detection test is used, addictions counselors must be aware of required and standardized procedures which promote reliable and accurate drug detection. These standardized procedures must follow strict specimen collection and appropriate notification processes. Specifically, the specimen collection process should ensure that specimens have little chance of being adulterated, and the notification process should occur within a time period that insures adequate detection.

Urine

Urine drug detection testing is typically used when concerns arise about immediate past drug use (e.g., 6 hours to 4 days). Depending on the suspected psychoactive substance used within the immediate past (e.g., alcohol), urine drug detection testing can be a cost-effective and easily administered means to testing clients. Contrary to popular belief, urine drug detection does not have to be witnessed. Instead, temperature strips attached to the specimen vial or digital thermometers can be used to ensure that samples are genuine (e.g., the client's actual urine sample) and unadulterated (e.g., not mixed with any of a variety of products commonly sold specifically to mask or evade psychoactive drug detection). Although some drug detection laboratories require urine specimens to be measured via digital thermometer with a temperature range between 96 and 99 degrees Fahrenheit, federal agencies such as the Substance Abuse and Health Services Administration (SAMHSA) have broader collection standards and indicate specimens can range between 90 and 100 degrees Fahrenheit. The more stringent temperature requirements reportedly increase reliable and accurate detection. Thus, persons adding masking contents into their specimen or using others' urine will typically have urine specimens that do not match the temperature standards.

Additionally, for detection of most psychoactive substances, except alcohol, a specimen should be required within 24 hours of notification. In other words, to insure reliable and accurate detection, clients need to provide an urine specimen within a day of notification. Should this not be required, clients abusing psychoactive substances could merely wait until after the substance has been completely metabolized out of the client's body. Clients doing this would simply pass the urine test without detection.

In the instance of alcohol, a urine test should be completed within 6 hours of notification. This is because, depending upon the amount of alcohol consumed, urine tests will only detect alcohol consumption up to 12 hours from the last use. Many times alcohol use will only be detected if the urine is collected within 6 hours of use.

Another complicating factor regarding using urine detection tests with alcohol is that although it can be determined that the client used alcohol within the immediate past, results cannot indicate whether or not the client was under the influence or indicate the blood alcohol levels attained as a result of the alcohol consumption. In other words, unless the client is a minor or required to be alcohol free by the courts, corrections agencies, the treating counseling agency, or the client's employer, merely knowing that the client has consumed alcohol within the preceding 12 hours does little good.

Most nonemergency, ambulatory, medical care facilities, as well as hospitals with occupational medicine programs and laboratory facilities, will provide urine drug detection testing. Additionally, there exist many relatively inexpensive over-the-counter home drug detection kits sold at local pharmacies. Most of these kits sell for less than $60. Some kits are even Federal Drug Administration (FDA) approved (e.g., Dr. Brown's Home Drug Testing System) and can provide results within 3 to 9 days from submission.

Hair

Werner Baumgartner developed hair drug detection testing in 1978 (Minnesota Poison Control, 2001). In 1986, hair drug detection testing became available for commercial use, and currently it is utilized by the courts and corrections systems to insure parolees and probationers remain substance free (Jordan, 1988; Minnesota Poison Control, 2001). The central premise of hair drug detection testing is that once psychoactive substances enter the bloodstream, substances or metabolites contained within the blood are deposited on individual hair shafts. Thus, this process creates a historical record of recent drugs used. Given that hair typically grows half an inch each 30 days, a one-and-a-half-inch hair sample is painlessly cut from the crown of a client's head and tested to determine what psychoactive substances have been used within the last 90 days. As with urine detection testing, hair drug detection testing is used when concerns arise regarding past psychoactive substance use. However, hair drug detection testing, unlike urine drug detection testing, provides a wider window. Thus, it is especially useful when concerns reflect substance use within the last 8 to 90 days. Additionally, unlike other forms of drug detection tests, it was uniquely created "to show whether drug use is frequent, or occasional, light or heavy" (Jordan, 1988, p. 68). Because clients are not required to urinate into a vial or have blood extracted, hair drug detection testing is less "personally invasive" and therefore likely more comfortable than urine or blood drug detection testing.

As with urine drug detection testing, hair drug detection testing cannot determine if a client who has used alcohol was impaired or indicate the client's blood alcohol level at the time of consumption. And although hair drug detection testing can usually identify psychoactive substances used within 90 days, it typically cannot identify psychoactive substances used within the last week. Hair detection drug tests typically cost between $125 and $175 per test and therefore are more costly than urine drug detection tests. Unlike urine tests, which can be home administered, hair drug detection tests most frequently require clients to travel to specific laboratory destinations for hair specimen removal.

Blood

Although the most intrusive and expensive drug detection testing type, blood drug detection testing is the most accurate. Unlike urine and hair drug detection testing, blood drug detection testing is used to detect immediate psychoactive substances within the client's body. In other words, this test is typically used to determine the specific amount of psychoactive substance in the client's body at testing time (e.g., blood alcohol levels) and can immediately indicate whether a client is under the influence. Often this method includes using gas chromatography (GC) to separate the psychoactive substances and compounds (e.g., masking agents used by clients to adulterate urine samples) within the client's sample of blood and then mass spectrometry (MS) to identify the isolated psychoactive substances (personal communication, R. Silverman, June 19, 2001). Because it is the most expensive and the most invasive drug detection testing method, it is used less frequently then the other testing types.

Breathalyzer

Breathalyzers come in many different types and, like blood drug detection testing, are used to assess current intoxication levels. Stated differently, Breathalyzers indicate if a client is currently under the influence. Breathalyzers are frequently used by police following vehicular accidents when drivers' are perceived as intoxicated. Two of the most frequently used Breathalyzer types include disposal, "blow pipe" alcohol detectors, and digital handheld Breathalyser. Typically, blow pipes are purchased to identify a specific alcohol percentage (e.g., 0.8%) and can be used to detect breath alcohol from .02% to .10%. Usually the counselor will break a plastic ampule within the blow pipe and the client will be required to blow through one end of the plastic tube for period of 10 to 20 seconds. Next, the counselor will shake the blow pipe and allow the crystals in the ampule to change color. Blow pipes are relatively inexpensive and usually can be purchased in quantities for under $5 apiece.

Digital handheld Breathalyzers are also easy to administer and read. Often these units will have liquid crystal (LCD) displays indicating the client's alcohol level from .0% to .15%. They are small, about the size of a computer mouse, and run on batteries. When used, clients are required to blow a steady stream of air through a strawlike tube for approximately 10 to 20 seconds. Often this type of Breathalyzer will emit a tone when enough air has been blown into the instrument to provide a reading. The Breathalyzer will then provide via the LCD display the client's alcohol level. These methods are summarized in Table 5.10.

Other Drug Detection Testing Methods

A number of other drug detection testing methods exist, but their use is not as prominent or is relatively recent. For example, there are aerosol products that can be sprayed onto backpacks, clothing, computer keyboards, or deck tops and change color to indicate residual cannabis or cocaine. Certain swab-type drug detection tests are similarly used. Here someone swabs items that the client touched and then forwards the swab to the test's maker for analysis. Additionally, there are bandage-type "patches" with tamper-proof seals designed to absorb perspiration. After being worn for approximately 1 week, the perspiration patch is sent to a lab for analysis to determine which psychoactive substance residues or metabolites were excreted via perspiration.

THERAPEUTIC USE OF DRUG DETECTION TESTING

The intent of drug detection testing is threefold. First, at the onset of treatment drug detection testing is used to identify which psychoactive substances the client has recently used and to further sunstantiate any abstinence claims. Using the case vignette of Diane, the college student described in the previous chapter who reported drinking to intoxication only one time per week, but whose roommate and boyfriend during the Phase 2 significant other interview reported that she was intoxicated nearly every night of the week and consumed a fifth of vodka every other day, the counselor might request a hair analysis at the onset of treatment. Given the robust rate of comorbid alcohol and cannabis use among college students and Diane's minimization of her alcohol consumption, the hair analysis would both rule out her use of other psychoactive substances (e.g., cannabis) and indicate the frequency of her alcohol use. Here, for example the counselor might say something like:

Counselor: Diane, one of the things I do at the onset of counseling is get a better understanding of what substances my clients have been using and to understand how frequently they use those substances. This understanding provides a baseline of information on which we can compare our future counseling progress. In other words, clients like to track their progress. Given that you are an education major, I'm sure this makes sense to you.

Diane: Sure, we do that with kids all the time. You know . . . using end-of-chapter tests and end-of-semester grades.

Counselor: Exactly. When you use end-of-chapter tests and end-of-semester grades you are identifying your students' progress. This is very similar to what we do in counseling. I believe you would agree that securing such an information baseline would be important.

TABLE 5.10. Drug Detection Types

Type	Used When Suspected Drug Use	Advantages	Disadvantages
Urine	Occurred within last 6 hours to 4 days	Broadly accepted as accurate Inexpensive Home testing kits available Available at most medical care facilities Digital thermometer and specimen temperature monitoring alerts counselors to adulteration.	Cannot provide information indicating if client was under the influence at time of use or substance amount used Information regarding evading and masking methods widely known and distributed via the web Somewhat personally invasive method of specimen collection
Hair	Occurred within 8 to 90 days	Broadly accepted as accurate Provides a 90-day historical record of all psychoactive substances used Less personally invasive than urine detection tests and Breathalyzers Can indicate whether client is frequent user and whether use patterns are light or heavy	Cannot provide information indicating if client was under the influence at time of use or amount of substance used. More expensive than urine detection tests and Breathalyzers May not detect psychoactive substances used within the preceding 8 days Requires the use of trained technicians to acquire specimen sample and, thus, travel to a laboratory or specimen selection facility
Blood	Is immediate and the client is currently suspected as being under the influence	Considered the most accurate detection method Can identify all psychoactive substances and their corresponding levels within the client's current blood Nearly universally Almost impossible to mask or adulterate specimen sample	The most personally invasive drug detection method, requires drawing of blood Most expensive drug detection method available Does not provide a history of drug use as the hair drug detection method does
Breathalyzer	Is immediate	Inexpensive Broadly accepted	Used only for alcohol

Diane: Sure, that makes sense. And I've done that by telling you that I've been getting drunk once a week over the past few months.

Counselor: Yes, you've done a very good job identifying your current alcohol use and describing the frequency of alcohol consumption. However, the persons you've identified as knowing you the best have indicated differently. Frankly, it would be important to get a baseline of the frequency of your alcohol consumption and further substantiate your report that you are not using any other substances.

Diane: So, you don't believe me?

Counselor: To the contrary, I believe that you are telling me exactly what you believe. You've told me you want things to change, and I believe you are committed to making those changes. Isn't that correct?

Diane: Yes.

Counselor: Good, one way we can help promote such change is via a hair analysis.

Diane: What's that?

Counselor: Hair analysis is a way of further substantiating what you've told me and creating a baseline of information regarding all the substances and the frequency of their use within the last 90 or so days. We can use the baseline data provided by the analysis to compare our future counseling progress.

Diane: So you'd know if I had used other drugs like marijuana or ecstacy by this test?

Counselor: Yes, but more importantly it will provide a baseline related to the frequency of your current alcohol use so we can compare your future progress. This will help us note your progress so we can help you obtain the goal you previously identified . . . that of being alcohol free.

Diane: What will it cost? I don't think I can afford it.

Counselor: The cost is about $135, and you can't afford not to do it. You are paying $68 an hour for counseling. If you were not serious about beating your drinking you wouldn't be paying that kind of money and you wouldn't be here. I believe you truly are committed to making progress and attaining your goals, Diane. You've told me you want to graduate from school, get married, and be successful. The hair analysis is just one part of helping ensure your forward momentum and goal attainment. Professionally speaking, I see it as part of your treatment. It is expensive. However, in comparison to failing school and not attaining your identified goals, it is a minimal cost.

Diane: But what happens if you learn that I've been smoking a little pot and experimenting with other drugs?

Counselor: It doesn't matter. The point is that we need to establish a baseline related to the substances you've been using and the frequency of use. Once we do that, we can create goals to help you increase the probability of beating the drugs and attaining the goals you want for your life.

This vignette demonstrates how drug detection testing provides a baseline on which forward progress and goal attainment can be measured. Rather than getting side-tracked by bogus client concerns regarding costs[17] or the identification of other previously nonreported psychoactive substance use, the counselor describes drug detection testing as part of the overall counseling process. Furthermore, the counselor does not accuse the client of lying or deceitfulness. Thus, the purpose is not to "catch" the client in a lie, but merely to authenticate the client's self-report and secure a recent psychoactive drug use history via drug detection testing.

Second, drug detection testing can be used should a counselor suspect that a client may have been using or is currently under the influence. Part of the therapeutic use of drug detection testing contained within this second area of intent revolves around the issue of accountability. For example, it is not all that uncommon for clients undergoing a driving under the influence (DUI) evaluation or for those attending a group substance abuse counseling session to present while under the influence of alcohol. Although these clients may deny any AOD use since their most recent DUI arrest or enrollment in court-mandated group counseling, they may have the aroma of alcohol "about them" and emanating from their breath, clothes, and perspiration. Additionally, they may have slurred speech, be unusually gregarious, and have dilated pupils. At this point, the counselor might then ask another counselor to speak with the client to determine if the original counselor's perceptions appear founded. Should the second counselor also believe the client is under the influence of alcohol, the client might be asked to use a Breathalyzer to document the concern and the client's alcohol level. Such an interaction is depicted below.

Counselor: George, upon entering the county's DUI offenders group you signed a contract indicating that you would not attend group while under the influence. Additionally, part of the court's conditions for your probation mandated that you not use alcohol or any other substances within 90 days of your release from incarceration. You also signed a release of confidential information as a condition of your probation indicating that you both authorized and required us to inform your probation officer should you be suspected of using and to secure a Breathalyzer test should we suspect you of being under the influence during group. Today, you have the smell of alcohol about you, your pupils are dilated, your speech is slurred, and you are extremely gregarious. Thus, you appear to be under the influence and as part of the conditions of your court parole and continued treatment with us, you will need to participate in a Breathalyzer drug detection test. Should you chose not to participate, we will still be required to inform your probation officer of the incident and indicate that you refused to participate in the Breathalyzer.

---

17. If the client's reported cost concerns were perceived as legitimate rather than merely a means of avoiding further drug detection, the counselor would need to identify other possible means to pay for the testing or might need to reevaluate the importance of the analysis in comparison to other pressing client needs.

George: You're wrong. I don't smell like alcohol, and I haven't had anything to drink since I was arrested three weeks ago. I'm just happy to be out of jail. That's why I'm acting so happy.

Counselor: I'm glad to learn this. However, I still need for you to complete the Breathalyzer. Given that you haven't used, the Breathalyzer will indicate that you are not under the influence, and it will support your statement. If that happens, we can get back to the group session and continue addressing the goals.

In cases like this one, it is best if the counselor can speak with the client privately and away from other group participants. Additionally, as demonstrated, the purpose is not to argue with the client about whether the client has used or not. Instead, the focus is to indicate that if the client hasn't used, the Breathalyzer will support the client's claim. Once noted as not being under the influence, the client can reengage in the group counseling process.

Accountability is an important issue with substance-abusing clients, because many have used their addiction as an excuse for inappropriate behaviors. Participation in counseling is not a right but a privilege. Therefore, if addicted clients fail to abide by the treatment rules, they can lose their treatment privilege. Additionally, drug detection testing can further teach accountability and increase client commitment to treatment by describing sanctions that will occur should a drug detection test indicate the client is using.

Often clients will spend many dollars each week on psychoactive substances of their choice and hours thinking about how to secure their drugs. It is not unusual for addictions counselors to require clients to identify a United Way Agency that they dislike the most and write a check to that agency in the amount that they typically spent in a week on their psychoactive substances of choice or make a pledge to provide volunteer work (e.g., mowing the lawn, cleaning the floors) equal to the amount of hours they typically spent thinking about how to secure their drugs within a typical "using" week. The check or volunteer working pledge is held and returned to the client if each of the client's drug detection tests return negative within the first six months of abstinence. However, should the client test positive for any psychoactive substance, the check and the client's volunteer working pledge will be mailed and the client will be required to meet the obligations before reentering treatment.

Third, drug detection use monitors continued abstinence and promotes abstinence recognition. This is exceedingly helpful to clients who are in the early and middle recovery stages. Often these clients will be nagged by concerned others who want to ensure that the client continues the abstinence process. The intentions of the concerned others is often good. However, their continued badgering tends to both provoke the client into stressful, defensive posturing (e.g., arguing with the accuser, returning to old substance using friends to escape the perceived "surveillance" etc.) and suggests the client is doomed for relapse (e.g., "If she thought I really could be substance free, she wouldn't be so worried about me").

Drug detection testing can be integrated into contingency contracting (Rinn, 1978) as a means of addressing such nagging. Here the emphasis is on successful monitoring of the client's continued abstinence. In other words, the client is told that the objective is to "catch you being clean." The goals are to support the client's abstinence and to let others know that they don't have to nag. Monitoring is especially helpful when working with recovering adolescents and their parents. Here, parents and adolescents jointly establish a clearly worded contract that describes expected (e.g., washing one's laundry) and unacceptable (e.g., marijuana use) behaviors and both sanctions for failing and rewards for passing drug detection tests. Additionally, adolescents agree to participate in random drug detection testing. They are told that the random screens can occur any day or night, and at any time. Parents and adolescents identify a time each day when all can meet for approximately 15 minutes.[18] During these meeting, adolescents verbally commit to remaining AOD abstinent and again agree to participate in random drug detection testing whenever it is requested by parents or counselors. Here, an adolescent might say something like, "Mom, I am committed to staying drug free. I will not use drugs today. I love you, Mom, and am committed to staying free from drugs for you, my little brother George, who may try to copy my behaviors, and for myself. I also agree to participate in drug screens whenever they are requested." At this time, parents can voice any specific concerns about upcoming events which may incite AOD relapse. For example, a parent may say, "Juan, I know that you have your final exams today and that you've been studying very hard to get into college. I'm worried that if you don't do as well as you wish, you may start drinking again." Next, adolescents verbally indicate how they will respond to the noted parental concerns. Here, Juan might reply, "Relax, Mom. I'm not going to fail the exam. I know the material and should do well. But if I don't, and I get all depressed, I'll talk to counselor Joe . . . especially if I get cravings to use." Then parents remind adolescents that the parents are committed to the adolescents and their recovery. Once adolescents indicate how they will respond, parents are not allowed to ask further questions. Adolescents then, in their parents' presence, take any prescribed medications for AOD-abusing symptomatology (e.g., Antabuse), and the parents place an "X" on a sobriety contract calendar (see Table 5.11). The intent is to ritualize this daily experience, encouraging parents and adolescents to direct this recovery experience and demonstrate their daily recommitment to each other.

One final note regarding drug detection testing: All one has to do is visit the Web or talk with a group of substance-abusing persons to learn the various myths and realities surrounding drug detection testing. From the products that can be placed in urine samples to ways of blowing into Breathalyzers, it seems nearly everyone has an idea of how to beat drug detection testing. Surprise is the ultimate method of ensuring that the samples taken are unadulterated and original. Thus, if a client is asked to provide a urine sample at 9 p.m. on Saturday night

---

18. According to our clients, meetings immediately before or following breakfast work best.

TABLE 5.11 Sobriety Contract

I, _____, agree to the following during the month of April . . .

   (A) Attend Al-a-teen each Wednesday night from 7 p.m until 8 p.m. at the Harris Street Baptist Church.

   (B) Not use any alcohol.

   (C) Not use any other illegal drug.

   (D) Not meet with, talk to, interact with, or mingle with Jane Smith or Joe Jones.

   (E) Attend school from 8:30 until 2:30 each weekday and complete my school assignments.

   (F) Attend family meetings each Tuesday night immediately following dinner.

   (G) Participate in all requested drug screenings and understand these screenings will occur randomly Monday through Friday, and will occur each Saturday and Sunday.

I understand that my failure to meet this agreement in part or whole will immediately result in my being placed in Dakota Half Way House for a minimum of 30 days. Furthermore, I will be granted free room and board, and television privileges from 8 p.m. until 10 p.m. on Sunday through Thursday evenings and from 5 p.m. until midnight on Friday and Saturday nights for completely complying with the above items.

---

another sample is warranted upon the client's return at 1 a.m., or she should be awakened and required to provide a third sample at 3 a.m. Clients often don't anticipate being asked to provide two or more samples on a given day. Choosing times immediately following when the client is using is key.

    Additionally, choosing a laboratory that alerts the counselor to substances commonly used to "clean" urine samples is important. The common rule I have with my clients is that if they take the time, effort, and money to purchase a product or substance that is added to their urine sample, it is the same thing as sending in a positive sample.

SUMMARY

This chapter reviewed fundamental psychometric properties which counselors must be familiar with when choosing standardized assessment instruments. Types of reliability and validity were summarized. The chapter then described three adult and two adolescent standardized AOD-specific instruments. These included the Alcohol Use Inventory, the Adult Substance Use Survey, the Substance Abuse Subtle Screening Inventory–3, the Adolescent Substance Use Survey, and the Substance Abuse Subtle Screening Inventory–Adolescent 2. Finally, readers learned about the four primary drug detection tests. These included urine, hair, blood, and Breathalyzer drug detection tests. Other drug detection tests types were succinctly discussed, and therapeutically efficient ways of using drug detection testing were described.

CLISD-PA TIER FOUR: STANDARDIZED AOD SPECIALITY INSTRUMENTS AND DRUG DETECTION TESTING SKILL BUILDER

This chapter described five standardized AOD speciality instruments and drug detection testing. Readers will next find five clinical vignettes. Please read the clinical vignettes and match each with the most appropriate standardized AOD speciality instrument profile. Additionally, indicate if drug detection testing should be used or how it might be integrated into the assessment and/or treatment process. Readers are encouraged to compare their responses to the authors' proposed answers on pages 188 through 192.

CLISD-PA Tier Four Skill Builder: Patrick

Patrick presents as an single, 28-year-old, Euro-American male. He is employed as a mason by a local construction company. Approximately 1 week ago, on the July Fourth holiday weekend, Patrick and three friends were traveling back from a beach concert and were stopped by law enforcement officers for speeding in a highway construction zone. Patrick reports he was "only driving 78 miles per hour in a 55 mile per hour construction zone." Police arrested Patrick and his friends for having open alcohol receptacles, approximately one quarter ounce of marijuana, and drug paraphernalia in his car (rolling papers, a roach clip, etc.). Although Patrick reports he had consumed "just two beers prior to driving" and had partially consumed a third prior to being pulled over, the police Breathalyzer test indicated he was "just under the legal limit" at the time of his arrest. Patrick was referred to your office by his attorney. Patrick reports he typically consumes a case of beer a week. "I mostly drink on the weekends" and "smoke a little weed most weekends," but he denies having alcohol or marijuana use problems. He reports work-related difficulties related to his AOD use: "I've gotten fired about every other month, because I use a little beer and pot to relax on the job." He also states, "I just can't find a woman who will put up with my drinking and drugging." Patrick reports that he was raised in a family that "grew pot as a cash crop" and that his mother, father, and siblings are "alcoholics." Patrick has been arrested on two previous occasions within the last year for driving under the influence.

Please see the standardized AOD speciality instrument profile that most closely resembles Patrick's presentation and indicate if drug detection testing should be done or how it might be integrated into the assessment and/or treatment process.

CLISD-PA Tier Four Skill Builder: Shawnelle

Shawnelle presents as a divorced 42-year-old African-American female. She is currently a human resources manager at a Fortune 100 company. Besides working her "normal" 60-hour week, she is enrolled in the company's Executive MBA Program with a major university. Her work in this program requires her to attend graduate classes from 8 a.m. until 9 p.m. each Friday and Saturday during the academic terms. Shawnelle is currently concluding the first year of the program with a 3.57 grade point average. She has another year of academic work before graduation. "I couldn't do it without my alcohol. I'm able to interact better with my peers and professors when I'm using alcohol. Additionally, without alcohol, I just can't think or perform as well. It helps me manage my moods and helps me cope." Shawnelle has a significant alcohol use history dating back to high school. She claims, "I can spot a party a mile away. Frankly, I've changed the word party from a noun to a verb." Shawnelle recently failed a Breathalyzer test which occurred as a result of her supervisor witnessing her consumption of vodka while on the job. Shawnelle reports she sneaks drinks at work to manage her "anxious mood" and states, "I can't stop thinking about drinking. I couldn't handle the anxiety and stress of my job without it. I'm constantly thinking about my next drink—sometimes, when I'm with an employee, I'll indicate I need a personal break. But the truth is I need a drink and will gulp some vodka so I can keep my composure." Shawnelle reports, "I lost everything significant to me because of alcohol—even my husband." She indicates that her husband divorced her two years ago due to her excessive alcohol use. Shawnelle states, "I'm ready to fight my alcoholism. If I don't stop it now, I'll lose my job. And that's the most important thing left in my life." Shawnelle flatly and adamantly denies the use of other drugs: "Nope, alcohol is my only lover. I don't use anything else."

On pages 158, please review Shawnelle's Alcohol Use Inventory Profile. Indicate if drug detection testing should be used or how it might be integrated into the assessment and/or treatment process.

CLISD-PA Tier Four Skill Builder: Krista

Krista presents as a 27-year-old Euro-American female. She is in her second year of a nursing program at a local college, but has taken an incomplete for the semester and withdrawn from classes due to her "plummeting" grade point average. Krista reports, "The emotional pain of not being able to be successful in my studies is killing me. I've even lost my best friends because they argue with me about how I act when I'm using . . . but I just don't care." She notes anxiety and worry about being able to complete her academic studies: "Sometimes I just get so anxious that I won't graduate that I just have to use more. Then I begin to feel depressed about my life and my future." Krista states, "I hurt my back a year ago and began taking painkillers. Once I began using I couldn't stop. I like to zone out and be by myself. The painkillers remove all the school pressures." Krista states that during her internship last semester she actually began stealing patient medications, "Sometimes my patients weren't in much pain and would ask for just a half a dose of pain medication . . . so I began collecting what they didn't use. Then it got to a point where I was actually stealing any painkillers I could find around the nurses' station or the patients' rooms." Krista also indicates that she began presenting at physicians' offices with lower back pain complaints so she could get painkillers. "It was pretty easy getting the stuff when I couldn't get enough at work. I would just go to a doctor's office and complain of a nebulous back pain and have my college health insurance pay for the drugs." Krista denies the use of nonprescription or illegal drugs and states, "Oh no. I could never use something that didn't go through FDA inspection. That kind of thing would be dangerous." She further denies the use of alcohol: "Don't use alcohol. My mom was an alcoholic and I don't want to be like her. Anyway, alcohol upsets my stomach." Krista indicates a loss of friends due to her drug use, "I simply prefer doing drugs by myself rather than being around people who want to do what they want to do. Since I've been doing the painkillers, I don't put up with people like before. Now I simply walk away from my ex-friends rather than argue." Krista denies any pending legal charges or current or past arrests, "Oh, gosh, no. I haven't even gotten a traffic ticket."

Review Krista's Substance Use Survey on page 159 (Table 5.4) and indicate if drug detection testing should be used or how it might be integrated into the assessment and/or treatment process.

CLISD-PA Tier Four Skill Builder: Billy

Billy presents as an intelligent and cordial 15-year-old Native American male. He has been in and out of juvenile detention centers and foster care homes since age 11. Two days ago he blacked out after huffing metallic paint and claims, "I'll never do that again. I can still taste the stuff. I burned skin off too, because I had to use turpentine to get the paint out of my nose. I'll stick to drugs I know how to use." Billy reports he sees his mother on weekly visitations, but indicates, "She really is an alcoholic and needs help. I can never tell if she will be drunk when I go to see her or not. As for my dad, he's totally out of the picture. I haven't seen him since he went to prison years ago." He denies any significant relationships with adults: "The only people I hang with are my age or slightly older. Anyone else is out to screw you." When asked about AOD use, Billy replies, "You think I'm dumb, man? Sure I've used alcohol, pot, 'shrooms,' ice, crack, crank, and heroin . . . who hasn't? But I'm not going to tell you I'm using it now. You think I want to go back to detention or something?" Billy does indicate that he has lots of friends who use AODs, and states, "I think its up to them if they want to quit or not. Society shouldn't tell them what to do. It's their lives, man, not the government's." Billy reports that he doesn't want to attend school and college isn't in his plans, "I can make more money peddling dope than most adults can working 9 to 5. And, it's easier too, because I get to be around people I like. I don't even need to wear a stupid tie or nothing."

Review Billy's Adolescent Substance Use Inventory profile on page 169 (Table 5.8) and indicate if drug detection testing should be used or how it might be integrated into the assessment and/or treatment process.

CLISD-PA Tier Four Skill Builder: Monica

Monica presents as a 16-year-old Hispanic-American female. She is an honors student who is enrolled in advanced-level and college-credit courses at the private high school she attends. Monica wants to be a trial lawyer like her mother and father, "My mother worked as an attorney in Paris, France, before she moved back to the States, and my dad graduated first in his law class." She was arrested for driving under the influence. The incident occurred immediately following a high school football game and dance. "I'm a cheerleader, so I've got to drink a little alcohol at school parties. I really don't think I was as drunk as they say. The police were just waiting for us to leave the dance. They always arrest teens driving expensive cars like my dad's Jaguar." Monica reports an "excellent" relationship with her parents and notes that she is an only child—"Why have the rest when you've already got the best." Monica denies AOD use following her arrest: "My dad said if I use again and get caught, I'll never get into a prestigious college. If that happens I'll never make it to law school." Monica states she once smoked a joint with her friends, "But that was when I was "15, young, and foolish . . . I'd never do it again." Monica denies any *DSM–IV–TR* criteria related to substance dependence and indicates, "Look, this isn't a big thing. I'm just here because my dad and mom think the judge will go lighter on me if I am in counseling. I really don't have a drinking problem. I'm just a social drinker who is underage."

Please review Monica's Adolescent SASSI-A2 profile on page 168 (Table 5.7) and indicate if drug detection testing should be done or how it might be integrated into the assessment and/or treatment process.

CORRECT RESPONSES

CLISD-PA Tier Four Skill Builder: Patrick

Patrick's clinical profile is contained within the SASSI–3 (Table 5.6). Both his Face-Valid Alcohol and Face-Valid Other Drug scales are elevated and match his face-to-face clinical interview statements that he uses alcohol and other drugs— especially on weekends. These elevated scale scores further match with his arrest record and statements indicating that he has driven while under the influence no less than three times within the last two years. Patrick also reported robust symptoms related to his AOD use at work and interpersonal problems. However, in the clinical interview he seemed to minimize this by verbally denying alcohol or marijuana use problems. Additionally, related to the Symptoms Scale, Patrick was involved with three peers who were also AOD abusing the night of his most recent arrest, and he reported that he was raised in a family where AOD use was prevalent. Patrick's Obvious Attributes Scale score is a little above the 50th percentile, possibly suggesting that he admits to some characteristics commonly associated with AOD-dependent persons and/or some personal flaws. However, it should be noted that his spiked Subtle Attributes Scale score suggests that he either may be attempting to present himself in a favorable light or may not fully recognize or admit the extent to which his AOD behaviors are problematic. His high Defensiveness Scale score in conjunction with the Subtle Attributes Scale score suggests he may have responded defensively to the instrument and attempted to deny the degree of his AOD difficulties. The high Defensiveness and Supplemental Addiction Measure Scale scores suggest that Patrick's defensiveness is related to his AOD use. Furthermore, his Family vs. Control Subjects Scale matches his clinical interview statements and supports his statements that he was raised in an AOD-abusing family. Finally, his Correctional Scale score supports his rather antisocial behavior of driving while under the influence, speeding, and being a part of a family that grew and sold marijuana.

Given that Patrick admits both alcohol and marijuana use, it would seem that urine drug detection testing may be appropriate during the course of his treatment to monitor and reward him for his abstinence and to insure that he does not use other psychoactive substances. Should the counselor be concerned that Patrick is not fully disclosing the types of psychoactive substances recently used, a hair detection test would provide a 90-day history of used substances.

CLISD-PA Tier Four Skill Builder: Shawnelle

Shawnelle's clinical profile is depicted in the Alcohol Use Inventory (Table 5.3). As clearly evident by her SOCIALIM, MENTALIM, MANAGMOOD, and ENHANCED Scale scores, her profile matches her clinical interview and supports her statements about using alcohol to socialize, manage her moods, and help her think and perform well mentally. Her GREGARUS Scale supports her verbal statements and suggests she clearly is a social drinker. And her COMPULSV and SUSTAIND Scale Scores match her clinical interview statements regarding continually thinking about her alcohol use and her need to use alcohol nearly continually to successfully manage and perform her work and academic activities. She even stated within the clinical interview that she feigns personal breaks so that she can consume vodka to manage her anxious moods. This again matches her elevated clinical profile scores on the COMPULSV, SUSTAIND, ANXCONCN, OBSESSED, and GUILTWOR Scales. Shawnelle's DISRUPT1 score suggests that she has experienced fairly significant alcohol use consequences. This is supported by her verbal indication that she has "lost everything significant to me because of alcohol—even my husband" and by the fact that she is currently facing potential loss of her job resulting from her alcohol use. Additionally, her spiked AWARENESS score matches her verbal statements in that she believes her alcohol consumption is negatively affecting her life. Concomitantly, her high RECEPTIV Scale score suggests she is in crisis and ready to begin the addictions treatment process. Again, these scale scores are supported by her clinical interview statements.

Given that Shawnelle reports her drug of choice is alcohol, urine drug detection tests seem a logical option for monitoring her abstinence and progress. However, depending on when Shawnelle reported for counseling, blood detection testing or Breathalyzer tests may be warranted. For example, if the counselor was an Employee Assistance Program (EAP) counselor who worked onsite at Shawnelle's office and if Shawnelle had been walked to the EAP by her supervisor, a Breathalyzer would seem a logical option to determine if Shawnelle was able to drive home safely. If her Breathalyzer test determined her alcohol level surpassed the legal limit, the company as well as the counselor might be held liable should Shawnelle or others be injured as a result of her being released from work for consuming alcohol and driving while intoxicated.

CLISD-PA Tier Four Skill Builder: Krista

The Adult Substance Use Survey depicts Krista's clinical profile (Table 5.4). Her INVOLVEMENT 1 scale suggests that she is a polysubstance user who has used several psychoactive substances at a moderate to extensive level. Based on Krista's self-report, she is using painkillers extensively—matching her INVOLVEMENT 1 Scale score. Additionally, there is strong congruence between Krista's verbal reports of academic and interpersonal problems (e.g., discontinuing her relationships) and her DISRUPTION Scale. Krista's SOCIAL score also matches her clinical interview statements. Although the scale is not used to diagnose antisocial personality disorder, her low–medium score seems to match what might be expected of a typical college student who has never had a run-in with the police but who may steal or lie in order to obtain drugs. Her MOOD Scale scores also match her clinical interview statements. Although not indicated as overwhelming, she does indicate worry and anxiety regarding completing school and possible feelings of depression. There also appears to be congruence between Krista's clinical interview presentation and her low DEFENSIVE Scale score. Within the clinical interview she appears to be admitting her psychoactive drug use with little if any guardedness. She freely discusses her concerns and openly admits to stealing painkillers without hesitation. Additionally, her GLOBAL Scale score matches her voiced concerns within the clinical interview. She clearly has indicating a lot of concerns and stressors both within the clinical interview and via her test endorsements. Finally, her INVOLVEMENT 2 and DISRUPTION 2 scale scores indicate she has moderate AOD use disruptions, considering that she scores higher than 50% of the clinical sample on DISRUPTION 2. This would support a pattern of substance dependence (personal communication, Wanberg, July 2001). Given that she is a college student and intelligent, this seems congruent with her scores. She likely has many coping strategies and skills that are founded upon her intellectual abilities and interpersonal skills. Additionally, there is good congruence between the evaluating counselor's rater score and Krista's overall GLOBAL Scale.

Urine and hair detection tests seem the most relevant means of monitoring Krista's progress and abstinence. Here the emphasis would be on using the detection testing as a means of identifying her abstinence. Hair analysis would also provide supporting evidence of her use of painkillers only.

CLISD-PA Tier Four Skill Builder: Billy

Billy's clinical profile is provided via the Adolescent Substance Use Survey (Table 5.8). Given that Billy is a 15-year-old male and only one standardized adolescent AOD speciality assessment instrument depicts a male client, this is the only appropriate response. Billy's INVOLVEMENT Scale scores match his clinical presentation. He is a polysubstance user who has been huffing paint, and based on his verbal responses and his endorsements on the Adolescent Substance Use Survey, Billy reports past alcohol, cannabis, mushrooms, amphetamines, and heroin use (personal communication, K. Wanberg, July 7, 2001). The fact that he reported having passed out while huffing paint doesn't provide sufficient information by itself to determine if huffing paint was a one-time occurrence or whether or not he frequently huffs. However, the Adolescent Substance Use Survey actually asks clients to endorse the number of times they have used specific psychoactive substances, and this would be most helpful in determining how to help Billy. Interestingly, Billy endorses only a "high–medium" number of Disruption Scale items. Therefore, he is indicating, at least to a moderate degree, some substance-use-related problems. Because Billy endorsed only 2 out of a possible 28 Mood Adjustment Scale items, there appears to be an absence of significant depression, worry, anxiety, irritability, anger, feelings of not wanting to live, or being unable to control his emotions. Based on his clinical presentation, Billy seems to have sufficient ego strength and does not voice concerns regarding his mental health. Of course, the lower scores on the Mood Adjustment Scale and the Disruption Scale may be affected by his defensiveness. His DEFENSIVENESS Scale score is high. Thus, based on the instrument, Billy appears to be quite defensive and guarded and likely would not readily admit to or disclose AOD use, symptomatology, or concerns. This matches with the clinical interview, when Billy said, "I'm not going to tell you I'm using [drugs] now. You think I want to go back to detention or something?" Billy's MOTIVATION Scale scores suggest he does not perceive his substance use as problematic or is uncommitted to making a change in his using behaviors. Billy's responses on the Overall Adolescent Disruption Scale may well be affected by Billy's defensiveness as well. Clearly Billy has been dealt an unfair hand. He reports an alcoholic mother and indicates that he has not seen his father since the father was incarcerated. Additionally, he has a checkered history of juvenile detention and foster care placements. Based on his self-report, one would anticipate that he would be defensive. If one were to look solely at Billy's Overall Adolescent Disruption Scale responses, he is not endorsing significant disruption and problems related to both his drug use and psychological adjustment. However, he is endorsing some disruptions, and the counselor may wish to look at the individual question stems and Billy's answers to determine if the majority of these endorsements are in a specific area (e.g., problems with family, school). Billy's final scale score (the Substance Use Survey Rater Scale) is a 14. This indicates a discrepancy between Billy's self-report and the counselor's evaluation assessment. Specifically, the counselor's use and disruption ratings are higher than Billy's self-report. This indicates that the counselor sees Billy as fitting a substance use diagnosis, and therefore Billy likely warrants counseling.

Hair drug detection testing seems appropriate with this client. Thereby, the counselor would be able to obtain a 90-day history of psychoactive drug use. Additionally, it would seem appropriate that regular urine analyses be conducted to monitor Billy's abstinence.

CLISD-PA Tier Four Skill Builder: Monica

Monica presents as a 16-year-old Hispanic-American female. Her clinical profile is depicted in the SASSI-A2 (Table 5.7). Some of the most striking features of Monica's clinical profile are related to her elevated Subtle Attributes and Defensiveness Scale scores. Persons with elevated Subtle Attributes scores may have difficulty recognizing and expressing feelings. Additionally, her elevated scores on this scale suggest she may lack awareness related to her AOD abuse and may be experiencing problems frequently encountered by AOD adolescents. Concomitantly, Monica's elevated Defensiveness Scale suggests she may be either attempting to present herself in a favorable, non-AOD-abusing manner, or she may tend to "avoid acknowledging, and possibly recognizing, personal limitations or problems" (SASSI Institute, 2001, p. 36). The elevations on these scales match her clinical presentation during the face-to-face clinical interview. For example, Monica stated, "I'm a cheerleader, so I've got to drink a little alcohol at school parties. I readily don't think I was as drunk as they say," and she described how the police "always arrest teens driving expensive cars." Such statements can suggest a number of things, including defensiveness and/or an unwillingness or an inability to admit to inappropriate AOD use. Additionally, Monica's Family–Friends Risk Scale scores suggest that she may be part of a family and/or social system that may trivializes AOD abuse and the consequences of same. Again, this was supported via the individual clinical interview when Monica stated, "Look, this isn't a big thing. I'm just here because my dad and mom think the judge will go lighter on me if I am in counseling." Such a statement suggests the possibility that those within Monica's immediate social milieu may be minimizing Monica's AOD-abusing behaviors and the potential need for counseling. Here the counselor may wish to review the specific endorsements that Monica made on this scale to determine if Monica perceives whether her parents and/or peers are identified as trivializing her AOD abuse.

Depending on the counselor's clinical judgment, the counselor may wish to use either hair or urine drug detection testing to identify whether Monica is using only alcohol. If one suspected Monica of being under the influence during session, drug detection options could range from Breathalyzer to urine or blood tests.

REFERENCES

Drummond, R. J. (1996). *Appraisal procedures for counselors and helping professionals* (3rd ed.). Englewood Cliffs, NJ: Prentice Hall.

Ghiselli, E. E., Campbell, J. P., & Zedeck, S. (1981). *Measurement theory for the behavioral sciences*. San Francisco: W. H. Freeman.

Horn, J. L., Wanberg, K. W., & Foster, F. M. (1990). *Guide to the Alcohol Use Inventory.* Minneapolis, MN: National Computer Systems, Inc.

Jordan, R. (1988). Hair analysis: A new turn in drug testing. *Risk Management*, 68–69.

Juhnke, G. A., Vacc, N. A., Curtis, R. C., Coll, K. M., & Paredes, D. M. (in press). *A National Survey of Assessment Instruments Used by Master Addictions Counselors.*

Lazowski, L. E., Miller, F. G., Boye, M. W., & Miller, G. A. (1998). Efficacy of the Substance Abuse Subtle Screening Inventory–3 (SASSI–3) in identifying substance dependence disorders in clinical settings. *Journal of Personality Assessment 71*, 114–128.

Miller, F. G., & Lazowski, L. E. (2001). *The Adolescent SASSI–A2 manual: Identifying substance use disorders*. Springhill, IN: SASSI Institute.

Miller, F. G., Roberts, J., Brooks, M. K., & Lazowski, L. E. (1997). *SASSI–3 user's guide: A quick reference for administration and scoring*. Bloomington, IN: Baugh Enterprises, Inc.

Minnesota Poison Control (2001). Available: http://www.mnpoison.org/drug_testing_kit.htm.

Rinn, R. C. (1978). Children with behavior disorders. In Hersen & A. Bellack (Eds.), *Behavior therapy in the psychiatric setting* (pp. 197–229). Baltimore, MD: Williams & Wilkins.

Rychtarik, R. G., Koutsky, J. R., & Miller, W. R. (1998). Profiles of the Alcohol Use Inventory: A large sample cluster analysis conducted with split-sample replication rules. *Psychological Assessment*, 1107–119.

SASSI Institute. (2001). *The Adolescent SASSI–A2 User's Guide: A quick reference for administration and scoring*. Springhill, IN. Author.

Wanberg, K. W. (1997). A user's guide to the Adolescent Substance Use Survey–SUS: Differential screening of adolescent alcohol and other drug use problems. Arvada, CO: Center for Addictions Research and Evaluation:

Wanberg, K. W. (1997b). *A user's guide to the Adult Substance Use Survey*. Arvada, CO: Center for Addictions Research and Evaluation, Inc.

Chapter 6

Personality Assessment and Therapeutic Feedback

Chapter 6 Outline:

Chapter 6 Learning Objectives:
After reading this chapter, you should be able to:

- Describe Tier Four of the CLISD-PA model.
- Understand the use of the Minnesota Multiphasic Personality Inventory–2 (MMPI–2) and the Minnesota Multiphasic Personality Inventory–Adolescent (MMPI–A)
- Explain why the MMPI–2 and MMPI–A are used by addictions counselors.

- Describe the instruments' basic validity, clinical, and supplementary scales.
- Explain how to provide therapeutic feedback based on the CLISD-PA model experience.

OVERVIEW OF TIER FOUR OF THE CLISD-PA MODEL

Tier Four of the Clinical Interviews, Standardized Speciality, Drug Detection, and Personality Assessment (CLISD-PA) model uses a standardized personality assessment instrument such as the Minnesota Multiphasic Personality Inventory–2 to provide an expansive image of the client's personality and commonly corresponding personality traits and behaviors. Moreover, Tier Four suggests relevant *Diagnostic and Statical Manual of Mental Disorders* (4th ed.)–Text Revision (*DSM–IV–TR*) personality disorders, as well as evident psychopathology (e.g., mild hallucinations, aberrant thinking, suicidal ideation, substance abuse 7), which may not be readily admitted to valued significant others—and especially not counselors assessing the client for substance abuse.

Some personality disorders may be comparatively indiscernible to laypersons or less experienced counselors. This is especially true when: (a) interactions are limited or infrequent, (b) the client is "therapy wise,"[19] and (c) the client's psychopathology severity is just above the diagnosis threshold and well managed. When interviewed within the Tier Two significant other interview, friends may reframe client psychopathology in more heuristic terms. For example, friends may state the client is "quiet," "dependable," and "a good listener." Less experienced counselors may also fail to identify the underlying personality disorder and instead solely focus on the client's self-reported substance abuse. Yet the client may minimally qualify for dual *DSM–IV–TR* disorders like dependent personality disorder and alcohol abuse. Successful treatment, then, requires specific interventions for each disorder.

Other personality disorders floridly manifest themselves and initially can even appear alluring—that is, until the noxious aspects can no longer be ignored and their frequency becomes unbearable. An example of this might include histrionic personality disorder. Here, others within the Tier Two significant other interview may heuristically describe the client as "charming," "fun," and "vivacious." Such descriptions are accurate depictions, because they have observed the client effortlessly flirt between social function conversations and interact in a fun manner with absolute strangers. However, these significant others may mistakenly dismiss the shallow, self-centered behaviors that they have not yet fully recognized as problematic or acutely experienced on a regular basis. Once again, entry-level counselors may not discern the client's degree of presenting psychopathol-

---

19. Typically, clients who are therapy wise have a significant treatment history. As a result of these treatment histories (and likely in combination with their frequent personality disorder), they understand how to present concerns in a manipulative manner.

ogy as problematic and may at first disregard the histrionic's behaviors as nervousness or AOD related.

Given the robust comorbidity between certain disorders (e.g., bipolar disorder, borderline personality disorder, posttraumatic stress disorder) and AOD abuse (personal communication, J. Oldz, July 12, 2001), and the potential for both significant others and less experienced counselors to minimize less evident personality disorder dysfunction and/or attribute presenting concerns as primarily related to AOD abuse, the Tier Four personality assessment can be used when addictions counselors suspect possible comorbid personality and substance-related disorders. Thus, a standardized personality instrument can either rule out or confirm the presence of such disorders and related psychopathology. Furthermore, standardized personality assessment instruments help assess the need for intensive treatment or restricted treatment environments (e.g., inpatient hospitalization). Conversely, should clients present as defended or should there appear confounding or insufficient information at the conclusion of Tier Three, the Tier Four standardized personality assessment is a logical progression. Additionally, as is the case with standardized AOD assessment instruments, pre- and posttreatment scores can be compared to determine treatment efficacy. Therefore, this chapter describes one adult and one adolescent standardized personality assessment instrument. Then it describes how counselors effectively use the assessment results in a therapeutic manner.

MINNESOTA MULTIPHASIC PERSONALITY INVENTORY–2 AND THE MINNESOTA MULTIPHASIC PERSONALITY INVENTORY–ADOLESCENT

Why the MMPI–2 and MMPI–A?

Despite the existence of many excellent personality assessment instruments that could be reviewed in this chapter, only two are described. These instrument are the Minnesota Multiphasic Personality Inventory–2 (MMPI–2) and the Minnesota Multiphasic Personality Inventory–Adolescent (MMPI–A). Clearly, counselors are encouraged to choose the personality assessment instrument which seems most appropriate based upon their: (a) formal clinical testing and assessment training, (b) professional competence, (c) professional ethics, and (d) clients' needs (Vacc, Juhnke, & Nilsen, 2001). However, three key factors suggest the MMPI–2 and MMPI–A are the most logical standardized personality assessment choices for addiction counselors.

First, Master Addictions Counselors (MACs) identified the MMPI–2 and MMPI–A as the most widely used and most important personality instruments for addictions counselors working with adults and adolescents respectively. In other words, seasoned addictions counselors, certified specifically in the addictions speciality area, indicated the MMPI–2 and the MMPI–A were the personality assessment instrument they used most. Furthermore, these addictions professionals advocated that counseling students be trained in both. Such results are similar to and support those made by other mental health professionals, who indicated extensive MMPI–2 use (Bubenzer, Zimpger, & Mahrle, 1990; Watkins, Campbell, & McGregor, 1988). No other clinical personality assessment instruments have received such distinction by MACs.

Second, the MMPI–2 and MMPI–A have clinical scales and supplemental scales important to addictions counselors. Specifically, the MMPI–2 and MMPI–A provide a broad-spectrum view of the client's personality and the client's presenting symptomatology—including AOD behaviors. Such a view is vital when establishing effective addictions treatment.

Third, the MMPI–2 and the MMPI–A are respected personality assessment instruments that have been extensively reviewed and researched. For example, a cursory literature review for the years 1998 to 2001 found the MMPI–2 and the MMPI–A cited within article titles over 700 and 90 times respectively. In other words, within a 3-year span, the MMPI–2 and MMPI–A were used nearly 800 times by clinical researchers as the instruments of choice for research with specific populations or were researched on. These numbers do not reflect the times the instruments were used within research without the instruments' names appearing in the article title. Therefore, the sheer number of citations clearly suggests the prominence of these standardized personality assessment instruments and the credibility they have within the profession.

General MMPI–2 Overview

The MMPI–2 is composed of 567 true–false items and was restandardized by Butcher, Dahlstrom, Graham, and Tellegen in 1989 (Green, 1991). The MMPI–2 was developed for clients 18 years of age and older with a sixth-grade reading level (Green). The instrument takes approximately 60 to 90 minutes to complete and can be ordered directly from National Computer Systems (NCS) (1-800-627-7271) in Minneapolis MN.

MMPI–2 Reliability and Validity

One week test–retest coefficients for the MMPI–2 validity and clinical scales were reported between .67 and .92 for men and .58 and .91 for women (Butcher, Dahlstrom, Graham, Tellegen, & Kaemmer, 1989). It should be noted that 11 of the 13 scales for men had test–retest scores of .75 or higher and 9 of the 13 scales for women had test–retest scores of .76 or higher (Butcher et al., 1989). Additionally, internal consistency coefficients (alphas) ranged between .34 and .85 for men, with 5 of the 13 scales having alphas of .74 or higher, and .37 and .87 for females, with 4 of 13 scales having alphas of .72 or higher. Satisfactory concurrent validity among 2- and 3-point personality patterns were also noted between the MMPI original and the MMPI–2 (Chojnacki & Walsh, 1992; Graham, Timbrook, Ben-Porath, & Butcher, 1991). Furthermore, the MMPI–2 demonstrated

Criterion-Related Predictive Validity by predicting clinical diagnoses among outpatient clients (Morrison, Edwards, & Weissman, 1994).

MMPI–2 Scales

The revised MMPI–2 has "8 validity scales, 10 clinical scales, 15 content scales, 20 supplementary scales, [five] PSY-5 scales . . . , 31 clinical subscales . . . , five superlative self-presentation subscales [and] various special or setting specific indices" (NCS, 2001). Clearly, one needs advanced clinical assessment training to administer the MMPI–2 and all of its available scales. However, for the purposes of this book, the validity scales, 10 clinical scales, 2- and 3-point codes, and supplemental scales commonly relevant to AOD-abusing clients are described.

Validity Scales

The MMPI–2 Validity Scales are akin to the steam engine that pulls the train. They establish the foundation for the interpretation of clinical and supplemental scales commonly relevant to AOD-abusing clients. These scales give the counselor information related to the client's endorsements. Specifically, the Validity Scales suggest whether the client appears to be responding truthfully to the question stems. They also suggest whether or not the client's endorsements appear suspect or invalid.

The Revised MMPI–2 includes three new scales and two scales that were moved to the validity scales. Specifically, the validity scales are composed of the following nine scales: (a) Cannot Say (?), (b) Variable Response Inconsistency Scale (VRIN), (c) True Response Inconsistency Scale (TRIN), (d) Lie Scale (L), (e) Defensiveness Scale (K), (f) Superlative Self-Presentation Scale (S), (g) Infrequency Scale (F), (h) Infrequency-Back Scale (F b), and (i) Psychiatric Infrequency Scale (F p).

The Cannot Say Scale indicates the number of items to which the client did not respond. These items were left blank. The scale suggests the degree to which the client is cooperating in the assessment process. Should a client fail to respond to 30 or more of the first 370 questions, the instrument is considered invalid and the counselor may wish to review the items to determine if they specifically relate to common topic areas such as suicide or aberrant thoughts.

VRIN and TRIN scales identify random and inconsistent endorsements. High scores on either scale suggest inconsistent client endorsements, with T scores of 80 and above indicating the profile is invalid and T scores between 70 and 79 suggesting the profile is suspect.

The F Scale identifies clients endorsing extreme responses. These responses are made in a pathological direction. Specifically, clients scoring extremely high on this scale (e.g., T scores of 110 and above) are endorsing robust problems and may well be making a cry for help, malingering, or randomly responding. Extreme scores suggest "everything" is wrong and tend to inflate the clinical scales.

It is unlikely that clients endorsing so much florid symptomatology would be able to complete the 567 MMPI–2 questions without significant troubles. Clients more likely providing a valid profile with significant symptomatology will have T scores between 65 and 80. However, at times, addicted clients initially entering treatment completely overwrought by interpersonal relationship losses, job or academic performance issues, financial stressors, and withdrawal symptoms will perceive that everything is wrong. This perception is likely what drove them into treatment. Thus, clinical judgment must be used when making such assessments. Finally, low T scores below 50 indicate the client has endorsed no significant symptomatology and may be an indicator of either having no recognized concerns or potential defensiveness.

Similar to the VRIN and TRIN scales, the F b Scale again reviews inconsistent endorsements. Here, however, the emphasis is on determining if the client endorsed differing symptomatology degrees on the front of the instrument in comparison to the back. Given the MMPI–2's length, clients may become tired and either begin to randomly respond to items on the back or may be unable to maintain their concentration. If scores here are markedly different than on the front, it may well suggest an invalid profile.

The L scale suggests the client's ability to present herself in a truthful, balanced manner. Clients endorsing an unusually high number of items (T score of 60 and above, raw scores of 5 or above) are likely attempting to present themselves in a most positive light and are denying the presence of even minor flaws. Clients endorsing such a significant number of positive items may be defensive or may present with a high degree of religiosity. Although clients scoring below a T score of 50 may be overly critical of themselves, it is more likely that they are indicating a willingness to admit minor faults and are likely presenting themselves in a truthful, balanced manner.

The K Scale indicates the degree of symptomatology or lack thereof endorsed by the client. Here, higher scores (T scores above 65) suggest the remarkable absence of symptoms or problems. In other words these clients are suggesting they have no reason for participating in counseling. Things are going exceptionally well. T scores between 56 and 64 suggest clients are defensive or denying the existence of problems. Two ways of using the K Scale to potentially identify persons attempting to present themselves in an overly positive manner are to evaluate scale combinations. For example, when both the L and K Scales have T scores of 50 or above and the F Scale has a T score below 50, this suggests the client has endorsed items in a fashion similar to those who are attempting to present themselves in an overly positive manner. Additionally, counselors can subtract the K Scale Score from the F Scale Score. Should this "subtraction score" be 13 points or more, there again exists a strong probability that the client is attempting to present in a favorable manner.

Conversely, clients admitting significant problems and/or concerns will score low on the K Scale (T scores below 40). These low-scoring clients may be crying for help. As in the case with elevated F scores, addicted clients entering treatment and facing significant interpersonal, legal, and environmental stressors, as well as withdrawal symptoms, may endorse few if any positives in their lives.

Butcher and Han developed the S Scale in an attempt to assess defensiveness (NCS, 2001). Five subscales comprise the S Scale. These include Beliefs in Human Goodness, Serenity, Contentment with Life, Patience/Denial of Irritability and Denial of Moral Flaws (NCS). Graham (2000, p. 36) stated the S Scale was developed

> to assess the tendency of some persons to present themselves on the MMPI–2 as highly virtuous, responsible individuals who are free of psychological problems, have few or no moral flaws, and get along extremely well with others. This manner of self-presentation is very common in situations such as personnel screening or child custody determinations.

Moreover, Graham further reported that a raw score of 29 or above distinguished between those clients responding honestly and those attempting to present themselves in a most favorable light.

VALIDITY SCALE SUMMARY

It quickly becomes apparent that addictions counselors reviewing the MMPI–2 Validity Scales can best judge how the client approached the test-taking experience by looking at the Validity Scales and their configurations in unison. For example clients scoring excessively high L, K, and S Scale scores and excessively low F Scale scores may well be attempting to present themselves in an extremely positive light (Table 6.1). Related to substance-abusing clients, these clients are

TABLE 6.1. Client Presenting in an Overly Positive Light

Scale	VRIN	TRIN	F	Fb	Fp	L	K	S
Score	55	57	43	49	49	73	91	66

denying the existence of any profound problems or concerns and are reporting that treatment is unwarranted due to this lack of problems. One might find that clients presenting with such scores have been mandated to counseling. Such scores can also be common among clients reapplying for their vehicle operating license after having it revoked. Contrastingly, addicted clients facing criminal charges with likely potential for long-term sentencing for possession and selling controlled substances, and admitting severe interpersonal, psychological, and financial stressors, may score excessively high on the F Scale, with very low L, K, and S scale scores (Table 6.2). These clients may be endorsing a high number of symptoms and be making a deliberate cry for help or may be feeling truthfully overwhelmed. Matching these scores with the counselor's clinical judgment based on the Tier One Individual Assessment and Tier Two Significant Assessment promotes the most accurate and helpful manner of intervening.

Clinical Scales

The MMPI–2 contains 10 clinical scales. These include: (a) Hypochondriasis, (b) Depression, (c) Hysteria, (d) Psychopathic Deviate, (e) Masculinity–Femininity, (f) Paranoia, (g) Psychasthenia, (h) Schizophrenia, (i) Hypomania, and (j) Social Introversion. Many times, these scales are referred to by the numbered order in which they are depicted on the clinical profile sheet. Thus, the One Scale is Hypochondriasis, the Two Scale is Depression, the Ten Scale is Social Introversion, and so forth. Additionally, typical T scores for the clinical scales will be between 50 and 65.

TABLE 6.2. Client Presenting in an Overly Negative Light

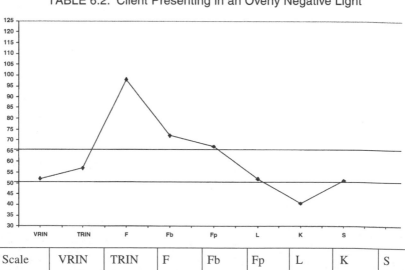

Scale	VRIN	TRIN	F	Fb	Fp	L	K	S
Score	51	58	100	74	67	52	42	51

THE ONE SCALE: HYPOCHONDRIASIS (Hs)

This scale denotes bodily aches, pains, and general physical concerns. Clients who score high on this scale, for example, T scores of 65 and above, are endorsing a significant number of somatic concerns and symptoms and may tend to use these complaints for attention or secondary gains (e.g., being relieved of charges as a result of their physical complaints). Long-term addicted clients beginning recovery may have T scores between 60 to 65 due to the physical discomforts associated with substance withdrawal (e.g., nausea, headaches, chills), increased physical activity after having a long-term sedimentary lifestyle, or newfound aware-ness of their body and its functioning. Additionally, many of these clients have failed to address basic hygiene as well as physical needs during their prolonged substance dependence. Thus, when initiating recovery they may have many noted somatic concerns. These concerns can range from pressing dental needs to derma-tology. Clients scoring below 40 on this scale are indicating a lack of physical alignments and may well be healthy, younger clients who truly are in the prime of their lives.

THE TWO SCALE: DEPRESSION (D)

As the name implies, the Two Scale indicates depressive symptomatology en-dorsed by the client. Addicted clients spiking this scale with T scores greater than 70 have likely been recently confronted with significant consequences resulting from their AOD use (e.g., arrest, incarceration, loss of significant or meaningful others) Additionally, they may be crying for help or entering into treatment and admitting the significant losses resulting from their AOD use. Sometimes they will report feeling so "totally overwhelmed" that they are unable to fully commit to abstinence and are at high risk for relapse. Others may see suicide as their only viable option. Thus, the presence of suicidal ideation and intent should be as-sessed with clients indicating depressed feelings on this scale and appropriate interventions should be implemented to insure the client's safety.

THE THREE SCALE: HYSTERIA (Hy)

Addicted clients scoring high on this scale with T scores above 70 tend to demand attention from others, act immaturely and selfishly, report broad and vague physi-cal complaints, and use AOD as a means to manage typical life stressors and concerns. Often they will initially present as socially able, talkative, and flamboy-ant. However, as others begin to know them, they will frequently be perceived as shallow and self-centered, and their once perceived alluring qualities will vapor-ize as the noxious personality characteristics become more frequent.

THE FOUR SCALE: PSYCHOPATHIC DEVIATE (Pd)

This is a crucial scale for addictions counselors to understand. Given that ad-dicted clients often: (a) illegally purchase, manufacture, or sell psychoactive sub-stances, (b) illegally or inappropriately use (e.g., drinking and driving, alcohol consumption while on the job, etc.), and (c) lie, cheat, steal, and perform sexual favors to secure psychoactive substances, it is logical that their endorsements on the Four Scale will exceed those of the general population. T scores of 65 and above suggest the addictive client may well be rebellious, may have difficulty with clients in authority as well as social rules, and may qualify for or have a personality characteristics similar to those diagnosed with antisocial personality disorder. Most often they are self-centered and unconcerned with the potential negative effect their behaviors will have on innocent others. Many will be adventure seeking and impulsive. This is especially true when psychoactive substance abuse is combined with their characterological disorder.

THE FIVE SCALE: MASCULINITY–FEMININITY (Mf)

This scale relates to stereotypical gender role affiliation. For males, T scores above 80 suggest possible sexual identity conflicts, masculine role insecurity, and "greater involvement with aesthetic and artistic interest than most men" (Butcher, 1999, p. 51). Furthermore, they may well be imaginative, persevering, and organized (Butcher, 1999). Low-scoring males with T scores below 35 likely present as "John Wayne" types who perceive themselves as robustly masculine and enjoy stereotypical masculine roles, recreation, and interests (e.g., football, NASCAR) (personal communications, J. Oldz, February 7, 1990). For females, T scores above 70 may suggest an interest in nonstereotypical work roles, interests, and behaviors. They may present as self-confident, adventuresome, and competitive. Females with T scores below 40 may fit the stereotypical "Southern belle" profile of robustly embracing traditionally accepted feminine roles and interests (personal communications, J. Oldz, February 7, 1990).

THE SIX SCALE: PARANOIA (Pa)

It is also important for addictions counselors to be knowledgeable about the Six Scale. Many addicted clients have legitimate reasons for their mistrust of persons they sell illegal drugs to—as well as rational suspicion related to police arrest. Often addicted clients have sound and compelling reasons for their blatant distrust. Given the significant sums of money and psychoactive drugs they have or make, they are in constant jeopardy of being robbed or incarcerated. Therefore, the Six Scale is often slightly to moderately elevated (T scores of 55 to 65) when comparing addicted populations to the general population at large. Additionally, some psychoactive substances (e.g., cocaine)—especially in large doses—increase paranoia. All of this can symbiotically increase Six Scale scores. For example, a cocaine-dependent drug dealer, working in a renowned high-crime area, carrying large sums of money and known by local law enforcement agents, likely will have an elevated Six Scale score. High T scores (e.g., 70 or above) may suggest someone with clearly aberrant thinking and faulty reference. Higher scores may also suggest someone as being psychotic with vivid hallucinations or delusions.

THE SEVEN SCALE: PSYCHASTHENIA (Pt)

Clients with T scores of 65 or higher on the Seven Scale typically present as excessively anxious and worried. Many will report they are unable to focus or concentrate and may have physical complaints of fatigue or exhaustion. They are often identified by others as extremely well organized, meticulous, and perfectionistic. Frequently they are highly self-critical and lack self-confidence. Some may attempt to self-medicate using substances like cannabis to reduce their anxiety and worry. Additionally, some high scorers may qualify for obsessive compulsive disorder.

THE EIGHT SCALE: SCHIZOPHRENIA (Sc)

Clients with *T* scores above 75 may well be endorsing psychotic experiences that could include florid hallucinations. Given that clients with such elevated scores would likely have difficulty remaining focused on a standardized assessment instrument composed of so many questions, such scores may also be indicative of clients who are making a cry for help. In other words, floridly psychotic clients would be so confused, it is more likely the client is making a deliberate cry for help. Substance-dependent clients who have extensive drug-use histories with psychoactive substances may also endorse mild to high elevations on this scale. For example, clients who have recently experienced a substance-induced delirium from psychoactive substances like cocaine, alcohol, or hallucinogens may have noteworthy scale elevations.

THE NINE SCALE: MANIA (Ma)

This scale describes manic behaviors or episodes. Clients with *T* scores above 80 may qualify for bipolar disorder and may present as grandiose with pressured speech and a history of inpatient hospitalizations. Non-bipolar disordered clients with *T* scores at 65 or above will typically present as impulsive, flamboyant, socially confident, and gregarious. Again, some psychoactive substances—especially when a long-term history of dependence is noted—can elevate Nine Scale *T* scores and even mimic bipolar disorder criteria. Such psychoactive-substance abusing clients may endorse items suggesting that they have experienced times, when under the influence, when they have boundless energy, an inability or an aversion to sleep, flights of ideas, pressured speech, and psychomotor agitation. Given high comorbidity between bipolar disorder and substance-related diagnoses (personal communications, J. Oldz, July 12, 2001) it is imperative that counselors determine if clients presenting with elevated Nine Scale scores qualify for a dual diagnosis (e.g., bipolar disorder and cannabis dependence).

THE TEN (ZERO) SCALE: SOCIAL INTROVERSION (Si)

This scale measures the degree to which a client interacts with others and feels socially comfortable. Clients scoring high on this scale (e.g., *T* scores of 70 and above) typically are uncomfortable in social situations and prefer to be alone or with a limited number of very close and trusted friends. Social interactions are often very difficult for these clients as they are often extremely shy and have difficulty voicing themselves. Concomitantly, they often feel anxious, acquiesce easily, and lack energy. Those scoring low on this scale (e.g., *T* scores below 45) frequently are seen as outgoing, extroverted clients who interact freely with others and may even be identified as brazen or audacious. Depending on the preferred psychoactive substances used (e.g., stimulants, hallucinogens, depressants), clients may endorse behaviors commonly associated with the substances frequently used. For example, a cocaine-dependent client who has a chronic and frequent history of daily cocaine use may score low on the Ten Scale. Therefore, it is incumbent on the counselor to determine if a low score appears to be associated with behaviors and feelings occurring when under the influence.

Code Types

When two or more clinical scales are elevated above typical scores (e.g., *T* scores of 65 and above), counselors can use the two or three highest scales to indicate "Two-Point" or "Three-Point" code types. For example, should a client's highest clinical scale be the One Scale (hypochondriasis) (e.g., *T* score of 75), with the second highest scale being the Three Scale (hysteria) (e.g., *T* score of 72), the counselor would indicate the client had a "One Three" code type. This would be written "13 code type."[20] Should the client's third highest score be the Eight Scale (e.g., *T* score of 71), the client would have a "One Three Eight" code-type, written "138 code type." Not all high clinical scale scores result in two- or three-point code-types. For example, there are no 16 or 20 code types. Most code types, and especially two-point code types, are interchangeable. In other words, the order of the highest and second highest scores have the same implications. For example, the previously noted 13 code type is often indicated as the 13/31 code type. Thus, no matter if the client's highest scale score was one or three, and the second highest score was three or one, the general information regarding the client would be similar. Additionally, should the first and second elevated clinical scales be equal, the results would be used similarly (e.g., 13/31 code type).

A number of two- and three-point code types are especially relevant to addictions counselors and warrant additional discussion. One of the most predominant features of AOD-abusing clients and their two- and three-point code types is their elevated Four Scale. Thus, a number of two and three point code types include the Four Scale as either the highest or second highest endorsed clinical scale. For example, clients with a 14/41 two-point code type often have a chronic history of AOD abuse that includes drinking sprees, family problems resulting from their AOD abuse, and problems with authority figures—especially parents related to AOD abuse (personal communication, J. Oldz, March 14, 1990). Clients with this code also are endorsing a high number of somatic complaints or concerns that may be rather vague and unspecific.

Clients with 24/42 two-point code types often report AOD abuse. Specifically, these clients frequently present as impulsive and angry clients with comorbid AOD abuse. Often they will attempt to self-medicate by using psychoactive sub-

---

20. Given that the Ten Scale is the highest clinical scale and it is noted as the "0" Scale, two- and three-point code types are written this way.

stances in an effort to cope with their anger. Typically, the Two Scale is elevated as a result of being caught or getting into trouble after acting impulsively—for example, after being arrested for driving under the influence (DUI).

Other two- and three-point code types commonly associated with AOD abuse include 46/64, 47/74, 48/84, 138, and 472. However, by far the most commonly occurring code types for AOD-abusing clients are 49/94 (personal communication, J. Oldz, March 14, 1990). Most often clients endorsing an excessive number of these items fulfill *DSM–IV–TR* (APA, 2000) antisocial personality disorder criteria and have a total disregard for others. They often demonstrate antisocial behaviors prior to AOD abuse and act even more impulsively when AOD abusing. Thus, they commonly are referred to counseling because of their law-breaking behaviors and concomitant drinking and drugging behaviors (e.g., driving while under the influence, domestic violence while under the influence). The prognosis for such clients is less than optimal. Most perceive they don't have a problem. When they do admit AOD abuse, they typically blame others for their drinking and drugging behaviors or perceive their AOD abuse as a viable coping mechanism.

Supplementary Scales

Three AOD-related supplementary scales are particularly important to addictions counselors. These include the MacAndrew Alcoholism Scale–Revised (MAC–R), the Addiction Potential Scale (APS), and the Addiction Acknowledgment Scale (AAS). Results from these scales when included with all previously attained information from the CLISD-PA assessment should provide an extremely thorough and accurate diagnosis. Moreover, related to Tier Four, these supplementary scales identify clients who have personality types that often abuse AOD or are at high risk for doing so.

The MAC scale was developed in 1965 (MacAndrew, 1965). It was later revised to 49 items and integrated into the MMPI–2. The scale should be viewed as reporting general AOD abuse and addicted behaviors (e.g., gambling, sexual addiction) vis-à-vis alcohol abuse only behaviors (Graham & Strenger, 1988). The majority of MAC-R items are not obviously transparent and often are not perceived by clients as associated with AOD use. Thus, guarded, AOD-abusing clients typically score in a relatively similar manner to others who are AOD-abusing. Raw scores of 28 and above are indicative of AOD-abusing clients. However, it should be noted that clients endorsing a significant number of MAC–R Scale items may be clients who are similar in personality (e.g., extroverted, confident) and may not actually be addicted. In other words, although AOD is exceptionally common among clients with such personalities, such endorsements do not mean that the client is addicted.

The APS is a 39 item scale designed to measure "personality factors underlying the development of addictive disorders" (Butcher, 1999, p.117). As with the MAC–R, scale items are subtle and not AOD transparent. Greater than 75% of the

APS scale items are independent from MAC–R items. Thus, clients who may not be identified on the MAC–R as responding similar to AOD-abusing clients may still be identified via the APS. *T* scores of 60 or more on this scale are noteworthy and can be used to provide additional support to previous AOD-specific standardized instruments and personality specific instruments.

The AAS is a 13-item scale that reflects the client's clear acknowledgment of AOD abuse problems. These scale questions are highly AOD transparent and specifically ask AOD-related questions. In other words, clients with elevated AAS scores (e.g., *T* scores of 60 or more) are frank and admitting they use AODs.

The Minnesota Multiphasic Personality Inventory–Adolescent (MMPI-A)

General MMPI–A Overview

MACs indicated they used the MMPI–A more frequently than any other adolescent personality assessment instrument (Juhnke, Curtis, Vacc, Coll, & Peredes, in press). The current instrument was first published in 1992 (Butcher et al., 1992). Four hundred seventy-eight true-false items comprise the instrument (Butcher et al., 1992). The MMPI–A was designed to be used with adolescents ages 14 to 18 with a grade 6 or higher reading level (Butcher et al., 1992). The instrument takes approximately 60 minutes to complete (Butcher et al., 1992). The MMPI-A can be ordered directly from National Computer Systems (NCS), 1-800-627-7271) in Minneapolis, MN.

MMPI–A Reliability and Validity

Reliability and validity of the MMPI–A validity and clinical scales appear adequate and reflect score characteristics similar to those within the MMPI–2. For example, MMPI–A validity and clinical scale test–retest correlations ranged between .49 and .84 (Butcher et al., 1992). Two-thirds of these scales (i.e., 10 scales) had test–retest correlations of .70 or higher. Internal consistency coefficients for the most part were adequate as well and ranged from a low of .35 on the Five Scale for a clinical sample of girls to a high of .90 on the F Scale for a normative sample of boys.

MMPI–A Scales

The MMPI–A is comprised of 8 validity scales, 10 clinical scales, 15 content scales, and 6 supplementary scales. The validity scales on this instrument are similar to those on the MMPI–2. For example, the Cannot Say Scale (?) identifies the number of unanswered items, and the Lie Scale (L) identifies naive client's attempting to present themselves favorably (Butcher et al., 1992). MMPI–A VRIN and TRIN scales measure inconsistent responses. The Infrequency scales (F, F1, and F2) measure attempts to present self in a negative manner, and the Defensiveness Scale (K) identifies clients attempting to present themselves in the most favorable manner. The 10 clinical scales are identical to those contained on the MMPI–2, which include: (a) Hypochondriasis, (b) Depression, (c) Hysteria, (d) Psychopathic Deviate, (e) Masculinity–Femininity, (f) Paranoia, (g) Psychasthenia, (h) Schizophrenia, (I) Hypomania, and (j) Social Introversion.

Clearly, differences exist between the MMPI–2 and the MMPI–A. For example, unlike the MMPI–2, the MMPI–A allows inferences based on T scores between 60 and 64 (Graham, 2000). However, the foundational basics of instrument interpretation and analysis remain very similar (e.g., greatest emphasis should be placed on T scale scores greater than 65). Again, as with the MMPI–2, addictions counselors may well find that adolescent clients who score high on either or both the Four Scale (Psychopathic Deviate) and Nine Scale (Hypomania) may have a greater likelihood of AOD abuse.

THERAPEUTIC FEEDBACK

Sincere Accomplishment Reviews and Compliments

Most people remember taking written examinations and returning the following class period to learn their fate. Often the major concerns didn't revolve around learning. Nearly everyone studied, attended lectures—at least to some degree—and learned something. Rather, the key anxiety-provoking components frequently revolved around the professor's interpretations of one's written responses, concerns regarding course failure, and, ultimately, rejection by the institution and significant others. Clients have similar concerns. The vast majority present themselves in a fairly accurate light. However, their concerns typically revolve around the interpretation of their assessment responses, failure to achieve their goal (e.g., obtaining help, getting their vehicular license back), and rejection by the counselor. Many fear they will be identified as "crazy" or "inferior." Thus, the first task after analyzing the assessment data is to help clients feel at ease and to help dispel potential fears. One way of engendering client comfort is to review the client's accomplishments via the assessment process and compliment the client's dedication to same. For example, in the case of Diane, the counselor might begin by stating,

Counselor: You have accomplished a lot in our assessment meetings together. You've told me about your experiences with alcohol and the problems resulting from those experiences. You've brought in your roommate, boyfriend, and mother to help me better understand your current circumstances, and you've enlisted their help in helping you maintain your sobriety. You've also completed some demanding tests and answered truthfully. These are major accomplishments, Diane. It truly is a privilege to work with someone so devoted to making her life better.

Diane: I don't think it was anything. I've got a long way to go.

Counselor: But the truth is you have done some very important things and you're making progress. A lot of people might have given up or refused to participate so fully. Not you, Diane, you fully participated and are consciously choosing to commit yourself to getting better.

In this exchange, we see the counselor reviews the work which the client has accomplished and gives a clear compliment. Diane has invested herself in the assessment process and has successfully utilized the assessment experiences. Diane belittles her behaviors and dismisses the compliment. Instead of accepting her self-abasing statement, the counselor responds by indicating that others might have given up, but that Diane is consciously choosing to make progress. Thus, the counselor reminds Diane of her attained progress and her active abstinence commitment. Concomitantly, the counselor demonstrates that Diane will be confronted should she chose to inappropriately belittle her accomplishments.

Conversely, it would be inadvisable to give hollow compliments or false statements. For example, if the client had refused to participate, a compliment like this one would be at best negatively perceived. The client would likely feel as though the counselor was attempting to manipulate her or that she had fooled the counselor. Either perception could negatively impact the counseling relationship.

In most situations the client has at least minimally participated in the experience. Thus the counselor should be able to positively reframe at least some portion of the client's behaviors into a compliment. Here, for example, the counselor might say:

Counselor: Maynard, based upon what you've stated, I know this assessment process has been challenging. You've indicated on a number of occasions that you didn't want to be here, and you did not want anyone you knew to participate in the significant other consultation meeting.

Maynard: Yeah, this whole thing is putrid. The judge makes me come. And I have to pay for an assessment I don't even want. The tests you made me take were really long and boring. I can't believe you made me read 567 questions. That stinks.

Counselor: Yes, the MMPI–2 is a long assessment instrument. But the point is that you completed it. You didn't give up.

Maynard: So what, man . . .

Counselor: So, you took the test and you completed the assessment. This suggests to me that you really want your license back.

Again, the issue isn't arguing with the client or giving an inappropriate compliment. Rather, the intent is to merely review what the client has done and provide a sincere compliment.

   Should the client's standardized instrument responses have been highly suspect or invalid (e.g., failing to answer 30 or more MMPI–2 questions) and the
client have refused to either retake the instrument or change responses accordingly (e.g., complete the previously unanswered questions), the counselor can
return to the unanswered questions and ask about specific questions to determine
if an underlying theme exists.

Counselor: Toni, although you originally agreed to take the MMPI–2 and you
answered most of the questions, I am unable to provide feedback until you complete the items which remain unanswered. Let's complete those unanswered questions now, so I can provide the best possible feedback in helping you.

Toni: Let's not. I'm tired of answering test questions.

Counselor: It is a long and tiring process, but you've taken the time to answer
most of the questions. Would you be willing to just take a look at the questions
that you didn't answer and see how many of those you can respond to right now?

Toni: No. I'm done reading the questions and filling in circles.

Counselor: Reading the questions and filling in circles is a long and tedious process. How about if we take just a few minutes right now, and I will read the questions. Certainly, you can tell me your answers?

Toni: I'm really not into it.

Counselor: I understand, but it will only take a few minutes, and I think it would
be helpful for you.

Toni: No way. I'm not going to answer any more questions.

Counselor: O.K., let's just take a few moments to discuss some of the questions
that you chose not to respond to. I noticed one of the questions to which you
didn't respond asked whether you have used alcohol excessively.

Toni: Yes, so what?

Counselor: Would you say that question is mostly true or mostly false?

Toni: I guess that is mostly true, I have used alcohol a lot. But, I don't think I've
used it excessively.

Counselor: That makes sense—especially given you have told me that you grew
up in a family where you considered most people to be high or drunk the majority
of the time.

Toni: Yeah, I guess that does make sense. I don't know if I use alcohol excessively, because I don't know what it's like for people not to use.

Counselor: Exactly. How could you possibly know if you were using alcohol
excessively when you don't know what it is like when people aren't using all the
time?

Toni: Makes sense.

Counselor: I also saw you didn't answer a question which asked if you enjoyed using marijuana. Do you enjoy using marijuana?

Toni: I don't know.

Counselor: During our initial meeting you indicated smoking marijuana daily. It seems to me that if you didn't enjoy it, you wouldn't be using.

Toni: All right, I enjoy it.

This verbal interchange demonstrates two important question review techniques. First, the counselor does nearly everything possible to encourage the client to respond to the unanswered question by herself. For example, the counselor begins by indicating most of the questions have already been answered. This implies that the client has completed the majority of work and that the major energy output is over. Moreover, it implies that she can complete the task with little effort—especially when compared to the energy already invested. Additionally, an invitation to complete the questions was made. Often such an invitation is sufficient, and clients will complete previously unanswered questions without further haggling.

Furthermore, when the client indicates she is tired of answering MMPI–2 questions, she is neither threatened by the counselor (e.g., "If you don't finish the test, I won't be able to score it and that will look bad for you") nor belittled (e.g., "Can't you answer a meager 567 questions?"). Instead, the counselor agrees that the process is tedious and offers a compromise. She will read the questions to the client, and the client can provide verbal responses. Again, the client denies. Thus, the counselor uses metacommunication. That is, she asks the questions by talking about the question. This seems to go well with Toni, and the counselor continues until the bulk of the questions have been completed. However, this might not always be the case. When the client simply refuses to answer the question, the counselor might say something like, "I'm confused" or "Help me understand." The following scenario depicts such an interaction.

Toni: Like I said, I'm not going to answer any more questions.

Counselor: I'm confused, Toni. You have invested so much time into responding to the questions already. How is it helpful for you to not complete the instrument.

Toni: I don't know and I don't care.

Counselor: Help me understand what I can do to help you finish these 32 questions so I can help you be as successful in your sobriety.

Toni: You sure are bullheaded. I said I'm not going to answer any more questions, and I mean it.

At this point in the Tier Four Assessment, the counselor clearly should have a good idea of the pressing addictions issues. Additionally, if the counselor had suspected a personality disorder and was using the MMPI–2 as a means of supporting her clinical judgment, the client's unwillingness to complete the instrument may well support the counselor's clinical judgment. Attempting to push the client further may damage the therapeutic relationship. Thus, the counselor would be advised to use other means to secure additional information necessary for treatment (e.g., police reports, driving records).

Eliciting Client Input

Once the counselor has provided a brief review of what has been accomplished and given a sincere accomplishment compliment, clients often begin to relax. Instead of charging into standardized test results and telling clients what is wrong with them and how pathological their drinking and drugging is, it is helpful to allow clients the opportunity to provide input into the experience. Therefore, the counselor might state something like:

Counselor: Laura Lynn, you've told me about who you are and invited me to meet people important to you. In both cases you received immediate feedback about what was said. This time, however, you took these two standardized assessment instruments. The first asked questions about your drinking and drugging behaviors and how these behaviors effect you. The second asked over 500 questions. Help me understand how you believe the instruments described you.

Laura Lynn: I bet they indicated I was some kind of insane alcoholic and a drug addict who needed help.

Counselor: They did suggest that you had both an alcohol and drug addiction problem, but they certainly didn't indicate you were insane. It might be helpful if we look at one issue at a time. What do you think the instruments suggested about your alcohol use?

Laura Lynn: Honestly, I believe it probably indicated that I have a severe drinking problem and that I've hurt others by my drinking—especially my lying about my drinking, my verbal assaults on loved ones when I'm drunk, and my failing to be what I promised to be to my significant other."

Counselor: It sounds like you have really thought this through, Laura Lynn. What else do you believe the instruments suggest about your alcohol abuse?

Laura Lynn: Probably that I've felt like killing myself, because I am so scared of losing Lucy and that I've let everyone in my life down—especially my children and my mother, Laraine.

Counselor: If the instruments could talk, Laura Lynn, what things do you think they would say that you need to do to maintain your alcohol abstinence?

Laura Lynn: Stop abusing alcohol.

Counselor: They likely would say that. But, how would they tell you to successfully achieve your sobriety?

Laura Lynn: I know that tests can't talk, but if they could, they would tell me to "lighten up on myself," "stop taking life so seriously," and "get into treatment."

Counselor: In what ways would the instruments suggest you could "lighten up on yourself"?

Laura Lynn: First, they would tell me to accept who I am as a person.

Counselor: What would that mean?

Laura Lynn: I guess like not feel that my divorce to Bill was wrong . . . you know, to admit that the relationship was bad and that I'm not straight. Bill didn't make me gay. I was trying to live a life that wasn't real. Next, I think the tests would say, "Let your mother deal with your being gay. It's not her life, but yours."

Counselor: How will you start doing those things? For example, how will you start letting yourself know and demonstrate through your actions that your divorce was right?

Laura Lynn: I need to stop using alcohol to give me permission to say what I want to say or to allow me to feel what I am feeling.

Counselor: Given that you've been using alcohol as a means to allow you to say things that you wanted to say and admit feelings that you had, how will you let others know you can do these things without having to use?

Laura Lynn: I think it's time I just tell it like it is.

This vignette depicts the therapeutic use of the client's perceptions related to the assessment instruments. This is a powerful therapeutic method and both allows the client to project what the client perceives the instruments specifically indicate about her and invites her to describe the treatment that will be most helpful.

Again, the vignette begins by dispelling the client's concern that she was identified as insane. This is critical. No one wants to be identified as insane. The client needs to hear and understand that the instrument does not note the client as being insane.

Insane is not a *DSM–IV–TR* diagnosis. It is a derogatory and useless descriptor most often used by lay persons to describe behaviors that appear inappropriate or illogical. However, clients displaying such behaviors often have very purposeful and credible reasons for behaving insanely. These reasons can range from keeping others from harming them, both physically and emotionally, to responding to internal turmoil and confusion. Even if a client was floridly psychotic, which likely will not occur because psychotic clients typically cannot respond to 500-plus multiple choice questions in a single setting, the label "insane" would be removed and the counselor would likely report something like, "Based on your responses it seems that you are seeing and hearing things which others don't." This is far different and more therapeutic than indicating someone is insane.

The counselor then validates the client's perception that the MMPI–2 suggests the client has both alcohol and drug addictions.[21] However, instead of diffusing the therapeutic potential of the feedback by discussing both addictions concomitantly, the counselor initially limits the discussion to alcohol. This is because the client identified alcohol as her first addiction. Next, the counselor asks the client what she believed the instruments suggested about her alcohol use. This is a subtle but noteworthy redirection. In other words, the client is encouraged to provide her input into the equation. This accomplishes two things. First, clients tend to accept instrument feedback when they have had the opportunity to "refine" and "improve" the results. Stated differently, clients buy into results they help generate. Thus, the client is able to project her perceptions of herself and her problems. Therefore, concerns and issues that may not be noted via the standardized test are not lost or left unnoted. Second, asking the client what she believed the instruments suggested about her alcohol use aids the counselor in assessing the veracity of the client's responses. Here, the client's perceptions either support or contradict instrument findings. For example, if the client scored very high on the Infrequency Scale (F Scale) but denied any problems or concerns, an incongruence would be noted and the counselor might say something like:

Counselor: Hmm, you verbally deny having any major concerns or problems. However, you have endorsed a number of concerns on the assessment instrument. For example, you've endorsed items on the instrument which suggest you feel blue most of the time, that you don't seem to care what happens to you, that you are under a great deal of tension at work, that your sleep is fitful and disturbed, and that you feel useless at times. Can you help me understand how it was you agreed with these statements on the MMPI–2, but now tell me that everything is all right?

Conversely, should the client's Infrequency Scale (F Scale) be very high, and if the client reports these same concerns via the clinical interview, and the client identifies specific situations which have engendered these concerns, it would seem likely that the veracity of the client's self-report would be supported.

Thus, the counselor can use previous client statements to augment the information provided via the standardized assessment instrument. Despite instrument findings, the most important factor is for the counselor to use her clinical judgment to integrate client input and assessment instrument findings into an accurate and useful diagnosis and treatment regimen.

The vignette also demonstrates how clients can be encouraged to identify ways of successfully describing their own needs and desired treatment. Here, the counselor asks what the instrument would say if it could talk. The counselor also asks what the instrument would say Laura Lynn needs to do to maintain her sobri-

---

21. Remember, standardized assessment instruments don't indicate the client has an addiction. Rather, the instrument merely notes that the client has endorsed responses in a fashion similar to those who have alcohol and drug addictions.

ety. Certainly, standardized instruments cannot personalize each individual client's treatment needs. However, giving the client the opportunity to describe things she can do to promote her treatment goals is an excellent place to start.

When Client Perceptions Don't Match the Assessments

Sometimes client perceptions contradict the counselor's clinical judgment and the assessment instrument results. An example is Arnie, a 38-year-old Euro-American male who adamantly denies AOD abuse or problems resulting from his daily alcohol and marijuana use. Arnie's driving license was revoked 3 years ago, because he was arrested 4 times within 6 months for driving under the influence (DUI). He has a checkered history of relatively minor offenses (e.g., drunk and disorderly conduct, urinating in public), which frequently resulted in county jail detention.

A Department of Motor Vehicles magistrate mandated Arnie's substance abuse assessment. Arnie indicated at the onset of the assessment process that he was participating only because he thought the assessment could reinstate his driving privileges. At the conclusion of Tier One, it was evident that Arnie qualified for both *DSM–IV–TR* alcohol and cannabis dependence and a personality disorder was suspected. These assessment results and the counselor's professional opinion were thoroughly discussed with Arnie. At that time the counselor also indicated that she would be unable to support Arnie's request for driving privilege reinstatement. Furthermore, the counselor encouraged Arnie to begin counseling and concomitant 12-step participation. However, Arnie did not agree with the diagnoses and continued to deny problems resulting from his daily alcohol and marijuana use. At the Tier Two conclusion, his significant others confronted Arnie about his addiction and advocated that he initiate treatment. Moreover, they described clear sanctions related to his continued use (e.g., Arnie's brother indicated he would call the police if he saw Arnie driving while his license was revoked—especially if Arnie was suspected as being under the influence). Arnie's Tier Three Substance Abuse Subtle Screening Inventory–3 (SASSI–3) supported the counselor's diagnoses. Given that Arnie readily admitted daily and extreme AOD use and refused abstinence recommendations, drug detection testing was not sought. SASSI–3 results were shared with Arnie. Yet, again, Arnie denied his daily and extreme AOD abuse as problematic, claiming "I'm not addicted" and "I don't have drug problems. My problems are because I have a screwed up family." The counselor continued into Tier Four due to Arnie's suspected personality disorder. Arnie's MMPI–2 results are profiled in Tables 6.3 and 6.4. Arnie's results suggest he responded in a fashion similar to persons attempting to present themselves in either a guarded or positive manner (low F, elevated L, and elevated K Validity Scale scores) and who likely qualify for a comorbid AOD diagnosis (elevated MAC–R Scale and elevated APS Supplemental Scale scores) and personality disorder (elevated 4 [Pd] and elevated 9 [Ma] Clinical Scale scores). An example vignette is provided next. It suggests how the counselor may wish to provide

TABLE 6.3. Arnie's Positive Light Profile

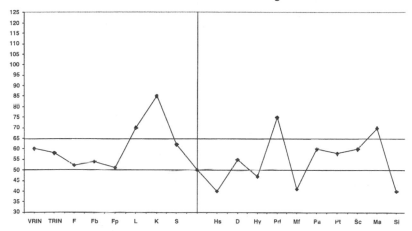

Scale	VRIN	TRIN	F	Fb	Fp	L	K	S	Hs	D	Hy	Pd	Mf	Pa	Pt	Sc	Ma	Si
Number							1	2	3	4	5	6	7	8	9	0		
Score	60		58	52	54	51	70	87	63	40	55	47	75	41	60	58	60	70	40

therapeutic feedback to a client who throughout the assessment process has denied his addictions despite significant contrary evidence.

Counselor: Arnie, you've provided a lot of information about your daily alcohol and drug use. As a matter of fact, from day one of our interactions, you were exceptionally frank. I appreciate your frankness, Arnie. A lot of people aren't so frank, but you don't appear to mince words.

Arnie: Thanks.

Counselor: You've also heard what your brother and wife said about your argumentative and dangerous behaviors, like driving when you are drunk. And we've spoken about how your responses to subtle or hidden-type questions on the SASSI–3 strongly suggested your AOD dependence. I have indicated that based on your statements, the statements of others, and your SASSI–3 assessment scores, it is my professional opinion that you qualify for both alcohol dependence and cannabis dependence. Furthermore, because of these results and your voiced refusal to discontinue drinking and driving, I cannot support your petition to reinstate your driving privileges.

Arnie: I know. You tell me that each time you see me, but you're wrong. I don't have a problem. I can drive fine when I'm high. Unlike most people, I don't get blurry vision.

TABLE 6.4. Arnie's Supplemental Profile

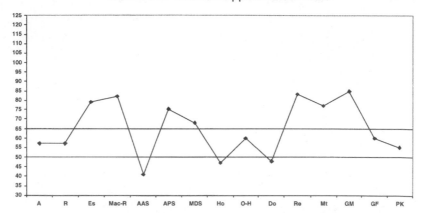

Scale	A	R	Es	Mac-R	AAS	APS	MDS	Ho	O-H	Do	Re	Mt	GM	GF	PK
Score	56	56	80	83	42	75	69	48	61	49	84	78	84	61	56

Counselor: Now you've completed one of the most widely used and respected assessment instruments which looks at your potential personality traits and behaviors. Help me understand how you believe the instrument described you.

Arnie: I bet it told you that I don't have a drinking problem and that I'm the kind of guy who keeps his word.

Counselor: Well, actually, Arnie, you are somewhat correct. Your endorsements suggest you were responding quite similar to people who are either attempting to present themselves in a positive way or people who are guarded.

Arnie: So you're calling me a liar?

Counselor: Based on your previous frankness and willingness to be truthful about your alcohol and marijuana use, I wouldn't call you a liar. However, statements made by your brother and wife, as well as your responses on the SASSI–3 and MMPI–3, suggest that you either don't want to or have a difficult time admitting some of the problems you are experiencing.

Arnie: So? People like you who work in offices and sit at desks all day don't understand what it is like for people like me. When I can find work, it doesn't pay much and I've got to do real work . . . shoveling and lifting work. I can't sit back and say, "Oh, I'm having problems" and whine about everything.

Counselor: Arnie, I'm sorry. It seems as though the results aren't what you expected or wanted.

Arnie: You can say that again.

Counselor: What did you want the results to suggest?

Arnie: That I should get my license back.

Counselor: Based on our previous conversations and feedback about the previous assessments, I thought it was clear that I could not support your petition.

Arnie: I know you said that, but I wanted this test to say I could get my license back. So, what did it say?

Counselor: Well, your responses are similar to persons who can be frustrated rather easily, who like adventure and excitement, and who don't like to be bored.

Arnie: That's me. I hate being bored.

Counselor: Your responses also suggest that you may have difficulties with authority figures and may have a history of legal or work problems.

Arnie: What else?

Counselor: And it suggests that you scored in a similar manner to people who have drug and alcohol problems.

Arnie: See, that's what I mean. I don't have any drug or alcohol problems.

Counselor: I'm confused, Arnie. You've indicated that you use alcohol and marijuana daily. Your family members have described problems resulting from your AOD abuse. Both the SASSI–3 and MMPI–3 have indicated that you have scored in a manner like those who qualify for alcohol and marijuana dependence. These things clearly indicate your need for counseling.

Arnie: No matter what you say, I'm not interested in counseling.

Counselor: I'm sorry to hear that, Arnie, because based on all the evidence, I truly believe you qualify for diagnosable disorders that can be treated effectively. When you are ready, I trust you will come back so we can work on your addictions and the behaviors that keep getting you in trouble.

This interaction depicts the importance of using all available data from each of the CLISD-PA tiers to support one's professional opinion. Again, it demonstrates how to begin therapeutic feedback with a compliment. Here, the counselor acknowledges Arnie's frankness. The compliment is then balanced by statements made by Arnie's significant others and his previous SASSI–3 scores, which suggest dependency diagnoses. The counselor later asks how Arnie believes the instrument described him. Arnie's voiced perception is opposite of the information provided thus far by the counselor and the opposite of the personality assessment instrument's findings.

Instead of indicating that Arnie's perceptions are completely inaccurate, the counselor reports that Arnie is "somewhat correct" and notes that Arnie's responses are similar to those who are attempting to present themselves in a positive manner or who are guarded. This is a very important point. First, the counselor does not say that Arnie is lying. Instead, she reframes potential falsification into more heuristic terms and provides two legitimate reasons why Arnie might have endorsed the responses that he chose. Second, the counselor accurately reports that Arnie's responses are similar to people who are attempting to present themselves in a positive light or who are guarded. Thus, the counselor is not saying that Arnie is positively presenting himself or guarded. No assessment instrument can indicate the client is a certain way. Instead, assessment instruments can only report that someone is responding similar to others (e.g., alcohol-abusing persons).

When confronted by Arnie, the counselor acts like Sargent Bill Friday on the old *Dragnet* police stories and reports "just the facts." These facts include: (a) Arnie's brother and wife described Arnie's daily AOD abuse, (b) Arnie openly admits to daily AOD use, and (c) the standardized assessment instrument results suggest he is not admitting AOD problems. Arnie becomes defensive and attempts to lure the counselor into an argument. Instead, the counselor apologizes that the results weren't what Arnie expected or wanted. Next, the counselor asks what Arnie wanted the results to report. When Arnie reports he thought the results would support getting his license back, the counselor reviews previous statements she had made to Arnie that specifically indicated the counselor would not support Arnie's license reinstatement. The counselor then presents Arnie's result in a straightforward and rather benign fashion. For example, instead of saying that Arnie was "antisocial," the counselor describes his yearning for excitement and his potentially checkered legal and work history.

When the counselor describes the personality instrument as suggesting AOD abuse, Arnie becomes angry. Again, the counselor does not argue with Arnie, but merely reports the previously established facts and statements that support the personality assessment instrument's results. Undaunted by Arnie's indications that he doesn't like results suggesting his AOD abuse or dependency, the counselor provides her clinical opinion that Arnie would benefit from and requires addictions counseling. When Arnie refuses, the counselor indicates she is sorry to learn the Arnie refuses to enter into treatment. Then she offers her professional opinion—Arnie qualifies for diagnosable disorders that likely can be effectively treated if he enters treatment. This statement is critical as it engenders hope and indirectly implies that the counselor is not unnerved by Arnie's addiction. Addicted clients often fear that they cannot successfully live without their addiction. Thus, this counselor is unabashedly saying, "You can make it, Arnie—when you are ready."

SUMMARY

This chapter described the fourth and last tier of the Clinical Interviews, Standardized Speciality, Drug Detection, and Personality Assessment (CLISD-PA) model. Readers gained a basic understanding of the Minnesota Multiphasic Personality Inventory–2 and the Minnesota Multiphasic Personality Inventory–Adolescent. Basic validity, clinical, and supplementary scales were described and readers learned via clinical vignettes how to provide therapeutic feedback to clients.

CLISD-PA TIER FOUR: PERSONALITY ASSESSMENT SKILL BUILDER

This chapter described the MMPI–2 and MMPI–A. Readers will next find three exercises designed to support and practice their learning. Readers are encouraged to compare their answers to the responses provided by the author on pages 223 through 226.

CLISD-PA Tier Four Skill Builder 1

Match each of the following scales to its correct definition.

Scale	This Scale Measures or Assesses . . .
A. VRIN	1. Gender roles
B. TRIN	2. Lying or balanced representation of self
C. F	3. Degree of symptomatology or lack thereof endorsed by the client; high scores are often associated with "defensiveness"
D. Fb	4. Somatic or bodily concerns
E. Fp	5. Depression
F. L	6. Mania
G. K	7. Social Introversion
H. S	8. Antisocial Behaviors
I. One Scale (Hs)	9. General or overall client endorsed psychopathology on the reverse of the MMPI–2
J. Two Scale (D)	10. Random and inconsistent endorsements
K. Three Scale (Hy)	11. Schizophrenia
L. Four Scale (Pd)	12. Excessive anxiousness and worry
M. Five Scale (Mf)	13. Beliefs in human goodness, serenity, contentment with life, patience/denial of irritability, and denial of moral flaws
N. Six Scale (Pa)	14. Random and inconsistent endorsements
O. Seven Scale (Pt)	15. General or overall client endorsed psychopathology
P. Eight Scale (Sc)	16. Paranoia
Q. Nine Scale (Ma)	17. Random and inconsistent endorsements
R. Ten Scale (Si)	18. Hysteria

CLISD-PA Tier Four Skill Builder 2

Carla presents as a 27-year-old college-educated Euro-American female. Early yesterday evening she was arrested on driving under the influence and attempting to resist arrest charges. The arrest occurred in her employing company's parking lot. Carla was driving the company minivan at the time of arrest. Occupants in the minivan included two employees who were supervised by Carla, plus Carla's immediate supervisor and the company's vice president for operations. All were returning to the company parking lot after celebrating Carla's first full week on the job. Carla was terminated by the company's vice president for operations as she was handcuffed and escorted to the transporting police vehicle.

As the "on call" counselor for Mountain Birch County Mental Health and Substance Treatment Services, you were contacted at 2 a.m. by the county jail's supervising deputy. The deputy requested you assess Carla regarding her voiced suicidal ideation. You interviewed Carla approximately one hour later at the county jail. During that interview, Carla was tearful and displayed psychomotor agitation. She complained of significant physical aches and pains. Specifically, she had: (a) nausea and a hangover from her alcohol consumption, (b) severe wrist bruising and swelling as a result of being handcuffed, and (c) facial lacerations and abrasions incurred during her scuffle with police while resisting arrest. Carla reported this was her first arrest. She denied significant past or present AOD abuse. "This is the first time I've gotten drunk since college. Even then, I only got drunk once or twice. I'm so ashamed and embarrassed." Carla stated, "I'll never get another job like this one. My parents and kids were so proud of me. What will my parents tell my kids about mommy being jailed?"

After posting bail, Carla was released and mandated for further evaluation and assessment by your agency. Specifically, your clinical supervisor requested that you provide Carla's substance abuse assessment. Carla completed all CLISD-PA model tiers, including the MMPI–2.

If the information just presented was accurate, and Carla was not AOD abusing, did not have a personality disorder, and was cooperative and truthful in responding to the MMPI–2 questions, depict how you would anticipate her MMPI–2 profile would look.

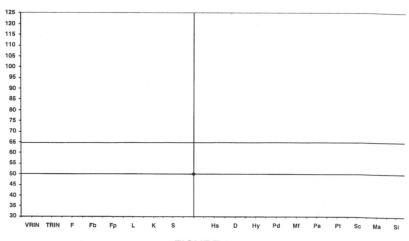

FIGURE 6.1

Now depict Carla's profile as if she lied about her AOD-abusing and arrest history, and assume she qualified for antisocial personality disorder.

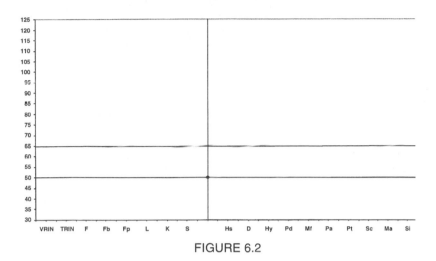

FIGURE 6.2

Describe the differences between the two profiles.

_____

_____

_____

_____

_____

Response to CLISD-PA Tier Four Skill Builder 1

The following scales are matched to the best definition. Note that responses 10, 14, and 17 ("Random and inconsistent endorsements") can be used interchangeably with scales VRIN, TRIN, and Fp.

Scale	This Scale Measures or Assesses . . .
A. VRIN	10, 14, or 17. Random and inconsistent endorsements.
B. TRIN	10, 14, or 17. Random and inconsistent endorsements.
C. F	15. General or overall client endorsed psychopathology.
D. Fb	9. General or overall client endorsed psychopathology on the backside of the MMPI–2.

E.	Fp	10, 14, or 17.	Random and inconsistent endorsements.
F.	L	2.	Lying or balanced representation of self.
G.	K	3.	Degree of symptomatology or lack thereof endorsed by the client; high scores are often associated with "defensiveness."
H.	S	13.	Beliefs in human goodness, serenity, contentment with life, patience/denial of irritability, and denial of moral flaws.
I.	One Scale (Hs)	4.	Somatic or bodily concerns.
J.	Two Scale (D)	5.	Depression.
K.	Three Scale (Hy)	18.	Hysteria.
L.	Four Scale (Pd)	8.	Antisocial behaviors.
M.	Five Scale (Mf)	1.	Gender roles.
N.	Six Scale (Pa)	16.	Paranoia.
O.	Seven Scale (Pt)	12.	Excessive anxiousness and worry.
P.	Eight Scale (Sc)	11.	Schizophrenia.
Q.	Nine Scale (Ma)	6.	Mania.
R.	Ten Scale (Si)	7.	Social introversion.

Response to CLISD-PA Tier Four Skill Builder 2

"Carla No Personality Disorder"

Although readers may have depicted any of a number of profiles similar to the one above, the emphasis here is on a few common themes. For example, related to the validity scales, if Carla was responding truthfully the majority of her validity scales would fall somewhere between T scores of 50 and 65. The validity scales T scores here suggest that she was relatively consistent in her responses (VRIN and TRIN scores are 52 and 57 respectively) and likely experiencing stressors and admitting immediate difficulties and troubles in her life (F score of 76). Given that she is answering truthfully and college educated, one would likely suspect that her L, K, and S scale T scores would be within these normal ranges as well. The elevated F scale T score suggests that she is experiencing noteworthy concerns and emotional stress. Additionally, these scores are similar to one another, suggesting that she did not respond significantly differently on the front in comparison to the back. Additionally, the elevated F scale T score is consistent to her reported distress resulting from her arrest and job loss. It is also consistent with her tearfulness and psychomotor agitation.

Related to her clinical scales, Carla's elevated Seven, Two, and One scales appear congruent with her recent arrest and job loss experience. The elevated Seven Scale suggests that she feels anxious and tense. Additionally, she may be ruminating on the embarrassment of her arrest, loss of her job, thoughts that she won't find another job of the same quality, and concerns of how her children will

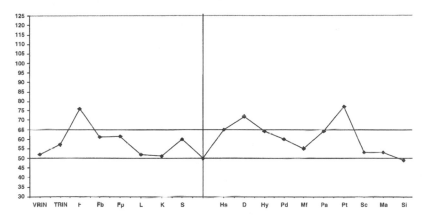

Scale	VRIN	TRIN	F	Fb	Fp	L	K	S	Hs	D	Hy	Pd	Mf	Pa	Pt	Sc	Ma	Si
Number									1	2	3	4	5	6	7	8	9	0
Score	52		57	76	62	62	52	51	60	65	73	64	62	55	64	78	52	52	49

FIGURE 6.3. MMPI–2 Carla No Personality Disorder

perceive her arrest. Her elevated Two Scale is also congruent with her recent experience. She has just lost her job and has been arrested; thus, she may well feel depressed regarding these experiences and losses. Additionally, given the extent of her physical injuries, the higher One Scale is congruent with her physical presentation as well.

"Carla with Antisocial Personality Disorder"

Similar profiles may be depicted here as well. For clearer instruction, the validity scales have remained consistent for both depictions. It is possible that if Carla qualified for an antisocial personality disorder, she might attempt to present either herself in a more or less favorable light. For example, if Carla thought it was in her best interest to present herself as a helpless victim, she might have endorsed more transparently pathological items. Thus, her F Scale would be elevated in a cry for help. Of course, the motive for this cry for help would likely be to escape punishment and gain leniency from the court.

It is just as likely that persons fulfilling antisocial personality disorder criteria would have little concern about being incarcerated. In other words, they don't fear incarceration and view it as an injustice placed on them. Therefore, such clients may have an elevated K Scale and a F Scale T score within the normal range. In other words, they don't experience distress symptoms.

More likely, the more noteworthy differences with someone fulfilling anti-

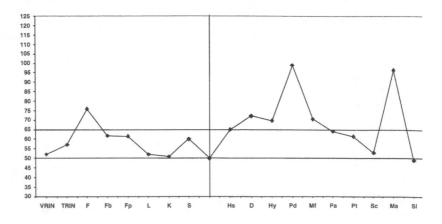

Scale	VRIN	TRIN	F	Fb	Fp	L	K	S	Hs	D	Hy	Pd	Mf	Pa	Pt	Sc	Ma	Si
Number									1	2	3	4	5	6	7	8	9	0
Score	52	57	76	73	65	52	51	60	65	73	69	99	70	64	63	53	96	49

FIGURE 6.4. Carla Antisocial Personality Disorder

social personality disorder criteria is that they will have elevated Four and Nine Scale *T* scores. In Carla's case, this elevated Four Scale *T* score matches with the situation which she just experienced. Basically, she was the life of the party and had everyone in the company minivan. Persons with such high scores are often perceived as intelligent, adventuresome, and gregarious. They can be socially charming and talkative. Given that she had only been there a week, some of her noxious behaviors hadn't yet been realized by those around her. She is likely impulsive and rebellious—especially toward others. Again, this is a match with the described arrest incident. Specifically, not only had she been drinking and driving—a blatant disregard for others—she attempted to resist arrest—a direct act of rebelliousness toward authority figures. Given that persons fulfilling anti-social personality disorder criteria are mostly free from feelings of depression and anxiety, Carla's profile might be seen as a little unusual. However, it is more likely that she is depressed that she was caught. In other words, she likely is not remorseful. Rather, she is merely "bummed" because she didn't get away with drinking and driving.

Differences between Profiles

The most likely differences between the two profiles will be the elevated Four and Nine scales on the second profile in which Carla fulfills antisocial personality disorder criteria.

REFERENCES

Bubenzer, D. L., Zimpfer, D. G., & Mahrle, C. L. (1990). Standardized individual appraisal in agency and private practice. *Journal of Mental Health Counseling, 12*, 51–66.

Butcher, J. N. (1999). *A beginner's guide to the MMPI–2*. Washington, DC. American Psychological Association.

Butcher, J. N., Dahlstrom, W. G., Graham, J. R., Tellegen, A., & Kaemmer, B. (1989). *Minnesota Multiphasic Personality Inventory–2 (MMPI–2): Manual for administration and scoring*. Minneapolis, MN: University of Minneapolis Press.

Butcher, J. N, Williams, C. L., Graham, J. R., Archer, R. P., Tellegen, A., Ben-Porath, Y. S., & Kaemmer, B. (1992). *Manual for administration, scoring, and interpretation: Minnesota Multiphasic Personality Inventory–Adolescent*. Minneapolis, MN: University of Minnesota Press.

Chojnacki, J. T., & Walsh, W. B. (1992). The consistency of scores and configural patterns between the MMPI and MMPI–2. *Journal of Personality Assessment, 59*, 276–289.

Graham, J. R. (2000). *MMPI–2: Assessing Personality and psychopathology* (3rd ed.). New York: Oxford University Press.

Graham, J. R., & Strenger, V. E. (1988). MMPI characteristics of alcoholics: A review. *Journal of Consulting and Clinical Psychology, 1,* 197–205.

Graham, J. R., Timbrook, R. E., Benn-Porath, Y. S., & Butcher, J. N. (1991). Code-type congruence between the MMPI and MMPI–2: Separating fact from artifact. *Journal of Personality Assessment, 57*, 205–215.

Green, R. L. (1991). *The MMPI–2/MMPI: An interpretive manual*. Boston: Allyn and Bacon.

Juhnke, G. A., Vacc, N. A., Curtis, R. C., Coll, K. M., & Parades, D. M. (in press). Assessment instruments used by addictions counselors. *Journal of Addictions and Offender Counseling*.

MacAndrew, C. (1965). The differentiation of male alcoholic outpatients from nonalcoholic psychiatric outpatients by means of the MMPI. *Quarterly Journal of Studies on Alcohol, 26*, 238–246.

Morrison, T. L., Edwards, D. W., & Weissman, H. N. (1994). The MMPI and MMPI–2 as predictors of psychiatric diagnoses in an outpatient sample. *Journal of Personality Assessment, 62*, 17–30.

Vacc, N. A., Juhnke, G. A., & Nilsen, K. Mental health services providers' codes of ethics and the Standards for Educational and Psychological Testing. *Journal of Counseling and Development, 79*, 217–224..

Watkins, C. E., Jr., Campbell, V. L., & McGregor, P. (1988). Counseling psychologists' uses of and opinions about psychological tests: A contemporary perspective. *Counseling Psychologist, 16*, 476–486.

Chapter 7

Conclusion

Most students entering my graduate counseling courses on assessment or beginning clinical supervision with me often view assessment as something that is "done" to clients. This view seems to match my early experiences as a counselor working within a large community mental health agency. For the most part, it seemed, clients were assessed and diagnoses were made in an effort to secure third-party reimbursement. Assessment and treatment were typically viewed as distinctly separate. Each was compartmentalized. And, except for paperwork contained within the client's folder, more affectionately know as "the jacket"—assessment information on the left, progress notes and quarterly and yearly treatment reviews attached to the right—little effort was made to join the client in developing current treatment based on past and present assessment information.

The intent of this text has been to break this flawed notion and proclaim the inseparability of assessment and treatment. As an egg is composed of a shell, a yoke, and an egg white, we cannot affect one part without influencing the others. As we continually ask clients and their significant others to join us in an ongoing review of their lives and to explain who they are, we as counselors more accurately understand how to help the person behind the symptomatology and the diagnosis. Only through continual assessment can we mobilize our clients' strengths and resources to foster daily success in their battle for sustained abstinence. Understanding what triggered their drinking and drugging yesterday or learning what helped them abstain earlier in the day helps us better prepare them for next addiction battle.

In this text I have described the CLISD-PA model and how to use this model without becoming lost in the assessment process or purpose. Readers have become familiar with common substance-related disorders and the *DSM–IV–TR* basics—including the Multiaxial System and diagnostics—and have learned how to use this four-tiered model to jointly develop effective client treatment. I have suggested how to effectively interview court-mandated clients and respond to their potential AOD denial. Additionally, I have provided a basic overview of AOD speciality, drug detection, and personality instruments. Specifically, readers have learned how and when to use these instruments to help clients attain their treatment goals. Finally, I have described how we must work with clients not as being the victims of their diagnoses but as the people behind the symptomatology. Only then can we be successful helpers.

I trust this text has been helpful to you as you help others. Ironically, I could not help you without the help of many others whom I owe sincere thanks. Among them are: Deborah, Bryce, Brenna, Gerald, and Violet Juhnke, my family members who provided significant support and encouragement throughout the writing process; Nicholas Vacc, William Purkey, Joe Oldz, and Alan Hovestadt, my mentors and past instructors; Ken Wanberg, Frank Miller, and the SASSI Institute associates, who helped me provide the most up-to-date and accurate information regarding their testing instruments; Jane Carroll, David Whittinghill, Monique Manhal-Baugus, Brian Glaser, Tim Julet, and Emily Epstein, my reviewers; and Emily Bowman, Lisa Crowley, and William Moats, my helpers.

Index